*Small Groups
and Political Behavior*

A STUDY OF LEADERSHIP

Books published for
The Center of International Studies
Woodrow Wilson School of Public and International Affairs

SMALL GROUPS
AND
POLITICAL BEHAVIOR

A Study of Leadership

BY SIDNEY VERBA

PRINCETON, NEW JERSEY

PRINCETON UNIVERSITY PRESS

1961

To Cynthia

ACKNOWLEDGMENTS

THE major intellectual debt of this work is to the many researchers in the field of small group analysis whose work I have summarized, analyzed, sometimes criticized, but I hope not distorted. Their names are cited in the footnotes and bibliography.

Many people helped in my understanding of political analysis and of small group analysis. I would like particularly to acknowledge the encouragement and guidance of Gabriel A. Almond from the inception of the study. John Kennedy gave me the valuable opportunity of observing and participating in the design and administration of some of the interesting small group experiments that he is conducting at the Princeton Psychological Laboratories. John K. Hemphill and Harold Guetzkow shared with me some of their experiences in small group experimentation. Others who read the manuscript at various stages and made useful comments are Marver Bernstein, Stanley Kelley, Jr., V. O. Key, Jr., James G. March, Herbert McCloskey, Carroll L. Shartle, and Fred L. Strodtbeck. The most valuable (and severest) criticism came from my wife, Cynthia, whose rigorous standards in matters of logic and style contributed substantially to the final product. Jean MacLachlan edited the book with her usual care and skill. The above-mentioned should be associated with whatever contribution the book makes. I alone should be associated with its faults.

I am grateful to the publishers for permission to quote from the following works: Muzafer Sherif and Carolyn W. Sherif, *Groups in Harmony and Tension* (New York: Harper and Brothers, 1953); V. O. Key, Jr., *Southern Politics* (New York: Alfred A. Knopf, 1949); and Kurt Lewin and Ronald Lippitt, "An Experimental Approach to the Study of Autocracy and Democracy," *Sociometry*, Volume I, 1938, J. L. Moreno, M.D., Editor.

During the course of this study I was on the research staff of the Center of International Studies at Princeton University. I am grateful to the Center and to Frederick S. Dunn, its director, for providing financial support, secretarial assistance, and a stimulating environment in which to work. Mrs. Gretchen McCabe and Mrs. Suzanne Patronsky typed the manuscript with patience and accuracy.

The above are my intellectual debts. All students of small groups know that task accomplishment depends upon socio-emotional support. It is for that support that I owe my greatest debt to my own small group—to Margaret and Erica, and even to Duffy, but above all to Cynthia.

S.V.

Princeton, New Jersey
March 1960

CONTENTS

*Small Groups
and Political Behavior*

A STUDY OF LEADERSHIP

Chapter I

INTRODUCTION

Recent theories and methods in the social sciences have not respected disciplinary boundaries. In political science, for instance, theories have been developed that cut across its traditional fields. Theories of the psychological roots of political behavior apply to the individual participant in the political system as voter, judge, administrator, political boss, or congressman. Theories of the structure and function of organizations apply to parties, bureaucracies, pressure groups, and courts of law. And theories of decision-making apply to decisions at all levels of government, state and national; and to decisions on all subjects of political concern, foreign and domestic. Furthermore, theories that cut across the boundaries traditionally separating political science into fields of study also cut across the boundaries that have divided political science from other disciplines interested in the study of human behavior. Theories of organizations apply to businesses as well as bureaucracies; theories of decision-making, to economic as well as political decisions.

This book will explore the relevance for political science of a theory and method that grew up under the aegis of the disciplines of sociology and social psychology. The theory is that of the behavior of small face-to-face groups. The method is that of the controlled experimental study of interaction in small groups.

Although one of its main purposes is to introduce to a political science audience a new and exciting field of research, the book will, it is hoped, be more than an essay in interdisciplinary contact. It will attempt to show that the small group approach, at first glance quite remote from the study of political affairs, has certain unique contributions to make to political science. Perhaps this work will help to reduce the gap between the study of small groups and the study of politics and, in so doing, enrich the theories and methods of political science.

3

Small group studies say little directly about the operations of political organizations or about the behavior of people in politics. The interests of the small group analysts have been quite different. They have sought to find uniformities of behavior within the confines of certain experimental situations. Therefore an analysis of small group research will present few facts about political behavior. But the immediate need in political research is not for more facts or more data: rather, it is for adequate conceptual schemes and systematic theories into which to fit the facts we have and the facts we shall gather in the future. Also needed are more precise and explicit techniques of data gathering so that the reliability and validity of the data we accumulate can be estimated. Small group analysis can contribute to these broad theoretical and methodological interests of political science.

In developing adequate and usable theories for the study of political behavior there is a need for the specification of the significant variables of the political system, ways of observing and measuring these variables, and propositions about their relations with other variables in the system. Ultimately, one would hope that these variables could be fitted into an overall systematic theory of politics. That goal is, however, well beyond the scope of this book. We shall be concerned only with certain variables and with bits of theory. This study will use the findings of small group research to deal with two crucial political variables—the primary group and leadership.

The importance of the primary group in politics is one of the central themes of this book. If we are to understand the political process, greater consideration must be given to the role of face-to-face contacts. Primary groups of all sorts mediate political relationships at strategic points in the political process. They are the locus of most political decision-making, they are important transmission points in political communications, and they exercise a major influence on the political beliefs and attitudes of their members. These various functions of the face-to-face group and the place of these functions within the political system will be discussed in greater detail in the next chapter.

The second theoretical contribution that this study hopes to make is to the analysis of political leadership. Here again, small group analysis will be found to be a useful tool. One of the great gaps in the study of politics—a gap that is just starting to be closed—is the absence of adequate theories and concepts for the study of political power. There is a lack of clear and unambiguous concepts for identifying the major variables in power relationships and of systematic theories for ordering the relations among these variables. Consequently, research on the power structures of political systems has been poorly integrated and non-cumulative. We shall use the methods and findings of small group research on leadership— a concept closely related to that of power, since leaders are usually defined as the major power-holders in a group—to attempt to add to our concepts and methods for the study of these significant political relationships. We shall present no complete and fully rounded theory of political power and leadership, but it is hoped that the small group approach will suggest new ways of thinking about these concepts and stimulate new approaches to the study of politics.

Small group studies of leadership will be related to the political process in two ways. First we shall consider the use of techniques and methods of measuring and identifying leadership in small group studies as tools for analyzing and improving methods and techniques in political studies. We shall then take up three problems in the leader-follower relationship that have received intense study within the small group literature and that also have great significance for leaders in actual political situations. The three problems are: the relation between affective leadership and instrumental leadership, the relation between the norms of the group and social change, and the effects of participation in decisions on the nature of the decision and its degree of acceptability. We will hope to demonstrate that the processes studied within the small group are of social and political importance, and that knowledge of them should operate to improve our understanding of political processes.

Each of these represents an aspect of the power relations

between leader and follower of the utmost political significance, but about which our theoretical models are inadequate.
The tension between affect and task accomplishment is a
problem faced by all political systems. Governments, political parties, and organizations of all sorts must satisfy both
the instrumental and the affective demands placed upon them.
It is not enough for a political system to be instrumentally
effective—maintain a satisfactory economic system, respond
to the demands of the various groups in the system, and so
forth—it must also gain and keep the allegiance of its citizens.
The citizens must give their loyalty to the particular political
arrangements in their nation not merely because these arrangements satisfy their instrumental demands, but because they
believe the political system to be legitimate *per se*. They support it because they feel they ought to support it. A system
that does not have this basic loyalty of its citizens may remain
stable for a time, but it will be hard-pressed to survive a
breakdown in its instrumental effectiveness. A system that
does possess this loyalty will be able to weather instrumental
crises more easily. Thus the United States and Britain, with
strong citizen allegiance to the governmental system, could
weather a severe depression with little fundamental change
in form of government, but the Weimar Republic, whose
legitimacy was questioned by large groups in Germany, could
not survive a similar instrumental crisis.[1] And it is in relation
to the maintenance of legitimacy that the affective outputs of
the system are of great significance. The symbolism of the
state, its holidays and slogans, and its ability to arouse the
emotional commitment of its citizens play a major role in
developing its legitimacy. In underdeveloped countries, the
affective side of the citizen-state relationship—the magnetism
of a charismatic leader, the excitement of a nationalistic
slogan—is a key aspect of the transition of these new nations
to unified nation-states. If the study of the relation between
instrumental and affective aspects of the leader-follower rela-

---

[1] See Seymour Martin Lipset, *Political Man: Where, How and Why
Democracy Works in the Modern World* (Garden City, New York: Doubleday and Company, 1960), Chap. 3.

tion in the small group can add to our theoretical understanding of this problem, it will certainly contribute to the study of politics.

Similarly, the relation between the norms of the group and social change is a political relationship about which we have inadequate theory. Most theories of group influence on voting behavior, for instance, stress the pressures on the individual voter to conform to the group of which he is a member. How then can we explain changes in group voting habits over time? If the members of the group, and especially the leaders of the group, are under pressure to conform to the group norm, how can a new norm be introduced? The entire question of the relationship between conformity and stability on the one hand (both needed in any political system), and non-conformity and change on the other (also needed), is one for which the theoretical tools of analysis are lacking. Again small group studies of leadership and group norms may help us fill the theoretical gap.

And lastly, small group studies of participatory leadership or the effects of participation in a decision on willingness to accept that decision can aid in the development of theories about the democratic political process—about the strengths of participatory systems and about their weaknesses.

Theories developed in the small group laboratory, while not directly transferable in a predictive sense to political processes, can be used to develop testable theories about politics. Furthermore, the political processes whose analogues we will study within the small group have wide generality. They are political relationships one would expect to find in all states, Western and non-Western, democratic and non-democratic; as well as in political parties and other organizations. And it is just this sort of theory on a high level of generality that is needed in political analysis.

The purpose of this book is methodological as well as theoretical. The method whose amenability to political research we shall examine is that of the controlled group experiment. There is a growing interest in the use of such controlled experiments for the study of political relationships.

7

Some scholars interested in attitude formation and voting decisions have found that the theories of attitude formation and change developed in small group research—often in laboratories far removed from the "real" problems of political, economic, and social behavior—are quite useful in understanding political behavior. There have been small group experiments explicitly designed to sharpen the conceptual tools of political science by studying problems of power and influence under controlled conditions. There has been a large-scale attempt to study the processes by which juries reach decisions through the use of experimentally created mock-juries. And there has been quite recently a rapidly growing interest in the use of small experimental groups for "political gaming," in attempts to see if one can create experimental models of international situations.[2]

In all these cases, the small group experimental method has been used for the creation of models of the political process and not for the study of actual political situations. Except under rare conditions, the political process itself cannot be subjected to experimental manipulation by researchers. If the small group experimental method is to contribute to the theory of politics, it will be because one can create useful models of the political process in the small group laboratory.

[2] For the studies of attitude formation, see Elihu Katz and Paul F. Lazarsfeld, *Personal Influence: The Part Played by People in the Flow of Mass Communications* (Glencoe, Ill.: Free Press, 1955), Part I. The study of power and influence is by James March, "Influence Measurement in Experimental and Semi-experimental Groups," *Sociometry*, *19* (1956), pp. 260-71. The jury studies include Fred L. Strodtbeck, "The Jury Project: Some Questions of Method Raised by Experimentation in an Institutional Study," Jury Project, The Law School, University of Chicago (September 1958), mimeographed; Fred L. Strodtbeck, "Sex-Role Differentiation in Jury Deliberation," *Sociometry*, *19* (1956), pp. 3-11; and Fred L. Strodtbeck, Rita M. James, and Charles Hawkins, "Social Status in Jury Deliberations," *American Sociological Review*, *22* (1957), pp. 713-19. On the use of experiments to study international affairs, see Morton A. Kaplan, *System and Process in International Politics* (New York: John Wiley, 1957), pp. xv-xvi; Harold Guetzkow, "The Use of Simulation in the Study of Inter-Nation Relations," *Behavioral Science*, *4* (1959), pp. 183-91; J. M. Goldsen, "The Political Exercise: An Assessment of the Fourth Round," The RAND Corporation, D-3640-RC, May 1956, mimeographed; Herbert Goldhamer and Hans Speier, "Some Observations on Political Gaming," *World Politics*, *12* (1959), pp. 71-83; and Lincoln P. Bloomfield and Norman J. Padelford, "Three Experiments in Political Gaming," *American Political Science Review*, *53* (1959), pp. 1105-15.

One task of this book will be to assess the usefulness of such small group models for the study of politics. In particular, we shall be interested in the problem of transferability from the level of the small group experiment to that of the political process. The specifically methodological chapters of this study (Chapters III and IV) will deal directly with this question. The more substantive chapters on leadership theory will also attempt to indicate what sorts of knowledge one can derive from the study of the small group by illustrating the types of propositions generated in small experimental group studies and the uses to which they can be put. It is thus hoped that the leadership sections of this book will contribute to an understanding of the methodological problem of the use of experimental research in the study of politics, as well as to the understanding of political leadership. Throughout we shall stress both the use and the limitations of the small group approach, for it is only when one has a clear understanding of the limitations of small group analysis that one can benefit fully from its use.

This book is conceived of largely as a contribution to political science. Most of the material, however, is derived from sources outside of what is ordinarily called political science. Our tour of the small group literature will take us through children's play groups, discussion groups among college students, family decision-making sessions, and into factories to see "human relations" programs in operation. And many of the methodological and theoretical propositions we shall suggest might apply as well to economic as to political organizations. If this is so, one might well ask: "Is this political science?" My answer would be, "I don't know. It depends on what you mean by political science. And though it matters if it is or not, it does not matter much."

In all the social sciences, one ought to work on significant social problems (and by that I do not necessarily mean social problems in the narrow policy-oriented sense), and employ for the analysis of these problems whatever approach seems most useful. Whether the problem falls into one academic domain or into another or into several at once is essentially a trivial question. Furthermore, if the theories developed have a wide range of generality, they will be all the more useful and fruitful. A theory of leadership that deals with problems faced by the leaders of states, the leaders of political parties, the leaders of business organizations (whether, for instance, the internal "politics" of a corporation is within the domain of political science is largely a matter of academic definition, not of social theory), and the leaders of other groups is a useful theory indeed.

But there are several senses in which this is a contribution to political science as usually defined, either as the study of the structure of power in a society, or of the "authoritative allocation of values," or, more narrowly, as the study of government and related institutions. Throughout, we have attempted to connect small group findings to political science as usually understood. Our discussion of the primary group in politics is not intended to be an exercise in family sociology, but an explicit discussion of the role of families, cliques, and other face-to-face groups in the political process. Similarly, the study of leadership is central to the study of politics no matter how defined. The leader-follower relationship is essentially a power or influence relationship and, as such, is a uniquely political relationship. Furthermore, the particular leadership problems we have chosen to deal with are problems of great political significance. And lastly, we have, wherever possible, drawn our examples of on-going social processes from the realm of what is conventionally called politics—political party behavior, voting behavior, and the like.

It is not the aim of this book to suggest that political science become an experimental science, or that small group analysis can replace the many other tools of analysis available for political research. The aim is merely to suggest that the small group approach has much to offer to the study of politics —that it can suggest new ways of looking at political relationships, and that it can give us some guidance in our attempts to understand the processes of politics.

What Is a Small Group?

This work will deal with "small groups," "face-to-face groups," and "primary groups." It is necessary, therefore, to look a little more carefully at what is meant by these concepts before plunging into the main body of the study. Since this is a study of studies, there is some difficulty in defining the small group. Among the many writers who have dealt with the subject there are many definitions, but certain significant elements are common to most of them.

FACE-TO-FACE CONTACT: One of the earliest sociological works on small groups defines the group thus: "By primary groups, I mean those characterized by intimate face-to-face cooperation and association."[3] This definition points to the key aspect of the small group as it has been analyzed in the many works on the subject since Cooley. This is the aspect of direct, face-to-face contact. What is called "interaction" by many of the workers in this field is some form of "face-to-face" communication. Homans' definition of the small group, while more elaborate than Cooley's, contains the same basic component: "We mean by a group a number of persons who communicate with each other often over a period of time, and who are few enough so that each person is able to communicate with all the others, not at second-hand, but face-to-face."[4] Again the major characteristic is face-to-face contact and communication.

One major implication of face-to-face contact is that the members of the group will have some awareness of each of the other members as separate and distinct entities. This has also been explicitly made the basis of the definition of the small group by another leading researcher in this field. Robert Bales writes that "A small group is defined as any number of persons engaged in interaction with each other in a single face-to-face meeting or a series of such meetings, in which each member receives some impression or perception of each

[3] Charles H. Cooley, *Social Organization* (New York: Charles Scribner's Sons, 1909), p. 23.
[4] George C. Homans, *The Human Group* (New York: Harcourt, Brace, 1950), p. 1.

11

other member distinct enough so that he can, either at the time or in later questioning, give some reaction to each of the others as an individual person, even though it is only to recall that the other person was present."[5] Thus a small group is one in which the members communicate on a direct face-to-face basis and are aware of each other as individuals, even if that awareness is limited to a recognition of the other's presence.

How SMALL? Groups in which face-to-face communication is possible among all members and in which all are aware of the others' presence must of necessity be small. But how small is a small group? Throughout the range of the literature on the subject there are groups of various sizes, from the two-person group on up. Clearly the maximum size that a group can attain and still retain the characteristics of a small group varies with the nature of the group, its task, the length of time it has existed, the membership, and so forth. However, few of the groups studied number more than twenty, and most are considerably smaller.[6]

GOAL ORIENTATION: For some writers, the essential characteristic of a group is its common goal. Before there can be interaction among the members of the group, before it can in fact become a group, there must be some common goal or purpose. In this sense, "Every group is an interest group. . . ."[7]

[5] Robert F. Bales, *Interaction Process Analysis* (Cambridge, Mass.: Harvard University Press, 1950), p. 3.

[6] James surveyed in a preliminary way the size of groups in which there was face-to-face contact. This was done by asking industrial firms for the usual size of "action-taking groups" and by observing informal groups at work and on the street. He found that most groups had between two and seven members. When the group size went over seven, it was difficult for all the members to maintain contact with all the others and the group tended to split into sub-groups. J. James, "A Preliminary Study of the Size Determinant in Small Group Interaction," *Am. Soc. Rev.*, 16 (1951), pp. 474-77.

[7] Raymond B. Cattell, "Concepts and Method in the Measurement of Group Syntality," *Psychological Review*, 55 (1948), pp. 48-63, reprinted in Paul A. Hare, Edgar F. Borgatta, and Robert F. Bales, eds., *Small Groups* (New York: Alfred A. Knopf, 1955), p. 107. See also C. A. Gibb, "The Principles and Traits of Leadership," *Journal of Abnormal and Social Psychology*, 42 (1947), pp. 267-84, reprinted in Hare, Borgatta, and Bales, eds., *op.cit.*, pp. 87-94.

Since all human behavior can be conceptualized as goal-oriented, it is valid and quite useful to think of group behavior in these terms. But goal orientation in itself does not differentiate the small group from the large organization or association.

VARIETY OF GROUPS: Small groups can be found in all shapes and forms, if not in all sizes. Within the small group literature are studies of families, informal work groups, boy scout troops, housewife discussion groups, research teams, airplane crews, submarine crews, college student groups hired for an experiment, therapeutic groups, committees of various sorts, mock and real juries, street corner gangs, groups of job applicants, children's play groups, classroom discussion groups, Princeton precepts, friends and neighbors. Some of these groups are brought together and, in a sense, created by the researcher. Others, such as families and work groups, are groups with a history of interaction before the researcher came on the scene and with expectations of further interaction after the researcher leaves.[8] Some significant differences between these two types of group will be dealt with later, but here the major assumption behind small group research ought to be mentioned—that despite the shapes and forms, origins and memberships of these groups, there are certain general behavioral characteristics of all small groups arising from their face-to-face interaction. One of the central tasks of this study will be to attempt to relate some of the general theories of small group behavior to the analysis of political behavior.

FORMAL AND INFORMAL GROUPS: The study of the small group has often been characterized as the study of the "informal" group as contrasted with the "formal" organization. And many of the small groups that have been studied have been informal in two senses: they have been informal in relation to the larger organization of which they are a part, and informal in their internal operation. In relation to the larger

---

[8] To avoid the complications associated with the term "real group," this type will be called an "on-going group."

organization, this means that they cannot be located on the organization charts, that their existence had not been planned by those who control the organization, and that many of the functions they perform that affect the larger organization are unplanned. Thus the formation of the informal work group found in the Hawthorne plant of the Western Electric Company had not been planned by the company hierarchy and, though this group functioned to affect the large organization—controlled output, influenced worker satisfaction, and the like—these functions had also not been planned.[9] Similarly, the face-to-face group, found by Lazarsfeld and his associates to have such a great influence on voting decisions, is an informal group in relation to the formal structure of the democratic election process. Just as the informal work group cannot be found in the organization charts of a business enterprise, so the face-to-face voting group exercises a form of influence on the voting decision, the existence of which has not been considered in the traditional theories of the way in which a democracy operates.[10]

In the same way, the internal operations of many small groups are characterized by their informality. This means that the structures (communications patterns, influence hierarchies, etc.) and/or the functions (limiting output, providing affective satisfactions, influencing votes, etc.) of the group have not been planned by its members.

But to maintain that all face-to-face groups are informal would be to ignore a wide variety of face-to-face groups whose operations affect the political system. Most of the literature in which the small group was "rediscovered," it is true, deals with informal groups whose existence is unplanned by the larger systems of which they are parts; this is perhaps

[9] The Hawthorne studies have been reported in numerous places. See, for instance, F. J. Roethlisberger and William J. Dickson, *Management and the Worker* (Cambridge, Mass.: Harvard University Press, 1947); and Homans, *op.cit.*

[10] See Paul A. Lazarsfeld, Bernard Berelson, and Helen Gaudet, *The People's Choice* (New York: Columbia University Press, 1948); Bernard Berelson, Paul Lazarsfeld, and William N. McPhee, *Voting* (Chicago: University of Chicago Press, 1954); and Bernard Berelson, "Democratic Theory and Public Opinion," *Public Opinion Quarterly*, *16* (1952), pp. 313-30.

why they had to be "rediscovered." But the theories of small group behavior with which we shall deal apply as well to face-to-face groups found within the formal structure of larger organizations (juries, committees, cells in the Communist Party, etc.) and to groups whose internal operations are governed by formal rules and procedures (chaired committees, courts, etc.). The key role played by informal groups ought not to obscure the significant part that these formal small groups play in larger social systems. The study of leadership in the small group will, therefore, deal with leadership in both formal and informal groups.

Although small groups are found in both the formal and the informal structures of organizations, there is a sense in which it is valid to link the small group phenomenon with the informal aspects of organizational behavior. Small group interaction, because of certain characteristics of face-to-face contact, will tend toward the informal end of the continuum that runs from the formal to the informal aspects of organizational behavior. That individuals in face-to-face contact have some impression of the other group members as individuals introduces into that interaction a certain diffuseness that is not necessarily introduced by other means of organizational communication in which contact is more limited. This is especially the case because of the increase in affective relationship that accompanies face-to-face interaction. And with the development of diffuse and affective contact, group behavior will become less directly connected with the formal structure of which it is a part. Patterns of interaction not specified in the organizational charts will begin to appear. Of course, the degree of affectivity and diffuseness varies greatly among different small groups. On the one hand, there is the family, deeply affective, diffuse, spontaneous, and long-lived; on the other, experimental groups and committees, with little affectivity or permanence. Numerous writers have pointed out the distinction between these two types of small groups, and we shall at several points in this study have to consider the differences between them. Both types, however, fall under the rubric of the small group, as that term is used here.

15

Certain significant characteristics of the small group have now been pointed out. But why, as a political scientist, study the small group? Can such a study tell us something about individual political behavior, about the working of political systems, and about the particular interest of this book, political leadership? And is the creation of artificial experimental groups a useful approach to the understanding of political affairs? These are the questions the present study will attempt to answer.

Plan of the Study

Chapter II attempts to demonstrate the relevance of small group analysis to political behavior by specifying the many significant roles that on-going face-to-face groups play in the political process. The small group is shown to be a key building block of political systems and a variable that cannot be ignored in political analysis.

Chapters III and IV deal with the experimental method as a tool for political analysis. Chapter III spells out the special characteristics of laboratory studies of group behavior, and Chapter IV deals with the problem of relating experimental studies to on-going social processes.

Chapter V compares and contrasts the concept of leadership used in small group studies with that used in political studies.

Chapters VI and VII deal with an aspect of the leadership process found in both small groups and on-going systems— the need to maintain instrumental achievement and affective satisfactions at the same time. The ways in which the process operates on the two levels are compared.

Chapter VIII uses small group analysis to explore the relationship between leadership and the norms of the group. Some attention is paid to the question of change in groups conceived of as being in a state of equilibrium.

Chapters IX and X deal with the "participation hypothesis," one of the most widely cited findings of small group research. Some of the difficulties associated with applying small group findings to political affairs are discussed.

Chapter II

THE PRIMARY GROUP AND POLITICS

To UNDERSTAND the processes of government, one must look beyond its formal structure. Realizing this, political scientists have studied non-governmental organizations—parties, pressure groups, and the like—as well as the impact of the individual personality on political affairs. But a significant level lies between that of the organization and of the individual personality: the level of the face-to-face group. These groups —families, committees, juries, informal discussion groups, face-to-face groups of all sorts—are basic units of the political system. Analysis of the many roles they play in the political process should further our understanding of that process.

The Rediscovery of the Primary Group

Social thought in the twentieth century has emphasized the contrast between the traditional, communal society and the modern, industrial society. In the small, intimate, traditional community, the member's participation is as a total individual; in the mass society, his participation is in large impersonal organizations and is limited to specific functions. The political process in the traditional society is characterized by the importance of family ties and personal loyalties. In the mass society, on the other hand, secondary relationships play the important roles. Communication is effected via the mass media. Impersonal bureaucracies and large organizations such as political parties and pressure groups perform the political functions carried on in traditional societies by families and cliques. This distinction between the modern and the traditional has proven particularly fruitful in characterizing the differences between the political process in Western nations and the political process in the new nations of Asia and Africa.[1]

[1] On the contrast between Western and non-Western political systems, see Gabriel Almond, "Comparative Political Systems," *Journal of Politics* 18 (1956), pp. 391-409; and Francis X. Sutton, "Social Theory and Com-

The distinction has, however, been modified by the "rediscovery" of the primary group in modern industrial societies. The "rediscovery" of the primary group refers to the realization by researchers that systems previously thought of as purely impersonal and formal are greatly influenced by networks of informal personal relations.[2] There are several significant aspects to this "rediscovery." In the first place, the researchers had not expected to find that primary relationships were important. For example, "Just as in the study of mass communications and voting intentions where the research blueprint gave no inkling of the possible relevance of interpersonal relations, so here, in the case of the mass production factory . . . nothing less than a *discovery* that the 'model' was wrong could have revealed that primary relationships were in operation and were *relevant to productivity*."[3] Secondly, these primary relationships were discovered in what might be called the heart of the modern industrial society—in those structures that most closely approach the ideal type of a rational-legal system. Primary relationships have been found to play a significant role in industrial plants, on the street corner of the large city, in modern armies, and as a mediator between the individual and the mass media.[4] What is especially important is that these primary relation-

parative Politics," a paper prepared for a conference under the auspices of the Committee on Comparative Politics of the Social Science Research Council, Princeton, N.J., June 1955. Mimeographed.

[2] The rediscovery of the primary group has been discussed in Edward Shils, "The Study of the Primary Group," in Daniel Lerner and Harold Lasswell, eds., *The Policy Sciences* (Stanford, Calif.: Stanford University Press, 1951); Katz and Lazarsfeld, *Personal Influence*, Part I; and Harold H. Kelley and John W. Thibault, "Experimental Studies of Group Problem Solving and Process," in Gardner Lindzey, ed., *The Handbook of Social Psychology* (Cambridge, Mass.: Addison-Wesley, 1954), Vol. II, chap. 21.

[3] Katz and Lazarsfeld, *op.cit.*, p. 36.

[4] See Roethlisberger and Dickson, *Management and the Worker*; William F. Whyte, *Street Corner Society* (Chicago: University of Chicago Press, 1943); Edward A. Shils, "Primary Groups in the American Army," in Robert K. Merton and Paul F. Lazarsfeld, eds., *Studies in the Scope and Method of "The American Soldier"* (Glencoe, Ill.: Free Press, 1950); Edward A. Shils and Morris Janowitz, "Cohesion and Disintegration of the Wehrmacht in World War II," *Pub. Opinion Q.*, 12 (1948), pp. 280-315; Lazarsfeld, *et al.*, *The People's Choice*; Berelson, *et al.*, *Voting*; and Katz and Lazarsfeld, *op.cit.*

ships—often informal and unplanned as far as the larger system is concerned—affect the operation of that system.

It would be futile to try to catalogue all the face-to-face groups in which decisions affecting the political system are made. All political systems tend to be formally divided into small units which reach significant decisions. These range from formally organized face-to-face groups at the highest levels of national policy-making—the Supreme Court or the National Security Council—down to the myriad committees and sub-committees in which important local government decisions are made. Added to these are numerous informal face-to-face groups ranging from the chance conversation with friend or neighbor that influences a citizen's vote to the informal channels of communication between the President and Congress. The bulk of significant political decisions, one might well argue, are made neither by individual, autonomous decision-makers (in our society, at least, Hitlers and Stalins are rare) nor by all the members of the political system, by the electorate, or by the rank and file of a political party. It is to the face-to-face group that one must look if one is to find the locus of decision-making in political systems.[5]

A brief glance at a typical political decision—a law passed by Congress, for instance—will suffice to illustrate the vast influence of formal and informal face-to-face groups on political decisions. Under our constitutional and legal system the authority of Congress to make laws derives from its conformity to a written set of rules found in the Constitution. According to this set of rules, the process by which a law is passed is highly formal and impersonal. The members of Congress

[5] The classic account by Robert Michels in *Political Parties* (Glencoe, Ill.: Free Press, 1949) of some of the reasons why decisions in large organizations tend to concentrate in a few hands is still pertinent. James, *Am. Soc. Rev.* (1951), presents some significant but preliminary evidence on this point. On the basis of a questionnaire sent to numerous business and governmental organizations, he found that "action-taking groups" (groups in which actual decisions are made) tend to number between two and seven members. Also relevant is the hypothesis suggested by Richard C. Snyder and Glenn D. Paige that "When crucial choices are forced on an organization from the environment the decisional sub-system will be characterized by smaller decisional units and a simpler role structure." ("The United States Decision to Resist Aggression in Korea," *Administrative Science Quarterly*, 3 [1958], p. 362.)

derive their authority to partake in the deliberations and decisions of that body from the fact that they are elected by the citizens of their respective states. As institutionalized, the electoral process epitomizes political decision-making in the "mass" society. Each citizen, as he enters the voting booth, faces the political system as a solitary, rational individual. The election clerk who counts the ballots is the only mediator between the voting decision and the governmental system, and his role is rigidly defined and his function a purely mechanical one. Similarly the process of decision-making in the Congress is highly mechanical and impersonal, as described in the Constitution. Each member has one vote and casts it as an individual. The votes are tallied and, if a measure receives a majority in both houses, it goes to the President. The process is formal and unambiguous.

Of course, the elective-legislative process of decision-making does not operate this way. At each stage, primary face-to-face contacts act as intermediaries in the decision. These face-to-face contacts are both formal and informal. Between the individual voter and the ballot box stands a wide variety of primary contacts that influence his vote. Districts tend to be formally divided into smaller sub-districts, precincts, and blocks, within which personal canvassing by the candidate or his supporters plays an important role. Candidates—especially for seats in the House of Representatives—often campaign on a "friends and neighbors" basis, asking support as long-term, well-known residents of the area. Furthermore, the voter is influenced by face-to-face contacts formally unrelated to the election process. These may take the form of political discussions with friends, family, or work associates.

Decisions within the Congress are even more obviously influenced by a wide variety of formal and informal face-to-face contacts. Both houses of Congress are divided into formal committees and sub-committees in which many more important decisions are made than are made on the floor of the House or Senate. In many cases basic legislative policy is made in a sub-committee with only a handful of members, the rest of the House acting largely as a rubber stamp. Or a sub-committee can exercise the authority of the Congress in its relations with an administrative agency without receiving any specific approval from the whole chamber. Informal face-to-face contacts (i.e., contacts not specified in the rules of Congress) also play a substantial role in legislative decisions. These include informal "cloak-room" politicking among the members of Congress as well as informal pressures upon individual congressmen from sources external to Congress.

The small face-to-face group certainly plays a significant role in the political process. Though there has been much written about the impact of particular face-to-face groups on politics, little attempt has been made to study systematically the ways in which primary relationships in general affect the political process. The rest of this chapter will attempt at least the beginning of such a systematic study.

The analysis of the role of the face-to-face group will proceed on two levels: the level of the political behavior of the individual, and the level of the political system as a whole. On the first level, we shall attempt to describe the way in which the face-to-face group influences the political behavior of its members. On the second level, we shall attempt to assess the overall impact on the operation of political systems of the presence of face-to-face groups as significant sub-units. The face-to-face group will thus be looked at in terms of its impact downward upon its individual members and its impact upward upon the larger political system of which it is a part. Through the processes of political socialization that take place within face-to-face groups, the norms and values associated with the political system are transmitted downward to the individual members of that system. Conversely, it is in face-to-face groups that individual political demands are reinforced and communicated upward to the political institutions of a society. The study of the face-to-face group should thus help to close a gap that has developed in the study of politics —a gap between the analysis of individual political behavior and the analysis of the operation of the political system. The intervening effects of face-to-face groups serve as a link between these two levels; and an analysis of these intervening effects should improve our understanding of the political process.

But before dealing with the impact of the face-to-face group on the political behavior of individuals and on the operation of political systems, we shall examine the special characteristics of the small group that give it such impact. For this we turn to a consideration of the pressures for conformity in the face-to-face group.

Pressures to Conform in the Face-to-Face Group

It is well known that the face-to-face groups to which an individual belongs exert a powerful influence over him; that he will accept the norms and standards of the group. It has in fact been suggested that "All other factors remaining equal, the control that is exercised by a group over an individual member is inverse to the size of the group."[6] Furthermore, ". . . a cardinal fact concerning the behavior of individual members in any collective situation stands out in high relief: the fact that once an individual identifies himself with a group and its collective actions, his behavior is, in a major way, determined by the direction of the group action, whatever this direction may be, good or bad, constructive or destructive."[7]

Numerous small group studies document the influence of the group on the individual. When the opinions of other group members are revealed to the individual, even if no other pressures are applied, he will change his views to conform more closely to that of the group. This takes place even in those cases where the group opinion is not objectively more correct than that of the individual or is objectively wrong. That individuals tend to conform to the norms of the group is one of the best documented generalizations in the small group litera-

[6] Richard T. La Piere, *A Theory of Social Control* (New York: McGraw-Hill, 1954), p. 101.

[7] Muzafer Sherif and Hadley Cantril, *The Psychology of Ego-Involvements, Social Attitudes and Identifications* (New York: John Wiley, 1947), p. 290.

ture. This conformity has been found in both on-going and experimental groups.[8]

Why should there be this tendency for the individual member to conform to the group? Several explanations may be offered. Festinger suggests that pressure to conform to the views of the group comes from the desire of the individual to reduce the unpleasantness of a situation of "cognitive dissonance" between his views and the views of the group. The opinions of those around us are used as a means of testing the validity of our own opinions. This is the case, as the Asch experiments suggest, even when there is a clear objective referent for our opinions, but it is more the case with those

[8] See Muzafer Sherif, "An Experimental Approach to the Study of Attitudes," *Sociometry*, 1 (1937), pp. 90-98; and Sherif, "A Study of Some Social Factors in Perception," *Archives of Psychology*, 27 (1935), No. 185. Experimental subjects were asked to judge the distance which a point of light in a darkened room moved. The light was in fact stationary but, owing to the so-called "auto-kinetic" effect, it gave the illusion of movement. When individuals were asked to judge the distance after another person had made his judgment, the individuals tended to change their previous judgments to conform to those made by the other group members.

In a study by Asch, the opinion of the group was objectively wrong. Yet, when faced with the unanimous opposition of group members, experimental subjects changed their judgment to conform to the group opinion even though the subject they were asked about was one for which there was a clear empirical referent—the length of lines. When asked to judge the length of the lines in private, individuals had a 99 per cent correct record of judgments. In the group situation, this figure fell to 68 per cent. See Solomon Asch, "Effects of Group Pressure on Modification and Distortion of Judgment," in Harold Guetzkow, ed., *Groups, Leadership and Men* (Pittsburgh: Carnegie Press, 1951).

For evidence of this proposition as applied to on-going groups, see, among others, Homans, *op.cit.*; Leon Festinger, Stanley Schachter, and Kurt W. Back, *Social Pressures in Informal Groups*, (New York: Harper, 1950), chaps. 5 and 6; and Shils, in Merton and Lazarsfeld, eds., *Studies in the Scope and Method of "The American Soldier."* Conformity in experimental situations is demonstrated in the work by Sherif and Asch cited above, and in K. Back, "Influence Through Social Communication," *Journal of Abnormal and Social Psychology*, 46 (1951), pp. 9-23; S. Schachter, "Deviation, Rejection and Communication," *ibid.*, pp. 196-207; and S. Schachter, *et al.*, "Cross-Cultural Experiments in Threat and Rejection," *Human Relations*, 7 (1954), pp. 403-40.

The standard procedure in experimental studies is to record the opinion or judgment of the experimental subject, expose him in some way to the opinion or judgment of the group (or some other form of group pressure), and then record his opinion or judgment again. The difference between his performance on the pre-test and on the post-test is assumed to have been caused by the intervening group interaction. See Chapter III for a fuller discussion of the experimental methods used; and Chapter VIII for a fuller discussion of group norms.

political and social opinions for which there is no clear and easy test except comparison with the opinions of our fellows. In such testing situations, there is pressure on the individual to change his opinion if it differs from the opinions of others around him. These pressures come both from the individual himself and from the other group members, since the condition of dissonance will be unpleasant to both the deviant and the other group members.[9]

Another formulation of the source of pressure to conform to the norms of the group is suggested by Argyle. For the individual group member, the internal pressure to conform comes from a ". . . need . . . for acceptance by groups." The external pressure that the group places on the individual derives from the threat posed by deviant opinions to the attainment of the group goal—especially in those cases where the attainment of the goal requires cooperative action.[10] Under either the Festinger or the Argyle formulation, deviance from group opinion will be followed both by pressures within the individual to change in the direction of the group norm, and by external pressures from the other group members on the individual deviant.

There is much evidence for both types of pressure in the small group literature. In the Asch and Sherif experiments just cited, there was no overt group pressure on the experimental subjects to change their opinions, except for the simple statement of group opinion. Yet the mere knowledge that the other group members had a different opinion led the experimental subjects to change.[11] The more attractive the group,

[9] See Leon Festinger, "A Theory of Social Comparative Processes," *Hum. Rel.*, 7 (1954), pp. 117-40; and Festinger, *A Theory of Cognitive Dissonance* (Evanston, Ill.: Row, Peterson, 1957).

[10] Michael Argyle, *The Scientific Study of Human Behavior* (London: Methuen, 1957), pp. 157-58.

[11] Asch lists three categories into which the yielding subjects (i.e., those who conformed to the incorrect majority judgment) fall. A few subjects actually saw the lines as being as the majority declared. Their perception of reality changed under group pressure. Of greater interest to us are the other two categories of yielding subjects. The largest number of yielders perceived that the length of the lines did not conform to the judgments being expressed by the majority, but decided that their own perceptions must be inaccurate and those of the majority correct. They were led to doubt their own perception by the group opinion. A third group perceived the lines

the greater will be the internalized pressures to conform. Back reports an experimental confirmation of this point. In highly cohesive groups (groups in which membership was highly valued) members were more likely to change their opinions in the direction of the group norm than in cases where group membership was not highly valued.[12]

There is also ample evidence for the existence of external pressures that the group places upon the individual deviant to bring him into conformity with the group norms. Evidence for overt pressures to conform and sanctions for conformity can be found in the fact that in experimental small groups more communication tends to be directed to deviants than to non-deviants, and that those who deviate from the group norm tend to be rejected by the group.[13] In studies of on-going groups, evidence for this rejection was found by Newcomb among college girls, by Kelley and Volkhart among members of a boy scout troop, and by Festinger, Schachter, and Back among residents of a housing project.[14] In all cases, those whose opinions differed from the opinions of the majority in the group tended to receive fewer choices from other group members when the group members were asked to select those whom they liked best. And, using experimental groups in this country and seven European countries, Schachter found that instructed group members who played deviant roles tended to be rejected by the other group members.[15]

---

correctly and believed that the group was wrong, but conformed to the group norm overtly so as not to appear different from the other group members and to avoid possible ridicule. In this last category, although the group made no overt attempt to enforce conformity (there was no ridicule of or threat of rejection for a non-conforming opinion), the experimental subjects had internalized the group pressures. Solomon Asch, *Social Psychology* (New York: Prentice-Hall, 1952), pp. 465-73.

[12] Back, *J. Abnorm. Soc. Psych.* (1951); and H. H. Kelley and E. H. Volkhart, "The Resistance to Change of Group-Anchored Attitudes," *Am. Soc. Rev.*, *17* (1952), pp. 453-65. See also Festinger, Schachter, and Back, *Social Pressures* . . . , p. 166.

[13] Leon Festinger and John W. Thibault, "Interpersonal Communications in Small Groups," *J. Abnorm. Soc. Psych.*, *46* (1951), pp. 92-99.

[14] Theodore M. Newcomb, *Personality and Social Change* (New York: Dryden Press, 1943); Kelley and Volkhart, *op.cit.*; and Festinger, Schachter, and Back, *Social Pressures* . . . , chaps. 5 and 6.

[15] Schachter, *J. Abnorm. Soc. Psych.* (1951); and Schachter, *et al., Hum. Rel.* (1954). Of course conformity is a two-way process. Not only does the

Groups influence the opinions and norms of the group members because of (1) the individual needs that the group fulfills (both affective needs and opinion evaluation), coupled with (2) the internal pressures within the individual to be accepted by the group and (3) the external pressures and sanctions that the group places on the non-conforming member. There are several other reasons why face-to-face contact can have a greater effect on opinions than other forms of contact. Studies of mass media have shown that audiences are highly selective; they will usually select only those communications that support their previous point of view.[16] Through selection, mass media communications can be kept from challenging an individual's opinions. But not so with the face-to-face group. One cannot as easily tune out or ignore communications that are hostile to one's point of view. Thus Asch points out that all the subjects in his experiment on the effects of group opinion on individual judgment—even those subjects who remained independent and did not change their opinion in the face of the unanimous group —felt anxiety when faced with the opposition of the group. Under the circumstances of the experiment in which the other group members were present, the group could be opposed but it could not be ignored.[17]

It was pointed out earlier that relations within small face-to-face groups tend to be diffuse. This diffuseness gives the small group a potentiality for influencing individual opinion that larger, more specifically goal-oriented organizations do not have. This diffuseness, coupled with the greater "presence" of face-to-face contact, is one of the reasons why primary contacts have such a great influence on voting choices.

The weight of personal contacts upon opinion lies, paradoxically, in their greater casualness and non-purposiveness in political matters. If we read or tune in a speech, we usually

group attempt to enforce adoption of its norms by members, but individuals tend to join groups in which the opinions, values, and norms are similar to their own. See J. A. Precker, "Similarity of Values as a Factor in Selection of Peers and Near-Authority Figures," *J. Abnorm. Soc. Psych.*, 47 (1952), pp. 406-14.

16 See, for instance, Berelson, *et al.*, *Voting*, chap. 11.

17 Asch, in Guetzkow, ed., *Groups, Leadership* . . . , p. 183.

do so purposefully, and in doing so we have a definite mental set which tinges our receptiveness. Such purposive behavior is part of the broad area of our political experiences, to which we bring our convictions with a desire to test them and strengthen them by what is said. This mental set is armor against influence. The extent to which people, and particularly those with strong partisan views, listen to speakers and read articles with which they agree in advance is evidence on this point.

On the other hand, people we meet for other reasons than political discussions are more likely to catch us unprepared, so to speak, if they make politics the topic. . . . Personal influence is more pervasive and less self-selective than the formal media.[18]

The pressures on the individual member that derive from participation in a face-to-face group can best be illustrated by a consideration of the process of decision-making in that group. Insofar as group membership is important to the members, there will be pressure for consensus in order to avoid overt conflicts within the group, conflicts that would be disturbing both to the group and to the individual member. Furthermore, the decisional process will tend to be such as to prevent overt conflicts from coming to the surface. Formal votes, for instance, will be avoided.

This pattern of decision-making is most evident in those cases in which group membership is highly important to the individual—in traditional groups, for instance, where relations among members are diffuse, deeply affective, and have existed for an extended period. Faris describes the process of social control in a community of 200 Englishmen living on the isolated island of Tristan da Cunha. There was no need for a police force or any formal means of securing obedience to community decisions. " 'What people will think' has the force of law, and the most extreme penalties were public teasing and the refusal to speak to an offender."[19] Similarly, decisions at meetings of traditional Japanese village councils have also been observed to be made without a formal structure. At some

[18] Lazarsfeld, *et al.*, *The People's Choice*, p. 152.
[19] Robert E. Faris, "Development of the Small Group Research Movement," in Sherif and Wilson, eds., *Group Relations at the Crossroads* (New York: Harper, 1953), p. 158.

point in the meeting, the chairman or some other group member merely announces the consensus of the group.[20] Though this process is characteristic of traditional systems, it is also found among those political groups in Western societies that have a history of long and intimate contact. Thus Duverger reports that among the many modern political parties run by a caucus, decisions are often made by tacit agreement, rather than by formal vote.[21] And, as McKenzie points out, the leader of the Conservative Party in Britain is selected by acclamation rather than ballot. He quotes the views of an MP that ". . . great leaders of the party are not elected, they are evolved. . . . The leader is there, and we all know it when he is there." If there is a serious division on naming the new party leader (as there was at the time of the selection of Bonar Law in 1911) the solution is usually a compromise candidate also selected by acclamation.[22]

Decisions by acclamation or consensus do not necessarily imply that there is no opposition to the group decision. Although consensus decisions that serve the interests of all group members are more likely in small intimate groups with a long history than in larger, less intimate organizations, the tendency for decisions to be made by consensus rather than by vote stems more from a desire to avoid challenging the solidarity of the group by overt dispute than from agreement with the decision. Even those who disagree will not do so openly

[20] Robert E. Ward, "The Socio-Political Role of the Buraku (Hamlet) in Japan," *American Political Science Review, 45* (1950), p. 1030. A similar point can be made about decision-making in primitive tribes. "Those who have lived among savage or barbarous peoples in several parts of the world have related how they have attended native councils where matters in which they were interested were being discussed. When, after a time, the English observer found that the people were discussing some wholly different topic, and inquired when they were going to decide the question in which he was interested, he was told it had already been decided and that they had passed on to other business. . . . The members of the council had become aware at a certain point that they were in agreement, and it was not necessary to bring the agreement explicitly to notice." William Halse Rivers, *Instinct and Unconscious* (Cambridge: Cambridge University Press, 1924), pp. 95ff., quoted in Erich Kahler, *The Tower and the Abyss* (New York: George Braziller, 1957), p. 8.

[21] Maurice Duverger, *Political Parties* (London: Methuen, 1954), p. 18.

[22] R. T. McKenzie, *British Political Parties* (London: Heinemann, 1955), pp. 52ff.

in order to preserve at least the semblance of group cohesion. The British MP quoted by McKenzie stated that "I think it will be a bad day [when we] . . . have solemnly to meet to elect a leader."[23] Where the solidarity of the group is highly valued, a formal vote with its revelations of division in the group will not be considered a desirable means of decision-making. As one of the members of the Nortons, William Whyte's street corner gang, put it: "It's better not to have a constitution and vote on all these things. As soon as you begin deciding questions by taking a vote, you'll see that some fellows are for you and some are against you, and in that way factions develop. It's best to get everybody to agree first, and then you don't have to vote."[24] Even in groups in which a formal voting process is institutionalized, members may not express views that disagree with the majority if the goal of group solidarity is highly valued. As Alpheus Mason points out: "During the early days of Taft's Chief Justiceship, it was not unusual for Justices to write on the back of circulated slip opinions: 'I shall acquiesce in silence unless someone else dissents'; or 'I do not agree, but shall submit.' For the sake of harmony, staunch individualists such as Holmes, Brandeis, and Stone, though disagreeing, would sometimes go along with the majority."[25]

The Small Group and Political Behavior

The fact that individual group members will, under certain circumstances, suppress their own views in order to conform to the dominant group position brings us to the first level of analysis of the impact of the face-to-face group on the political process—its impact on the attitudes, opinions, and behavior of group members. The face-to-face groups to which an individual belongs exert a major influence on him. This influence may be looked upon as taking place in two time

---

[23] McKenzie, op.cit., p. 52.
[24] Whyte, Street Corner Society, p. 96.
[25] Alpheus T. Mason, The Supreme Court from Taft to Warren (Baton Rouge, La.: Louisiana State University Press, 1958) p. 58. Of course when the external issues of the cases themselves become more important than the maintenance of internal solidarity large numbers of dissenting opinions appeared.

periods. In the first place, the primary group plays a major role in the political socialization of the individual before he enters the political process. It forms the predispositions that an individual brings with him into his participation in political affairs. Secondly, the primary groups to which an individual belongs continue to shape his political behavior after he has begun to participate in the political process.

An individual does not enter the political arena totally unprepared. The nature of his first political act—whether it be a vote or the equally significant political act of not voting when the opportunity arises; obeying a law or disobeying a law; showing interest in political affairs or avoiding political affairs—will to a large extent have been determined by the set of predispositions he brings with him from his experience in primary groups. "Whatever changes the New Age may bring, person-to-person relationships and primary groups will remain the basic character-forming agencies of society."[26] Primary group experiences influence an individual's political behavior in several ways. In such groups individuals develop non-political personality traits and general expectations from interpersonal relations. These traits and interpersonal expectations first receive specifically political content when the individual faces a particular political situation. Or the influence of the primary group can be more directly and manifestly political. Within the primary group, individuals may learn generalized attitudes toward government and the state. These general attitudes include trust and confidence in government, respect for the state and its symbols, respect for law, and the like. On the other hand, the political attitudes learned in the primary group may be quite specific. These may be support for a particular party or issue.

THE POLITICAL PERSONALITY: The influence of personality traits on political behavior has been stressed in political science for a number of years. The early works of Harold Lasswell, as well as recent works on the authoritarian personality,

[26] Karl Mannheim, *Freedom, Power and Democratic Planning* (London: Routledge and Kegan Paul, 1951), p. 181.

suggest that much political behavior is a projection of private needs and emotions onto the political sphere.[27] What is of particular interest here is the way in which the authority system in the primary group (what one might call the political system of the family) influences the expectations of the individual in regard to authority in the larger political system. Within the primary group, the individual receives training for roles that he will later play within society. This training consists in both the teaching of certain standards of behavior that can be applied to later situations and, perhaps more significantly, the playing of roles in the family and in other primary groups that are similar to roles later to be played in the political or economic system.

The type of political structure the child experiences in the family will affect the type of participation that the child will have in other social structures. In a study of ethnocentrism among children, Else Frenkel-Brunswik found that the degree of prejudice among children was related to the family atmosphere. Ethnocentric children tended to come from families in which the authority figure (the father) was strict and rigid, and in which the parent-child relationship was one of dominance and submission. Unprejudiced children came more often from families characterized by a more affectionate and less rigid relationship. It is especially significant that the prejudiced and non-prejudiced children had expectations in non-family role relationships similar to those developed in the family. When asked to describe the "ideal teacher," the two types of children gave quite different answers. Frenkel-Brunswik cites the typical responses of two non-prejudiced boys:

> Would carefully listen to your viewpoints and explain what's wrong and what's right about it, and let you argue it out instead of flatly telling you you are wrong. . . . If she can relate her own experiences in relation to some topic you are studying, it is interesting. Has the personality to keep order in the classroom and not afraid the pupils will dislike her if she does. Should accept a joke, but not let it go too far.

[27] Harold Lasswell, "Psychopathology and Politics," in *The Political Writings of Harold Lasswell* (Glencoe, Ill.: Free Press, 1951); and T. W. Adorno, *et al.*, *The Authoritarian Personality* (New York: Harper, 1950).

Fair in her attitude toward all pupils, doesn't favor one, explains the lessons and helps you within reason.

On the other hand, a highly ethnocentric girl replied: "Someone that is strict. If she asks for homework, you have to have it done. Most teachers are not strict enough. If the assigned work is not in you should be given a zero. She shouldn't let the class get out of hand."[28] Similarly, Baldwin, in a long-term and continuing study of power structure in the home, found that where the political system of the home was an open one—free communication in both directions between parents and children, some participation by children in family decisions, "fair" (not arbitrary) behavior on the part of parents—the children were better prepared to show initiative and participate fully in other role systems.[29]

Numerous writers have attempted to trace styles of political participation and types of political expectations back to early experiences in the family. Both Mannheim and Fromm emphasize that a stable and independent "democratic" personality, upon which at least to some extent democratic government depends, develops basically in the primary group.[30] Perhaps the major body of literature dealing with the impact of family training on political behavior is that of the "national character" school.[31] A large group of anthropologists and psychologists have attempted to find certain dominant psychological patterns within national societies. The patterns that characterize the "modal" person in that society are developed during earliest childhood experiences. Early childhood experiences may result in a personality that desires a submissive

[28] Else Frenkel-Brunswik, "Further Explorations by a Contributor to 'The Authoritarian Personality,'" in Richard Christie and Marie Jahoda, eds., *Studies in the Scope and Method of "The Authoritarian Personality"* (Glencoe, Ill.: Free Press, 1954), p. 239.

[29] A. Baldwin, "Socialization and the Parent-Child Relationship," in D. McClelland, ed., *Studies in Motivation* (New York: Appleton-Century-Crofts, 1955).

[30] Mannheim, *Freedom, Power . . .* , p. 181; and Erich Fromm, *Escape from Freedom* (New York: Farrar and Rinehart, 1941), pp. 287ff.

[31] For a general discussion of this school, see Nathan Leites, "Psychocultural Hypotheses About Political Acts," *World Politics*, 1 (1948), pp. 102-19; and Margaret Mead, "The Study of National Character," in Lerner and Lasswell, eds., *The Policy Sciences.*

relationship to authority,[32] a personality that alternates between acceptance and rejection of authority,[33] or a personality that thrives on signs of love and acceptance.[34] And these different personalities result in different political behavior in later life. Germans raised in authoritarian families, for instance, will want and expect political leaders to stand in such an authoritarian relationship to them.[35]

Many of the studies of the effects of early family experiences on political behavior have generalized too easily from childhood experiences to adult attitudes. The step from early socialization to political attitudes is a long one and, as we shall suggest below, can be fully understood only in terms of the intervening effects of other intermediate face-to-face contacts and of the political system itself.

TRAINING FOR POLITICAL PARTICIPATION: Small group experiences in childhood not only provide certain generalized expectations from political relationships; they also provide training for participation in these relationships. Much of this training of course takes place within the family, but it takes place in other face-to-face situations as well—in the classroom and, especially during adolescence, in the peer group. Furthermore, the training for political participation that takes place in face-to-face groups continues beyond childhood and adolescence.[36]

Participation in decisions in small face-to-face groups where

---

[32] David Rodnick, *Postwar Germans* (New Haven: Yale University Press, 1948); and Bertram Schaffner, *Fatherland: A Study of Authoritarianism in the German Family* (New York: Columbia University Press, 1948).

[33] Geoffrey Gorer, *The People of Great Russia* (London: Cresset Press, 1949); and Dinko Tomasic, *The Impact of Russian Culture on Soviet Communism* (Glencoe, Ill.: Free Press, 1953).

[34] Geoffrey Gorer, *The American People* (New York: W. W. Norton, 1948).

[35] Rodnick, *op.cit.* The same point is made by Fromm, *op.cit.*; Schaffner, *op.cit.*; and Kurt Lewin, *Resolving Social Conflicts* (New York: Harper, 1948).

[36] Cf. A. S. Maslow, "Power Relationships and Patterns of Personal Development," in Arthur Kornhauser, ed., *Problems of Power in American Democracy* (Detroit: Wayne University Press, 1957). The influence of the peer group is discussed in Sherif and Cantril, *Psychology of Ego-Involvements*, pp. 156-347. John Dewey argues that democratic techniques must permeate the family, the school, and the community to be effective. (*The Public and Its Problems*, Chicago: Gateway Books, 1946, chaps. 5 and 6.)

the individual can have some grasp of the alternatives available for choice is a preparation for participation in decisions that are more complex, less immediate, and engage only a small part of an individual's attention. According to Bryce, "An essential ingredient of a satisfactory democracy is that a considerable proportion of the people should have experience of active participation in the work of small self-governing groups, whether in connection with local government, trade unions, cooperatives or other forms of activity."[37] Some writers have in fact maintained that democracy is possible only in situations in which relations are predominantly face-to-face in nature.[38]

Much of the literature on the authoritarian family suggests that a democratic political system is difficult, if not impossible, to achieve unless there is experience in democratic participation within the family. Levy, for instance, on the basis of his studies of Nazis and anti-Nazis, concluded that democracy could not be introduced into Germany simply by removing authoritarian controls, since there was not sufficient training for democratic participation among the German people.[39] Similarly, it can be argued that an absence of participation in decisions in other face-to-face situations outside the family will affect the level of participation in the broader political system. Crozier, on the basis of a study of administration in

[37] James Bryce, *Modern Democracies*, Vol. I (New York: Macmillan, 1921), p. 132.

[38] G. D. H. Cole, for instance, maintains that men "can control great affairs only by acting together in the control of small affairs, and finding, through the experience of neighborhood, men whom they can entrust with larger decisions than they can make rationally for themselves. Democracy can work in the great States (and *a fortiori* between great States or over Europe or the world) only if each State is made up of a host of little democracies, and rests finally, not on isolated individuals, but on groups small enough to express the spirit of neighborhood and personal acquaintance. . . . Democracies have either to be small, or to be broken up into small, human groups in which men and women can know and love one another." G. D. H. Cole, *Essays in Social Theory* (London: Macmillan, 1950), pp. 94-95. Cf. J. J. Rousseau, *The Social Contract* (London: Everyman's, 1931), p. 55.

[39] David M. Levy, "Anti-Nazis: Criteria of Differentiation," in Alfred H. Stanton and Stewart E. Perry, eds., *Personality and Political Crisis* (Glencoe, Ill.: Free Press, 1951). The importance of primary group participation as a basis for a democratic political system is stressed in Lewin, "The Special Case of Germany," in *Resolving Social Conflicts*.

French government agencies and industrial organizations, notes a complete absence of participatory leadership. Social distance between different levels in the various organizations is great, and there is little communication. Organizational relations are characterized by a "fear of face-to-face contacts" and a "constant recourse to impersonality."[40] Charles Micaud, who cites the Crozier work, suggests that this lack of face-to-face participation is one reason for the combination of a highly centralized state and highly atomized society in France. Lack of participation leads to an *espoir millénariste* and a desire to escape from political activity. If there were greater participation in primary groups, there might be greater political participation.[41]

Participation in decisions on levels below that of the political system is a requisite or, at least, a desirable adjunct to a democratic political system. In the first place, insofar as significant political decisions are made in such sub-groups, effective participation in the political system will not exist

---

[40] Michel Crozier, "La France, Terre de Commandement," *Esprit*, 25 (1957), pp. 779-98; and Crozier, "Pour une Sociologie de l'Administration Publique," *Revue Française de Science Politique*, 6 (1956), pp. 750-69.

[41] Charles Micaud, unpublished manuscript on the French Left, chap. 2. Micaud cites Charles Bettelheim and Suzanne Frère, who point out the low level of participation in face-to-face relations in *Une Ville Française Moyenne: Auxerre en 1950* (Paris: Armand Colin, 1950). Only 18 per cent of the men and 38 per cent of the women of Auxerre visit each other. They do belong to a large number of interest groups, but these are centrally organized with headquarters in Paris. This is supported in Roy V. Peel, *The Political Clubs of New York* (New York: Putnam's 1945), who found that France had none of the diffuse, social-political local clubs found in American cities. A similar finding is reported by Lawrence Wylie, *Village in the Vaucluse* (Cambridge, Mass.: Harvard University Press, 1957). See also Edward C. Banfield, *The Moral Basis of a Backward Society* (Glencoe, Ill.: Free Press, 1958), for a similar, but more extreme, situation in a southern Italian village.

The view that the type of participation in the face-to-face group will be similar to the type of participation on other levels is supported by some findings in a different context from the one discussed above. It has been found in military and industrial situations that leaders of lower-level, face-to-face groups tend to stress participation of the group members in decisions if the leaders in the hierarchy above them also stress participation. The style of leadership in the higher levels of the organization is directly related to the style on lower levels. See Stanley Seashore, "Administrative Leadership and Organizational Effectiveness," in Rensis Likert and Samuel P. Hayes, eds., *Some Applications of Behavioral Research* (Paris: UNESCO, 1957), p. 57; and Edwin A. Fleischman, "Leadership Climate, Human Relations Training and Supervisory Behavior," *Personnel Psychology*, 6 (1953), pp. 205-22.

unless members can participate on these lower levels. Further-more, participation in decisions is much easier within smaller units. In larger units, the organizational necessities associated with a larger structure make participation difficult, if not impossible. Bureaucratic structures, introduced to bring rationality into the organization, limit participation. The decision process and the effects of decisions are less visible. Communication on an organization-wide basis requires the use of formal media, more easily controlled by the hierarchy. And the complexity of decisions is likely to limit the ability of the individual members to comprehend the issues involved.[42] Evidence of the rarity of participation by members in organization decisions is found in numerous studies.[43] The proposition is also supported by the finding in numerous small group studies that as the size of the group increases, there is a tendency toward less free participation on the part of group members and toward the concentration of group activities in the hands of a single leader.[44]

The most complete study of the relationship between the existence of small sub-units in which individuals can participate and organizational democracy is that of the International

[42] These reasons why participation is difficult, if not impossible, in large organizations are essentially the ones suggested by Michels, *Political Parties*, pp. 2-44, 130-35, 185-204, and *passim*. Cf. Seymour M. Lipset, Martin A. Trow, and James S. Coleman, *Union Democracy: The Internal Politics of the International Typographical Union* (Glencoe, Ill.: Free Press, 1956), pp. 9-10.

[43] Michels (*op.cit.*) is still the classic study on the German Socialist Party and trade unions. See also Duverger, *Political Parties*, pp. 151-68; Oliver Garceau, *The Political Life of the AMA* (Cambridge, Mass.: Harvard University Press, 1941); and David Truman, *The Governmental Process* (New York: Alfred A. Knopf, 1951), pp. 139-55.

[44] Carter and his associates found that as group size is increased from four to eight members, a more restricted atmosphere develops. "In the group of four, each individual has sufficient latitude of space in which to behave and thus the basic abilities of each individual can be expressed; but in the larger group only the more forceful individuals are able to express their abilities and ideas, since the amount of freedom in the situation is not sufficient to accommodate all the group members." Launor Carter, *et al.*, "The Relation of Categorization and Rating in the Observation of Group Behavior," *Hum. Rel.*, 4 (1951), p. 250.

Similar results are reported by Bales, *et al.*, "Channels of Communications in Small Groups," *Am. Soc. Rev.*, *16* (1951) pp. 461-68; and by F. F. Stephan and E. G. Mischler, "The Distribution of Participation in Small Groups: An Exponential Approximation," *Am. Soc. Rev.*, *17* (1952), pp. 598-608.

Typographical Union carried on by Lipset, Trow, and Coleman. Unlike most other unions, the ITU has maintained a democratic system. This is attributed by the authors to the existence of numerous formal and informal sub-groups to which the members belong. Most of these sub-groups are formally apolitical and deal with social affairs, but they perform a number of important political functions. They are centers of communication about what is going on in the union. Through them, members develop interest in union affairs and are drawn into participation in union politics. Participation in the sub-units also trains potential leaders for union office—training that otherwise would have to take place within the organizational hierarchy. Thus a pool of potential leaders not necessarily committed to the existing leadership is developed. Furthermore, the sub-units serve as possible alternate power centers to challenge the leadership hierarchy. The maintenance of democracy in the large organization—the ITU—is, therefore, highly dependent upon the existence of sub-groups in which members can participate, even though these groups are not formally political.[45]

SMALL GROUP ROLES AND POLITICAL ROLES: Though experiences within primary groups profoundly influence political behavior, one cannot accept any simple primary group monism and look for the explanation of all political behavior within the family, the peer group, and other primary groups. Political behavior is not determined solely by the predispositions that an individual brings into the political process from his experiences and training in primary groups. It is also affected by the way in which the political system interacts with these predispositions. The political system can channel political behavior in a number of directions. Insofar as political predispositions are molded in childhood, they are developed in essentially non-political situations. The point is obvious but significant. It means that predictions that can be made about adult political behavior on the basis of childhood experiences will be limited to a rather general set of predis-

[45] Lipset, Trow, and Coleman, *op.cit.*, chaps. 4-9.

positions that an individual brings into the political process—
in a sense, to an individual's psychological orientation to
politics. We may be able to predict some of the psychological
satisfactions that he will seek from political participation, but
we will know little about the political content of that participation. This content will depend, among other things, upon
the position of the individual within the political structure and
the alternatives that the political structure offers him. As Shils
has pointed out in his commentary on the Berkeley studies of
authoritarianism, similar authoritarian personality traits may
be directed toward the Left (Communism) or the Right
(Fascism), depending upon the political environment in
which the individual finds himself.[46]

The limitation in the range of choices that any political
system offers an individual means that particular predispositions and expectations developed in early primary group
situations may be directed into diverse political activities,
depending upon the political environment. But the range of
choices within the political system may also direct the individual seeking to satisfy expectations developed in the primary
group in another direction—out of politics. This situation
will arise if the political system cannot satisfy the needs developed in primary groups. Much of the literature that attempts to link childhood experiences and political behavior
assumes that the political system will be congruent with the
patterns in the primary group and will satisfy the needs developed there. Authoritarians will find an authoritarian political system, and non-authoritarians will participate in democratic relationships. But this assumption is not necessarily
valid. This can be seen if we compare the relationship between
family training and political participation in France and Germany. According to Schaffner, the political orientation of the
German people is a reflection of the respect for authority
learned within the family. Thus the Germans readily accepted
Hitler, "whose manner was that of the traditional German
father: it inspired confidence."[47] The French family system,

---

[46] Shils, in Christie and Jahoda, eds., *Studies in the Scope* . . . , p. 24.
[47] Schaffner, *Fatherland*, p. 75.

according to Rodnick, has a similar pattern and develops expectations similar to those of the German family. "Individuals [are] conditioned to expect guidance and a dependency relationship from their authority figures."[48] But, unlike the German political system, the French system has produced (at least, until recently) no authority figures who inspire such confidence. The individual cannot find satisfaction in the political sphere for needs developed in the family. "The reaction against authority has been because it has been weak rather than because it has been strong."[49]

Similar role experience in primary groups may, therefore, lead to quite different political behaviors. The question as to whether there is pressure toward homogeneity among the various political systems to which a person belongs is still open. Do those who experience one type of authority in the family, school, and peer group desire the same type of authority in their economic and political relations? Some of the evidence we have cited suggests that such will be the case, but it may well be that in certain situations there is a high degree of autonomy among the various authority systems in which a person participates. Further research is needed on the relationship between primary group training and political predispositions.[50]

POLITICAL ATTITUDES AND THE SMALL GROUP: The impact of the primary group on politics has been discussed so far in

[48] David Rodnick, *An Interim Report on French Culture* (Maxwell Air Force Base, Ala.: Human Resources Institute, 1953).

[49] *Ibid.* This section does not necessarily agree with the accuracy of the descriptions by Schaffner and Rodnick. Their works are used merely as examples of the type of interaction that may take place between primary group training and political structures to influence the political behavior of the individual.

[50] The problem of connecting roles in small face-to-face groups with roles in larger systems is a thorny one about which little is known. Roles in face-to-face groups—say, the role of participant in decisions or the role of leader—may be quite different from participant or leadership roles in larger systems. Authority patterns in a small group where all members communicate directly are clearly not the same as authority patterns in systems in which communication is indirect and authority figures are distant. The question of moving from analysis of roles on the small group level to analysis of roles in larger systems will be discussed below. See also Talcott Parsons, "The Small Group and the Larger Social System," in Roy R. Grinker, ed., *Toward a Unified Theory of Human Behavior* (New York: Basic Books, 1956).

terms of the political structure of the primary group. Participation in families, peer groups, work groups, and other formally apolitical groups influences the individual's style of political behavior by developing certain expectations of political roles and certain skills for political role-playing. But the impact of the face-to-face group on political affairs can be more direct and have a more specific political content. The explicit political attitudes with which an individual comes into contact in the face-to-face group have a significant impact on his political views and behavior. This is especially so in the light of the strong influence that the primary group has on the attitudes of its members. This primary group influence does not involve the development of a political "personality" or of generalized role expectations that receive political content only when brought into contact with the political system, but the impact of the primary group may be on quite general political attitudes as well as on specific political opinions. Thus children may learn by direct teaching, or by observing the political attitudes and behaviors of their parents, certain general attitudes toward the state, toward law, and toward other political groups. They may learn to have trust and confidence in political figures, or to look with distrust and disdain on politics. They may learn respect or disrespect for law. This aspect of political socialization has been little explored, but there is reason to believe that it is very significant. French *incivisme* was explained by Rodnick in terms of the disappointment of the individual Frenchman at not finding in the political system the strong authority figure that he had been led to expect by his experience in the family; and by Crozier and Micaud in terms of the lack of primary group training for participation. But *incivisme* is probably also influenced by the explicit attitudes toward the political system that young people hear from the adults around them. Wylie reports that the children in the French village he studied ". . . constantly hear adults referring to Government as the source of evil and to the men who run it as instruments of evil. There is nothing personal in this belief. It does not concern one particular Government composed of one particular group of men. It concerns Government everywhere and at all times—French Governments, American Governments, Russian Governments, all Governments. Some are less bad than others, but all are essentially bad."[51]

The development of political attitudes begins in the family. The relations between the attitudes of parents and those of their children have been most widely explored in the fields of intergroup relations and voting behavior. Studies of grade-school children as well as of college students have found that the racial attitudes of parents are a major influence on the attitudes of children.[52] Voting behavior is also influenced by early family experiences: "Indeed it would not be inappropriate to consider the family as the primary unit of voting analysis. . . ."[53] The panel studies of voting behavior indicate that between two-thirds and three-quarters of the American voters vote for the party for which their fathers voted.[54] The family may also influence the general tendency of an individual's political affiliation, rather than the specific party for which he votes. Thus members of the Communist Party show a tendency to come from radical and left-wing, but not necessarily Communist, families.[55] The emphasis in much of the

[51] Wylie, *Village in the Vaucluse*, p. 208. It is interesting to note that this political education is effective despite the fact that it is in direct conflict with the teachings of the school civics textbooks. *Ibid.*, pp. 106-7. This is another example of the greater effectiveness of informal as against formal communications.

[52] The study of grade-school children is by E. L. and R. L. Horowitz, "Development of Social Attitudes in Children," *Sociometry*, 1 (1938), pp. 301-8. The college student study is by G. W. Allport and B. M. Kramer, "Some Roots of Prejudice," *Journal of Psychology*, 22 (1946), pp. 9-39. These and other corroborative studies are discussed in John Harding, *et al.*, "Prejudice and Ethnic Relations," in Lindzey, ed., *Handbook . . .* , Vol. II, chap. 27.

[53] Berelson, *et al.*, *Voting*, p. 93.

[54] *Ibid.*; and Lazarsfeld, *et al.*, *The People's Choice*. Of course, since children usually share certain politically relevant characteristics with their parents—residence, class, religion, ethnic group—the relationship between vote of father and vote of child may not be due to family influence. The Elmira voting study attempted to test the relative weight of family influence and social characteristics. Among those having family influences and social characteristics that led in different political directions (members of the working class whose fathers had voted Republican; members of the middle class whose fathers had voted Democratic), family influence was found to play as large a role as social position. Berelson, *et al.*, *Voting*, pp. 88-93.

[55] Gabriel A. Almond, *The Appeals of Communism* (Princeton: Princeton University Press, 1954), pp. 221-24.

41

literature on the connection between family experience and such implicit personality-oriented attitudes as authoritarianism may have led to an underestimation of the more manifest and direct political training that an individual receives in primary groups. On the basis of an analysis of numerous studies of political socialization, Herbert Hyman concludes that socialization into party affiliation seems to take place earlier than that into ideological orientation. Similarly, while there is little evidence for an implicit personality-oriented authoritarianism among children, studies have found that manifestly political authoritarian attitudes (say, opposition to civil rights) are more highly developed at a young age.[56]

The influence of the primary group on voting extends beyond that of the family during childhood. The face-to-face contact that a voter has during a campaign has a significant effect on his voting choice. This was the "discovery" made in the Erie County voting study; that not only does one's class, religion, occupation, and residence affect one's voting choice, but the small face-to-face groups in which one participates play an important role.[57] A major finding in relation to the role of the small face-to-face group in voting and other decisions is that the mass media of communication, rather than acting directly upon the individual audience member, act upon individuals through a "two-step communication process." Certain community members, it was found, are more receptive to the communications of the mass media. These "opinion leaders," in turn, pass on the content of these media to those with whom they have face-to-face contact.[58] The discovery of the intermediary role of face-to-face communication between the individual and the mass media serves as a strong qualification of the conception of modern society as a "mass society"—a place where lone individuals stand naked and defenseless before the mass media. The two-step process

[56] Herbert Hyman, *Political Socialization* (Glencoe, Ill.: Free Press, 1958), p. 47.
[57] Lazarsfeld, *et al.*, *op.cit.*, chap. 15, and Berelson, *et al.*, *op.cit.*, pp. 137-38.
[58] See Elihu Katz, "The Two-Step Flow of Communications," *Pub. Opinion Q.*, 21 (1957), pp. 61-78.

of communication has been found in voting and community studies in this country. It has also been found as a major determinant of the lack of impact of hostile propaganda on the *Wehrmacht* and as an important technique of propaganda and agitation in the Soviet Union.[59]

The face-to-face communication groups found by Lazarsfeld and his associates in the voting studies and the Decatur study, as well as the primary group in the *Wehrmacht*, are informal parts of the communication process. These groups did not come together with the explicit purpose of linking the individual and the mass media. They are not planned parts of the communication process. But, as was mentioned earlier, face-to-face groups are not necessarily informal. Their communication functions may be explicitly planned. One of the major sources of the strength of the Communist Party, it has been suggested, is the fact that it is organized on the basis of cells, for which the optimum size is about 15-20 members.[60] The strength of the cell system lies not only in its greater adaptability to clandestine action, but in the greater influence that such small meetings can have on the attitudes of the members. For many members, Micaud points out, the cell is a substitute for primary ties in family or church. Furthermore, it performs the intermediary function in the two-step process of communication. The Party literature is available in the cell, and its transmission in the small group context gives it an especially strong impact.[61]

The process of transmitting communications from the mass media through the face-to-face group is not merely one of amplification. Communications from the group's external environment do not reach the group unchanged by the process of face-to-face transmission. The views of the opinion leader will, of course, affect the content of the transmitted message. So will the nature of the group. Communications that chal-

---

[59] Shils and Janowitz, *Pub. Opinion Q.*, *12* (1948); and Alex Inkeles, *Public Opinion in the Soviet Union* (Cambridge, Mass.: Harvard University Press, 1950), chaps. 5-8.

[60] Duverger, *Political Parties*, pp. 28-30.

[61] Charles Micaud, "Organization and Leadership of the French Communist Party," *World Politics*, *4* (1952), pp. 318-55; and Inkeles, *op.cit.*, p. 84.

lenge the solidarity of the group, for instance, tend to be rejected by group members.[62]

The participation of an individual in politically relevant face-to-face groups affects not only the content of his political attitudes, but the intensity of these attitudes as well. There are two variables to be considered here: (1) the range of primary groups in which there is political participation; and (2) the homogeneity of that participation. The wider the range of primary contacts that are politicized, the greater the intensity of political participation. In a survey in France, voters were asked: "Before voting, do you discuss the election with others in your circle?" The percentage answering "yes" is shown in Table 1, broken down into party affiliation.[63] The

TABLE 1. PER CENT SAYING THEY DISCUSS POLITICS

Party preference	With family	With friends	With colleagues
Communist	68%	65%	69%
Socialist	53	49	42
Radical	58	49	31
MRP	51	43	40
Moderates	53	53	36
RPF	58	51	32

interesting point of these figures is that not only do the Communist supporters report discussion within the family more frequently than do the supporters of the other parties, but unlike the other parties there is no falling off in the frequency of discussion among Communists as one moves from family to friends to colleagues on the job. The political intensity of the Communist supporter is manifested in the high degree of politicization of the range of primary groups to which he belongs.

Secondly, the greater the homogeneity of primary group contacts, the greater the intensity of political participation. In *Voting* it was found that voters with friends of various political persuasions were less strong in their voting inten-

---

[62] See Shils and Janowitz, *op.cit.*

[63] From Jean Stoetzel, "Voting Behavior in France," *British Journal of Sociology*, 6 (1955), p. 119.

tions than those whose friends were all of the same persuasion. McCloskey and Dahlgren report similar findings, both for relations within the primary group and for those among primary groups. The greater the political homogeneity of a particular primary group—for instance, the more solid a family is in one political direction—the more likely the individual is to be a stable voter in that direction. And the greater the political homogeneity among the family of origin, the present family, and the peer group, the more likely the individual is to be a stable voter in that direction.[64]

The Small Group and the Political System

That the face-to-face group plays a significant role in the political process is now clear. The process of decision-making in small groups has been described, as has the influence of the small group on the political attitudes and behaviors of its members. What remains is to consider the small group from the point of view of the operation of the political system as a whole. That face-to-face relationships have an impact on the political system because these groups influence the attitudes of their members is not to say what that impact is likely to be. To relate the face-to-face group to a theory of the political system, we shall look at (1) the effect of the discovery of "pre-modern" primary structures in the modern political system on the theoretical distinction between modern and traditional political systems; and (2) the relationship between face-to-face contacts and political stability.

FACE-TO-FACE GROUPS IN TRADITIONAL AND MODERN SYSTEMS: The discussion so far indicates clearly that there is no absolute distinction between modern and traditional systems in terms of the absence or presence of significant primary structures. In both systems, primary, face-to-face contacts play an important role. But if the contrast between the traditional and the modern was once too sharply drawn, the discovery of these pre-modern primary structures in modern

[64] Berelson, *et al.*, *Voting*, p. 98; and Herbert McCloskey and Harold E. Dahlgren, "Primary Group Influence on Party Loyalty," *Am. Pol. Sci. Rev.*, 53 (1960), pp. 757-76.

society does not justify the opposite conclusion that an analysis of primary group phenomena cannot be used to distinguish these two types of system. Though both types of system contain primary structures, distinctions can be drawn in two ways: (1) in terms of the *types* of politically significant primary structures; and (2) in terms of the relative *importance* of primary and secondary structures.

(1) *Types of primary structure*: Though primary structures persist in modern systems, they tend to be penetrated and modernized by the larger organizations of which they are a part. It was a significant finding of the "rediscovery" of the primary group that these groups regulate behavior within the larger systems to which they belong. But the primary group is in turn regulated by these larger systems. Though the primary groups discovered in the modern factory and army are often informal and unplanned in relation to the larger organization, the structure of these groups is greatly influenced by the framework set for them by the organization. The composition and location of these informal primary groups are largely determined by the formal structure of the organization. Informal groups in factories or in the army usually develop only where the formal organizational structure facilitates frequent contact—at certain locations in the plant or in the squads of the army. Thus, to a large extent, the formal rules determine who interacts with whom. More important is the fact that the formal organization impinges on the informal, internal interaction of the group. If, for instance, some of the members of the informal face-to-face group have higher statuses within the formal organization, this will affect the structure of interaction as well as the degree of solidarity within the group. Similarly, the degree to which the group members are oriented to the norms of the formal organization in contrast to those of the group—for instance, are interested in promotional opportunities—affects interaction within the group.[65]

Relations within primary groups tend to be affective, diffuse, and particularistic. But they differ greatly in the extent

[65] See Leonard R. Sayles, *Behavior of Industrial Work Groups: Prediction and Control* (New York: John Wiley, 1958), chap. 3.

to which they approach this pattern. The informal, face-to-face group in a modern organizational context is pre-modern in orientation when contrasted with the secondary system of which it is a part, but it tends to be quite modern when contrasted with primary groups in a traditional society. The work group discovered in the Western Electric Hawthorne plant is in this respect quite different from the traditional family. And within the industrial society there is wide variation in the degree to which primary structures approach the traditional pattern. Thus the street corner gang studied by Whyte is much more inclusive and intimate than the industrial work group in the Bank Wiring Room of the Hawthorne plant. The commitment of the individual member is much greater in the former group. In contrasting the modern and traditional systems it is thus important to note what types of primary groups are politically relevant.

(2) *The relative importance of primary structures*: The relative importance of primary structures differs from society to society, with a tendency for them to be more important in traditional societies. This can be measured in two ways: (1) the relative weight given to primary and secondary group norms; and (2) the relative degree to which political functions are performed in primary and secondary structures. Though in both the traditional and the modern societies, primary groups are significant reference points for norms and attitudes, the weight of loyalty to primary norms differs. Ike writes of the situation that would arise in Japanese politics if an individual were caught between ". . . conflicting loyalties: loyalty to his political principles and convictions and his obligation or *on* to an individual"—*on* being the sense of obligation developed in an intimate face-to-face relationship. In a conflict situation of this sort, the dominant norms in Japanese society would require that the individual fulfill his personal, particularistic obligation rather than follow the universalistic criteria associated with his loyalty to the rules of the impersonal political system. If he did not follow the norms associated with his loyalty to an individual, he would

be ". . . subjected to social disapproval and criticism."[66] One can imagine a similar conflict in the American political system between obligation and loyalty to one's primary group—family and friends—and loyalty to the abstract rules of political principle. And no one can deny that often the particularistic criteria will prevail, and that bureaucrat, voter, or legislator will behave according to standards other than those prescribed by the rules of the formal political system. But though such behavior is likely to exist, it would receive blame in the United States, rather than the praise it receives in Japanese politics. Thus, though primary loyalties exist in both systems, the weight placed on these loyalties differs.[67]

In the modern system, furthermore, the number of significant political functions performed within primary groups will not be as great as in the traditional system. Face-to-face groups will tend to share the performance of political functions with secondary structures. Thus, while in the modern system the face-to-face group plays a significant role in political communication as a mediator between the mass media and the individual, it shares the communication function with these media. And insofar as primary groups in modern systems tend to be more functionally specific, greater demands are placed upon secondary structures to regulate the relations among these groups.

Thus an analysis of primary group phenomena as they appear in traditional and modern systems is still useful in drawing distinctions between these two systems if the types of primary structure and their relations with the larger system are elaborated.

The next question we shall deal with in placing the analysis of the primary group within the context of the political

[66] Nobutaka Ike, *Japanese Politics* (New York: Alfred Knopf, 1957), pp. 31-33. Cf. Chitoshi Yanaga, *Japanese People and Politics* (New York: John Wiley, 1956), p. 69.

[67] Apter points out the extent to which primary groups are more important in a traditional system such as that of the Gold Coast than in a Western system. David Apter, *The Gold Coast in Transition* (Princeton: Princeton University Press, 1955), p. 288. But even among primitive societies, the weight given face-to-face loyalties varies with, among other things, the size of the tribe. See I. Schapera, *Government and Politics in Tribal Societies* (London: Watts, 1956).

system is the relationship between face-to-face contacts and political stability. Do face-to-face groups act to support the political system, or are they destructive and subversive forces from the point of view of the central political structure? Clearly a question of this sort when asked in such general terms can only be answered in such terms. The specific content of the impact of any face-to-face group—the particular attitude influenced, the particular decision made—depends of course upon the specific group and the specific situation. It is, however, possible to describe some general effects that the face-to-face group has as both subverter and supporter of the political system, as well as to suggest some variables that affect the direction in which primary group pressures will go.

THE SMALL GROUP IN CONFLICT WITH THE POLITICAL SYSTEM: The face-to-face group may conflict with the larger political system of which it is a part in several ways. In the first place, the very existence of primary groups which have an effect on the political system may be regarded as a source of conflict with the development of a rational, efficient system. Secondly, the face-to-face group may support particular behaviors or attitudes that are deviant in terms of the norms of the larger system. We shall look at these in turn.

(1) *The "irrationality" of small group behavior*: It was once a common view among sociologists, as Shils has pointed out, to consider the primary group and modern society ". . . logically antithetical and empirically incompatible. . . . The persistence of traditionally regulated informal and intimate relations was regarded as an archaism inherited from an older rural society or from a small-town handicraft society."[68] This view that informal relations are *per se* in conflict with larger structures is found among those administrative theorists who view organizations as essentially rational and formal. Though the organization planner will have to consider the informal relations that exist within an organization, he will look at them as deviations from the formal pattern and will try to

---

[68] Shils, in Lerner and Lasswell, eds., *Policy Sciences*, p. 44.

minimize them. Urwick describes the process of designing an organization:

> He [the planner] should never for a moment pretend that these difficulties don't exist. They do exist; they are realities. Nor, when he has drawn up an ideal plan of organization, is it likely he will be able to fit in all the human material perfectly. There will be small adjustments . . . in all kinds of directions. But those adjustments are deliberate and temporary deviations from the pattern in order to deal with idiosyncrasy. . . .
>
> What is suggested is that problems of organization should be handled in *the right order*. Personal adjustments must be made insofar as they are necessary. But fewer of them will be necessary and they will present fewer deviations from what is logical and simple, if the organizer first makes a plan, a design. . . .[69]

Insofar as the face-to-face groups in larger structures are informal—that is, perform unplanned functions—they are here looked on as in conflict with what is felt to be the essential planned rationality of the larger structure.

Similarly, it was pointed out earlier that the face-to-face voting groups are informal in the sense that their function in influencing voting decisions is a form of influence which has not been considered by traditional theories of the way in which a democracy operates.[70] In this sense, face-to-face contacts in voting can be considered to be in conflict with the operation of a "rational" democratic system in which voting choices are made on the basis of principle or a rational calculation of interests, or both. V. O. Key contrasts the voting decision made on the basis of party or issue with that made on a "friends and neighbors" basis. The support of a candidate by his "friends and neighbors who know him" is an indication of ". . . the absence of stable, well-organized, state-wide factions of like-minded citizens formed to advocate measures of a common concern. In its extreme form, localism justifies a diagnosis of low voter interest in public issues and a susceptibility to control by the irrelevant appeal to support the hometown boy. . . . If the factions within the Democratic Party of Alabama

---

[69] L. Urwick, *The Elements of Administration* (New York: Harper, 1953), pp. 36-39.

[70] Berelson, *Pub. Opinion Q.* (1952); and Berelson, *et al., Voting*, chap. 14.

amounted to political parties, a candidate's strength in the vote from county to county would not be appreciably influenced by his place of residence. A well-knit group of voters and leaders scattered over the entire state would deliver about the same proportion of vote to its candidate wherever he happened to live. A concern for issues (or at least group success) would override local attachments. In well-developed two-party situations, localism is minimized, if not erased, by a larger concern for party victory. The classic case is that of Duchess County, New York, the home of Franklin D. Roosevelt, a Democrat of some note. The county, traditionally Republican, stubbornly held to its party attachments and repeatedly failed to return a majority for even its most distinguished son. Radically different voting behavior characterizes battles within the Alabama Democratic primaries. A candidate for governor normally carries his own county by a huge political majority, and the harshest criticism that can be made of a politician is that he cannot win his own beat or precinct. If his friends and neighbors who know him do not support him, why should those without this advantage trust a candidate?"[71]

In this view, personal influence in the voting decision is looked at as the antithesis of a voting decision made on the basis of party or issue; the passage cited above would seem to reflect a belief that such face-to-face influence is inconsistent with political choices made on a rational democratic basis. This view of a conflict between the primary group and the rational political system or the rational organization may, however, be more a reflection of an artificial, rational model than a reflection of actual conflict between primary and secondary structures.[72]

(2) *Deviant small groups*: Face-to-face participation will also be in conflict with the larger political system if the particular norms of that system differ from those of the face-to-face

[71] V. O. Key, *Southern Politics* (New York: Alfred A. Knopf, 1949), pp. 37-38.

[72] As the studies of Berelson and Lazarsfeld have shown, face-to-face contact is not necessarily in conflict with political choice on the basis of party or issue. Even decisions based on party or issue are made in a face-to-face context.

group. Thus conformity to the face-to-face group, when that group is a deviant one, will mean non-conformity to the norms of the larger system.

> I . . . have been, am still, a criminal. But there is a sense in which I have been an almost abjectly law-abiding person. From my very first years I adapted myself wholeheartedly to the community I lived in, accepting its values, obeying its imperatives, observing its customs. Submissiveness could go no further. If, then, law-abidingness is acting according to the dictates of the community you were born into, there never was a more law-abiding person than myself.
>
> But, unfortunately or otherwise, the community I was born into was a small one at variance with the larger community containing it. In obeying the laws of the criminal quarter I incurred the disapproval of the law courts.[73]

Similarly, the people with radical family backgrounds who join in radical political movements will be conforming to their primary group background, though they are deviants from the point of view of the larger political system.

Conversely, the absence of strong face-to-face commitments on the part of the individual strengthens the norms of the general political system. As illustrated in the Elmira voting study, in a dominantly Republican community, this dominant norm has its least effect where the face-to-face group is "solid"; that is, where one participates in face-to-face groups of homogeneous political composition. Where the face-to-face group is "solid,"

> . . . the strong community majority for the Republicans has little effect because it has little access to persons within homogeneous Democratic groups.
>
> But when the primary environment is internally *divided*, the effect of the distant community can be seen. Then the Republicans get a higher proportion of the vote. . . . The impact of the larger community is thus most evident among voters with discordant or disagreeing primary groups. When the voter's close associates do not provide him with a single, clear political direction—when instead they offer an alternative—then wider associa-

[73] From an autobiographical novel by Mark Benney, *Low Company* (New York: Avon, 1952), quoted in Morton Grodzins, *The Loyal and Disloyal* (Chicago: University of Chicago Press, 1956), p. 42.

tions in the surrounding community reinforce one position over the other.[74]

Attachments to face-to-face groups may thus lessen the impact of the overall political culture on the individual. This fact is especially relevant in totalitarian societies. Insofar as such societies demand total loyalty to the state, loyalties to primary groups are in conflict with the dominant political norm. Attachment to a family or other primary group places an area of behavior outside government control. Thus, in Soviet theory, loyalty to primary groups is "deemed intolerable."[75] "Family circles" (informal cliques of local officials) have often come under severe criticism in the Soviet Union because of the many illicit activities that go on in them. Fainsod reports the exposure of such a "family circle" in Smolensk which had been formed for the self-protection of the local leaders against the demands placed on them by Moscow. The important point about these "families" is that while they were for the central government "the mortal enemy of control," they performed significant functions for the members in providing them with a sanctuary. The main reason why the "family" system grew in the local area studied by Fainsod was an "almost desperate desire for relaxation and security" in the

[74] Berelson, *et al.*, *Voting*, pp. 100-1.

[75] Raymond Bauer, Alex Inkeles, and Clyde Kluckhohn, *How the Soviet System Works* (Cambridge, Mass.: Harvard University Press, 1956), p. 81. See also Margaret Mead, *Soviet Attitudes Toward Authority* (New York: McGraw-Hill, 1951), pp. 55-57. On the attempts of totalitarian societies to atomize interpersonal relations below the level of the state, see Robert Ā. Nisbet, *The Quest for Community* (New York: Oxford University Press, 1953), chap. 8; and Hannah Arendt, *The Origins of Totalitarianism* (New York: Harper, 1951).

That attachment to a primary group is a possible challenge to the state has long been realized. Thus Plato argues in *The Republic* that communal property and families will prevent the guardians of the state from having divided loyalties. They can then serve the state better. "Both the community of property and the community of families, as I am saying, tend to make them more truly guardians; they will not tear the city in pieces by differing about 'mine' and 'not mine'; each man dragging any acquisitions which he has made into a separate house of his own, where he has a separate wife and children and private pleasures and pains; but all will be affected as far as may be by the same pleasures and pains because they are all of one opinion about what is near and dear to them, and, therefore, they will all tend towards a common goal." *The Republic*, Book V, Jowett translation.

face of the overwhelming production demands of the central government.[76]

THE SMALL GROUP AND POLITICAL STABILITY: Face-to-face groups are not necessarily in conflict with the political system. They also perform significant supportive functions. The norms they support, for instance, may be norms that are congruent with those of the larger system. They may supply the individual member with affective outputs, the absence of which might place burdens on the political system. And they are a source of flexibility in running the system. Let us look at these functions in turn.

(1) *Socialization for citizenship*: The major supportive role played by the primary group is the socialization of children to take adult roles in the political process. We have emphasized above some ways in which socialization into deviant political roles may take place. But it is highly probable that unless a large proportion of the population is socialized into behaviors that support the political system, that system will be highly unstable. In any case, even totalitarian states, afraid of competition from the family for the loyalty of their citizens, have had to revise doctrine so as to accept the basic role the family plays in socialization.[77]

Political socialization, furthermore, continues beyond childhood. Face-to-face contacts have a continuing effect on the individual's political attitudes and behavior. These face-to-face groups may, it was pointed out, support norms that are deviant from the point of view of the political system. They may, on the other hand, foster norms that are supportive of that system. What determines whether the pressures placed upon the individual in his face-to-face contacts—both as a child and later —will act to further the goals of the larger system? The ques-

[76] Merle Fainsod, *Smolensk Under Soviet Rule* (Cambridge, Mass.: Harvard University Press, 1958), pp. 48-50, 92, 111. See below for a discussion of some of the positive functions these same groups perform. See also Barrington Moore, *Terror and Progress: USSR* (Cambridge, Mass.; Harvard University Press, 1954), p. 161. Moore writes: "From the point of view of the rulers, a 'good' friendship clique is one that aids in the execution of policy, while from the point of view of the population a 'good' clique is one that aids in the evasion of policy."

[77] See Moore, *op.cit.*, pp. 158-60.

tion is a difficult one, but some tentative hypotheses may be offered.[78]

(a) Insofar as the leaders of the political system can directly penetrate and control the interaction process within the face-to-face group, the norms set by that process will tend to support the larger system. The ability of the totalitarian system to influence norm-setting within the family is the clearest example. In the first place, the political system may directly penetrate the family communication process. Interviews with Soviet *émigrés* reveal that it is a norm of Soviet family conduct that one does not express non-conforming attitudes in front of the children because of the possibility of inadvertent betrayal. Thus, even if the political system cannot completely control the norms held by adult family members, it can limit their transmission to the children. Secondly, insofar as the political system firmly controls the other norm-setting institutions to which the child is exposed—the school, the media, and so on—the parents are limited in the choice of norms that they may pass on to the children.[79]

(b) The greater the degree of cultural fusion between the primary and secondary structures, the more the norms of the small group will support the larger system. The fusion of the standards of the small group and the larger system may come from the "modernization" of the primary group by the larger system, or it may come from the diffusion upward of the primary group's particularistic and diffuse values into the political system. Whichever the direction of influence, this interpenetration of the two systems will increase the probability that the face-to-face group will further norms that support the political system. Almond suggests that it is the degree of fusion between the informal, traditional group component and the modern, secondary component of the political system that differentiates French from British politics. In the former the two compo-

[78] For a similar discussion in the context of organization theory, see James March and Herbert Simon, *Organizations* (New York: John Wiley, 1958), pp. 78-81.
[79] See Kent Geiger, "Changing Political Attitudes in Totalitarian Society: A Case Study of the Role of the Family," *World Politics*, 8 (1956), pp. 187-205.

nents are isolated and antagonistic; in the latter they are fused and supportive.[80]

(c) The more the face-to-face group perceives itself as participating in the decisions of the political system, the more the sub-group will tend to support the norms of the political system. The "participation hypothesis" is one of the basic hypotheses of small group research. It appears to have a wide range of political applicability, though its generality may be limited to cultures with value systems that support such participation. Two later chapters are devoted to this hypothesis; we will merely cite it here.[81]

(d) The more the face-to-face group perceives itself as receiving valued outputs from the political system, the greater will be its support of that system. This hypothesis merely states that those who perceive themselves as being highly rewarded by the activities of the political system are more likely to support that system.

(2) *The small group as a source of affect*: Just as the face-to-face group may support the political system by its furtherance of supportive norms, so may it support that system by providing affective outputs to its members. Relations in large organizations that engage only a part of the individual and that are specifically goal-oriented afford the individual insufficient emotional and affective ties.[82] The political system can offer some satisfaction for the individual's affective needs through emotional attachments to the symbols of the state, to a charismatic leader, or to some "cause" for which the state stands. But the specific demands that the larger system places upon the individual and the distance of the center of authority from the individual make it difficult for the system to satisfy his affective needs adequately. Argyris suggests that there is an inevitable conflict between the formal organization and what he calls the "healthy" personality, and that the more intimate face-to-face group in organizations is an adaptive

[80] Gabriel A. Almond and James C. Coleman, eds., *The Politics of the Developing Areas* (Princeton: Princeton University Press, 1960), pp. 24-25.

[81] See below, Chapters IX and X.

[82] Cf. Nisbet, *Quest for Community*; and Kahler, *The Tower and the Abyss*.

mechanism whereby the affective gap is filled.[83] In political systems, such "gap-filling" face-to-face groups may also be found. Local political organizations, for instance, give the individual a feeling of attachment to the political system that is not gained from participation in the larger, more formal processes. Writing of the political clubs of New York, Peel states: "Since in the modern democratic state the participation of the individual in the actual working of government is reduced to a minimum, the [local political] clubs might give him what the primaries, general elections, initiative, referendum, recall, assembly and petition have failed to give him—the feeling that he is an important part of the self-governing community."[84]

The important point is that affective ties to the primary group have significant latent effects on the political system. Loyalty to the face-to-face group may lead an individual to behave in such a way as to support the larger system. Thus, studies of wartime behavior in the American and German armies indicate that soldiers were motivated to fight by loyalty to the primary group. The results as far as the larger systems were concerned were the same whether the soldiers fought for the democratic or the Nazi ideology. The affective security and emotional rewards given by the primary group were directly related to the soldier's ability to act effectively in regard to the larger system. As Shils and Janowitz point out: "It appears that a soldier's ability to resist [enemy propaganda] is a function of the capacity of his immediate primary group (his squad or section) to avoid social disintegration. When the individual's immediate group and its supporting formations

[83] Chris Argyris, *Personality and Organization* (New York: Harper, 1957), p. 139 and *passim*. The fact that in large organizations affective satisfactions can be found within informal small groups is one of the major findings of the rediscovery of the small group.

[84] Roy V. Peel, *The Political Clubs of New York* (New York: Putnam's, 1945), p. 136. Rousseau maintained that a large state could not be proportionately as strong as a small one. One of the reasons he advanced for this is that in a large state an individual will not have the face-to-face contacts that make his political participation affectively satisfying. In large states, he wrote, ". . . the people has less affection for its rulers whom it never sees, for its country, which, to its eyes, seems like the world, and for its fellow citizens, most of whom are unknown to it." *The Social Contract*, Everyman's ed., p. 38.

met his basic organic needs, offered him both affection and esteem from both officers and comrades, supplied him with a sense of power, and adequately regulated his relations with authority, the element of self-concern in battle, which would lead to disruption of the effective functioning of his primary group, was minimized."[85] And it is important to note that though the attachment to the primary group was essentially a non-political attachment, it functioned directly to support the political goal of the organization. "The solidarity of the German army was discovered by these studies . . . to be based only very indirectly and very partially on political convictions or broader ethical beliefs. Where conditions were such as to allow primary group life to function smoothly, and where the primary group developed a high degree of cohesion, morale was high and resistance effective or at least very determined, *regardless in the main of the political attitudes of the soldiers.*"[86] Thus, in this case, the unplanned functions of the small group served the purposes of the formal organization by performing functions of which the formal organization was incapable.

The proposition that satisfactory affective ties within the primary group will lead to behavior on the part of the individual that supports the larger political system finds confirmation in a number of studies that link radical behavior with the absence of such ties. Several authors have argued that one of the major appeals of participation in the Communist Party is that its deep political ties satisfy affective needs left unsatisfied by the secondary relationships in an industrial society. The Communist cell often replaces weakened face-to-face ties in family or church.[87] A lack of face-to-face ties has been shown to be related to political instability in a number of other

[85] Shils and Janowitz, *Pub. Opinion Q.*, *12* (1948), p. 281; and Shils, in Merton and Lazarsfeld, eds., *Studies in the Scope. . . .*

[86] *Ibid.*, p. 314. Italics mine.

[87] See Philip Selznick, *The Organizational Weapon* (New York: McGraw-Hill, 1952), pp. 283-87; Almond, *The Appeals of Communism*, pp. 272-79; and Micaud, *World Politics* (1952).

A similar argument is made by Fromm in *Escape from Freedom*, and by Mannheim in *Man and Society in the Age of Reconstruction* (New York: Harcourt, Brace, 1950).

situations. Ringer and Sills found that political extremists in Iran tended to have fewer family, religious, and friendship ties. They engaged in individualistic recreation and reported that they received communications through the mass media rather than through visiting and talking.[88] Davies and Wada, in a study of the background characteristics of rioters and non-rioters, present tentative evidence that rioters tend to have fewer family and other primary group ties.[89]

Even the face-to-face group whose norms conflict with the formal organization may perform supportive affective functions. Thus Argyris has shown that even those informal work groups whose norms (limiting production) operate to hinder the goal attainment of the larger organization perform positive functions for that organization by satisfying needs of the workers that the organization itself cannot satisfy.[90] Similarly, Fainsod suggests that the "family group" in Russia, even though it fosters behavior overtly opposed to the central regime, performs a supportive function by serving as an "escape valve." He suggests that the Bolshevik attempts to transform the country rapidly under harsh conditions despite the opposition of many Russians would have led to stronger negative reactions than the formation of "family groups" if these informal, self-seeking groups had not developed.[91]

(3) *Source of flexibility:* Lastly, face-to-face communications may aid the achievement of the goals of the larger system by introducing an element of flexibility into the operation of the formal system. Over-conformity to the rules and directives of the formal system is a form of deviant behavior that can harm the larger system. And as Blau points out, the over-conforming bureaucrat—the stickler for rules—may behave in that manner because of ". . . lack of security in important social relationships within the organization."[92] The face-to-face

[88] Benjamin B. Ringer and David L. Sills, "Political Extremists in Iran: A Secondary Analysis of Communications Data," *Pub. Opinion Q., 16* (1952-53), pp. 689-701.

[89] James C. Davies and George Wada, "Riots and Rioters," *Western Political Quarterly, 10* (1957), pp. 864-74.

[90] Argyris, *Personality and Organization*, chap. 4.

[91] Fainsod, *Smolensk . . .* , p. 450.

[92] Blau, *Dynamics. . .* , p. 188.

group, often developing outside the structure of the formal organization, allows a flexibility in interpreting rules not possible within formal bureaucratic channels. Formal systems will, therefore, develop a tolerance for these informal structures. Thus, though the Soviet system is officially opposed to informal arrangements among administrators, it has become tolerant to some extent of these arrangements as a means of introducing flexibility into an otherwise highly formal and bureaucratized structure.[93] And the discovery of the importance of the informal organization in American administrative studies has led to attempts to put the informal structure to the use of the formal organization.

Conclusion

The case for the primary group as a subject of political study has now been made. Face-to-face relationships—their absence or presence, the kinds of relationships—play a significant role in the political process. But the specification of the small groups that affect politics and the type of effect they have is only a first step in increasing our knowledge of political affairs through small group analysis. Small groups have a characteristic that differentiates them from most other subjects of political analysis—they can be studied by techniques and methods not available for use with larger social systems. Small groups can be created by researchers in experimental laboratories, and can be manipulated in ways not possible in other systems.

On-going small groups are important in the political process. Can studies of experimental small groups increase our understanding of that process? This chapter may be looked at as one part of a two-part justification of the study of small group experiments by a political scientist. It has attempted to show the relevance of the small group to political affairs. We have still to justify our interest in the experimental method as an approach to small groups. To that task we now turn.

[93] Bauer, Inkeles, and Kluckhohn, *How the Soviet System Works*, p. 79; and Fainsod, *op.cit.*, p. 151.

Chapter III

EXPERIMENTS AND
THE POLITICAL PROCESS
1: THE CULTURE OF THE LABORATORY

THE renewed interest in the small group brought about by the "rediscovery" of these groups coincided with a developing interest in another type of small group study—the study of human behavior using experimentally created laboratory groups. The use of controlled experiments to study relationships *among* individuals, not merely the responses of individuals to certain stimuli, raises the question of the usefulness of such methods for the study of political affairs. Political affairs, many have argued, are too complex to be studied in the laboratory. The political scientist cannot isolate a segment of the political process that interests him, bring it into his laboratory and subject it to the controlled manipulations that a medical researcher applies to his guinea pigs. With some rare exceptions to be discussed below, the political process cannot be manipulated by the political researcher.

If the political system cannot be studied "on the scene" by the experimental method, can the researcher create his own miniature political process in the laboratory? There the practical and social objections to the manipulation of the political process do not apply.[1] Cut off from the uncontrollable bustle and flux of the political process, the experimenter can create the situation he wants; can observe, using precise observational methods, interpersonal relationships as they occur; and can prevent the intrusion of extraneous variables from marring the elegant connections between the variables he is studying. Furthermore, the use of small groups in a controlled laboratory situation allows the researcher to be both precise

[1] The most striking illustration of the social difficulties of experimentation in an on-going social situation is in the violent reaction to attempts to "bug" actual jury proceedings as one step in the validation of some experiments with mock juries during the University of Chicago Law School's jury studies. See Strodtbeck, "The Jury Project" (September 1958).

61

and complete: two goals of research that are often difficult to achieve simultaneously. Political scientists often fluctuate between making precise studies of some partial, isolated aspect of the political process and imprecise studies of the total political process. Thus, to study the decisional process in political systems we may gather precise data about one aspect of that process (the social backgrounds of political decision-makers, perhaps), or we may attempt to describe the total process by which a particular decision was made. The first approach, while lending itself to precise measurement and allowing systematic comparisons from country to country, is insufficient as a means of explaining how decisions are made in political systems. It deals only with the background characteristics of decision-makers and not with other relevant aspects of the decision-making process. On the other hand, the case study method tends to involve imprecise observations. Each case is "unique"; comparative studies and the development of general theories of decision-making are hindered. It represents a significant convergence of the interests of political scientists and small group researchers that both have considered the possibility of developing techniques of research that are at once precise and inclusive.[2] In this respect, the use of the small experimental group has a special advantage: the precision with which the situation is defined, the limited number of members of the group, and the techniques that are available to the observer allow an analysis of total group situations with a high degree of precision.

But the search for precision in the laboratory situation raises a major question: once we have moved into the laboratory to study relationships in simplified, artificial situations, can we move back to the world of actual political affairs? Can one, on the basis of experiments in a laboratory situation, explain and predict behavior in non-laboratory situations? Small

[2] A leading example of the attempt within political science to systematize the study of a large social process is Richard Snyder, H. W. Bruck, and Burton Sapin, *Decision-Making as an Approach to the Study of International Politics* (Princeton: Organizational Behavior Section, Princeton University, 1954). The works of Bales and Lewin and their associates dealt with below are examples of the attempt to achieve both completeness and precision in small group research.

experimental groups are, after all, quite different from the on-going groups and organizations that populate the political system. But, to revert for a moment to our analogy between medical and political science, guinea pigs are also quite different from the human beings whose bodily functions are the basic interest of the medical experimenter. Guinea pigs and artificial small groups are used in the laboratory because of the social difficulties involved in dissecting "on-going" human beings or organizations.[3] That the small experimental group and the on-going groups and organizations whose behavior we want to understand are different does not mean that we cannot learn about the latter from the former. But it does mean that the connection between the two levels of analysis is a difficult one that will have to be made with care. And the connection becomes more difficult as the small group situation becomes more and more artificial in the name of precision. One of the subjects this chapter will explore is the conflict within small group research between relevance and precision; between the desire, on the one hand, to have experimental groups that are similar enough to on-going groups to allow easy extrapolation from the artificial to the real situation, and the desire, on the other, to have groups in which the relations are so precisely defined that the connection between variables is clear and unambiguous. We shall be especially interested in seeing if the precision of the experimental method requires that we pay the price of relevance. The laboratory method for the study of political affairs will be useful if it serves to "narrow the gap between being precise about the trivial and trivial about the important."[4]

The Experimental Method

CONTROL: The most significant characteristic of the experimental method is the control that the experimenter has over the situation. By manipulating certain carefully selected variables and by controlling, ideally, all others, he can achieve

---

[3] Medical researchers can of course dissect cadavers, but the political scientist has the historian to do this for him.

[4] Harold Lasswell, "Current Studies of the Decision Process: Automation v. Creativity," *Western Political Quarterly*, 8 (1955), p. 386.

clear and unambiguous connections between the independent variables he controls and the dependent variables he is studying. "A laboratory experiment may be defined as one in which the investigator creates a situation with the exact conditions he wants to have and in which he controls some, and manipulates other, variables. He is then able to observe and measure the effect of the independent variables on the dependent variables in a situation in which the operation of other relevant factors is held to a minimum."[5] Furthermore, the experimenter, having planned the experimental situation, is able to apply more precise observational tools and techniques than he could use in less controlled situations; and the results of his study can be verified by replications of his work. According to Woodworth, the advantages of the controlled experiment are:

1. The experimenter makes the event happen at a certain time and place and so is fully *prepared* to make an accurate observation.
2. Controlled conditions being *known* conditions, the experimenter can set up his experiment a second time and repeat the observation; and, what is very important in view of the social nature of scientific investigation, he can report his conditions so that another experimenter can duplicate them and check the data.
3. The experimenter can systematically *vary* the conditions and note the concomitant variation in the results.[6]

If an experimenter wants to test the effect of an independent variable (let us say the style of leadership of the group leader) on a dependent variable (say, the productivity of the group) he must be careful to see that the various groups that receive the experimental treatment (the various leadership styles) differ only in that respect. Perfect equivalence of the groups except for the experimental variable is, of course, impossible. "The ideal of the experiment is never attained. It would mean that the whole universe proceeded uniformly

[5] Leon Festinger, "Laboratory Experiments," in Festinger and D. Katz, eds., *Research Methods in the Behavioral Sciences* (New York: Dryden Press, 1953), p. 137.

[6] R. S. Woodworth, *Experimental Psychology* (New York: Henry Holt, 1938), p. 2.

while we varied one ingredient."[7] But if experimental groups cannot be identical except for the experimental variable, the researcher must see that as far as possible the groups do not differ from each other in some variable that will systematically influence the results. Thus, the group receiving authoritarian leadership cannot be made up of high-school students, and that receiving democratic leadership, of college students. Or the members of one group cannot be more intelligent, better trained, or better acquainted with each other than the members of the other group. This problem is handled in literature by matching the members of the various groups in terms of as many characteristics as possible that might possibly affect the results. The subjects of the small group experiments have usually been male college students, of average intelligence, who do not know each other before the experiment begins.

Another way to eliminate the possible effects of external variables is to submit all groups studied to all experimental treatments. Thus, in their classic experiment on the effects of group climate on children's groups, Lippitt and White subjected all the groups they studied to all three leadership styles.[8] The reactions of the groups cannot then be attributed to other group characteristics. The problem of the order of treatment is handled by systematically varying the order in which the various leadership styles are used on the various groups. Furthermore, it is standard practice to see that the instructions to the groups are standardized, that the appearance and behavior of the experimenter do not vary from group to group, and that the groups meet under identical physical conditions.

EXPERIMENTS AND SURVEYS: Perhaps the particular characteristics of the experimental method can be made clearer by comparing it with a method with which it has a number of logical similarities and that is more familiar in political re-

[7] A. D. Ritchie, *Scientific Method*, quoted in Barbara Wooton, *Testament for Social Science: An Essay in the Application of Scientific Method to Human Problems* (London: Allen and Unwin, 1950), p. 28.

[8] Ralph White and Ronald Lippitt, "Leader Behavior and Member Reaction in Three 'Social Climates,' " in Dorwin Cartwright and Alvin Zander, eds., *Group Dynamics* (Evanston, Ill.: Row, Peterson, 1953), chap. 40.

search—the survey method. Both the experimental method and the survey method attempt to isolate the relations between two or more variables by holding all others constant. The difference between the two methods of research lies not in the logic of trying to isolate variables, but in the fact that the laboratory experimenter can control these variables by manipulating them in advance, while the survey researcher must attempt to control them by statistical means after the survey is completed.[9]

As has been pointed out, the goal of the experimental method in group studies is to isolate the effect of a particular treatment on group behavior. In the ideal experiment, the experimental group and the control group will differ only in respect to that treatment. In survey analysis, the logic is similar. The researcher, on the basis of his survey results, attempts to divide his sample into two groups that differ in only one respect to see the way in which that single difference affects some other dependent variable (an attitude, for instance). Thus a sample can be divided by occupation of respondent to see the way in which occupation affects voting behavior. However, if the researcher wants to avoid a spurious correlation between occupation and voting, a correlation that might be caused by the association of other factors with occupation, he must control for a variety of other factors. Thus occupational groups will have to be sub-divided by religion, residence, education, and so forth. If wage-earners are more likely to be Catholic and professionals more likely to be Protestant, religion will have to be kept constant so that voting behavior can be related to occupation without the contaminating effect of religion. Essentially, this is the same problem that faces the experimental researcher, who must control all conditions that might affect the result of the experiment. One major difference between the two types of research is that in the survey situation, where conditions cannot be manipulated in

[9] This difference has led Greenwood and Chapin to call the survey study an *ex post facto* experiment. Ernest Greenwood, *Experimental Sociology: A Study of Method* (New York: King's Crown Press, 1945), pp. 29-30; and F. Stuart Chapin, *Experimental Designs in Sociological Research* (New York: Harper, 1947), chap. 5.

advance by the researcher, but rather groups must be matched by sorting after the survey, there is no way to be sure that all possible variables that would have significant effects on the results have been held constant.[10]

The logic of the experimental method is not unique to the laboratory and the sample survey. If the historian wants to explain historical event Y as having been (partially or completely) determined by a previous historical event X, he must try to predict what would have happened if event Y (what might be called the independent variable) had not taken place. This can be done, as Max Weber does it, through the use of comparative history. To trace the effect of Protestantism on the development of a capitalist economy, he compares economic development in Western nations that have a Protestant ethic with development in those countries where such an ethic did not exist.[11] Or, instead of comparing two historical systems, one can compare historical developments with a hypothetical system in which independent variable Y does not exist. Raymond Aron, for instance, asks how the historian can evaluate the impact of the Austrian ultimatum to Serbia in July 1914, on the outbreak of World War I. Did this event cause the war, or were the causes more long-term, so that any one of a number of incidents could have touched it off? "We cannot repeat the experiment, eliminate the incident of July, 1914, so that history may take another course—which might confirm or refute the hypothesis of 'inevitability.' All we can do is perform mental experiments. We try to combine the fundamental data of the situation with a variety of accidents to conclude that in the largest number of cases (or in all, or in only a few) the event would have occurred."[12]

[10] This is especially true for two reasons. (1) In survey research one can deal only with those variables contained in the survey; i.e., if no question is asked in the survey about religion, one cannot control for that factor. And (2) if one tries to isolate too many factors at once, the numbers in any one cell become too small for statistical manipulation. On this general subject, see Patricia C. Kendall and Paul F. Lazarsfeld, "Problems of Survey Analysis," in Merton and Lazarsfeld, eds., *Studies in the Scope* . . . , pp. 136ff.

[11] Max Weber, *General Economic History* (Glencoe, Ill.: Free Press, 1927), chap. 30.

[12] Raymond Aron, "Evidence and Inference in History," *Daedelus* (1958), pp. 11-39.

The experimental method differs from the survey and the survey from the historical method not so much in the logic of explanation as in the control over the situation that the researcher exerts and, consequently, in the precision of the explanation. One major difference between the logic of the survey and the experiment must, however, be pointed out. In the experimental situation one can locate the causal relationship between two variables, something that is not always possible in a survey. Since the experimenter introduces the independent variable into a situation where it had not previously existed, he knows that the independent variable determines the dependent variable, and not vice versa. But to demonstrate in a survey that two variables correlate does not indicate which variable determines the other. Thus political attitudes correlate with occupation. But is it that the economic interests and the personal contacts of those in certain occupations engender particular political attitudes, or is it that those with particular political attitudes tend to go into certain occupations? Common sense and what we know of attitude formation suggest the former explanation; but the logic of the survey method does not favor one explanation over the other. If, on the other hand, we had been able to perform an experiment—if we could have taken several matched groups of people whose political attitudes were known, assigned them to different occupations, and at some later date studied the changes, if any, in their political attitudes—we would know the direction of the influence. The political attitudes of the subjects could not influence their occupational choice, since that was determined by the experimenter's fiat. However, differential changes in the political attitudes of the various groups of subjects could be traced to the occupation into which they were placed because (assuming the experiment is a "perfect" one) only this variable differentiates the various groups.[13]

[13] This subject is treated most fully in Herbert H. Hyman, *Survey Design and Analysis* (Glencoe, Ill.: Free Press, 1955), Part III.

The Culture of the Laboratory

In a desire to achieve something approaching perfect control, small group researchers have been led to create their own carefully controlled cultures in the laboratory. These laboratory cultures have a special character due largely to the artificial situation created by the experimenter. Of course, that experiments are artificial is implied in the notion of the experimental method. Nor is it unexpected that, as will be shown below, the behavior of individuals in these laboratory situations differs from what it would be in real life. One does not expect the laboratory situation to duplicate the real world. The function of the experiment is not to duplicate but to simplify so that precise relationships between variables can be discovered. Festinger writes: "There is frequently a tendency in social psychology to criticize laboratory experiments because of their 'artificiality.' A word must be said about this criticism because it probably stems from an inadequate understanding of the purposes of a laboratory experiment. A laboratory experiment need not, and should not, be an attempt to duplicate a real-life situation. If one wanted to study something in a real-life situation, it would be rather foolish to go to the trouble of setting up a laboratory situation duplicating the real-life condition. Why not simply go directly to the real-life situation and study it? The laboratory situation should be an attempt to create a situation in which the operation of variables will be clearly seen under special identified and controlled conditions. It matters not whether such a situation would ever be encountered in real life. In most laboratory experiments, such a situation would certainly *never* be encountered in real life. In the laboratory, however, we can find out exactly how a certain variable affects behavior or attitudes under special or 'pure' conditions."[14]

But surely the recognition that experimental groups differ from real-life groups is not the end of the problem. If one wants to apply the experimental findings to the real world, one must look more carefully at the nature of this artificiality.

[14] In Festinger and Katz, eds., *Research Methods* . . . , p. 139.

Unless one only wants to understand and predict behavior in other experimental groups on the basis of experimental studies—and that is clearly not the use that political science will make of these studies—the differences between the experimental and the real-life situation must be explored more fully so that the gap between the two can be bridged.

That the experimental situation represents a simplification of situations that obtain in the real world does not eliminate the possibility of applying these findings to the real world—as long as the nature of the simplification is known. In moving from the laboratory to explanation and prediction about behavior in the real world, it is necessary to specify the differences between the two. Two sources of difference are (1) the absence in the experimental groups of certain variables, the presence of which in the real situation significantly affects behavior (some of these missing variables might be emotional commitment and expectations of further contact); and (2) the presence within the experimental small group of certain hidden variables, not intended by the experimenter. These variables may be brought into the experimental situation by the group members from their roles outside of the laboratory. Such variables might be a personal idiosyncrasy of one of the members or a characteristic that all members shared that systematically distorted the direction of their behavior. Some of these variables that differentiate the small experimental group from on-going social situations will be discussed in greater detail below.

If the differences between the real world and the experimental situation are known, the application of the laboratory findings to the real world can be made in one of two ways. On the one hand, the differences may be eliminated by trying to build them into the experimental situation. Several examples of this attempt to make the experimental situation more "real" will be discussed below. While this solution has a number of advantages, it may conflict with the desire of experimentalists for greater control and precision. On the other hand, the differences can be taken into account when applying the findings of experimental research to the real world. Experimental studies will predict that under certain conditions certain behaviors will take place. If in the real world, under slightly different conditions, different behaviors take place, we can then, if we know what the different conditions are, explain to some extent the reasons why the behaviors predicted on the basis of the small group experiment and the behaviors observed in the real world did not coincide. This task is quite complex, given the complexity of actual social situations—a complexity that led to the use of experimental groups in the first place. But a constant movement from the laboratory to the real situation—using the small group experiment as part of a research chain, in order to suggest propositions about the real world, and to test propositions derived from field studies—will make this task easier and more rewarding.

The way in which the small group in the laboratory differs from groups in real life must now be considered more carefully. Many of these special characteristics of the culture of the experimental small group, it will be seen, are the result of attempts to make the small group situation a closely controlled and limited one. Has precision been introduced at the expense of relevance, or are there ways of achieving both precision and relevance? A study of the special laboratory culture may bring us closer to an answer to this question. The special characteristics of the small group may be found in the population from which the group is chosen, the techniques of observation used, and the setting of the experiment. Each of these characteristics will be considered in turn.

POPULATION: The subjects that populate the experimental small groups have an important effect in determining the peculiar culture of the laboratory. In contrasting the experiment with the sample survey, it was pointed out that the experimenter can control the experimental conditions by carefully matching groups. But carefully matched groups raise the problem of generalizability. The sample survey justifies its generalizations from a sample to a larger population on the basis of certain laws of probability. The experimentalists have, on the other hand, not shown as much interest in the population from which they draw their samples, or in the method by which the subjects are recruited from that population. And both the population base and the methods of choosing subjects may bias the results in a particular direction.

A typical experiment in which matched groups are used is that conducted by Bell and French.[15] They were interested in the question of whether leadership was specific to one group, or whether the individual who took a leadership role in one group was more likely to assume that role in another. The dependent variable was the leadership position of an individual in a five-man group. The independent variable manipulated by the experimenter was the composition of the group. The subjects in the experiment took part in six different discussion groups, the groups being systematically varied so that each consisted of five subjects who had not been together in a previous session. In order to isolate this one variable—the membership of the group—from all others, the experimenters had to see that the groups did not differ in other characteristics. One way to eliminate the effect of other characteristics would be to use a large number of groups chosen at random from a large population. In this case, other variables could be assumed to vary randomly and not influence the results. But this technique, used by the survey researcher, is much too cumbersome and expensive for small group research. The survey researcher who selects potential respondents on the basis of some sound sampling technique has but to present these respondents with a questionnaire. The experimentalist would have to seek them out and bring them to a central place at a designated time to take part in an experiment. Under these circumstances it is little wonder that the experimentalist has chosen a more practical method and has used subjects more easily available. The groups used by Bell and French were made up of male students in an introductory psychology course, who were previously unacquainted and who were matched in terms of intelligence and other factors.

[15] G. B. Bell and R. L. French, "Consistency of Individual Leadership Position in Small Groups of Varying Membership," *J. Abnorm. Soc. Psych.*, *45* (1950), pp. 764-67, reprinted in Hare, Borgatta, and Bales, eds., *Small Groups*, p. 275.

This allowed the findings of the experiment to be quite precise; but the findings, to quote the authors, ". . . cannot be generalized to all types of groups."[16]

The fact that the generalizability of the experimental results is so seriously limited by the group used represents one of the special problems of experimentation with groups of individuals. The natural scientist can, with greater confidence, assume that the particular piece of metal he examines is representative of all pieces of metal of that type. Experimentalists in biology can make the same assumption, though with somewhat less confidence. But in group experimental work, in which the personal idiosyncrasies of the members, their previous histories, and their experiences in other groups affect the way in which they act in experimental groups, the creation of representative groups—i.e. experimental groups from whose behavior one can generalize to a wide range of other groups—is particularly difficult.

The need for easily available subjects has turned the study of small groups largely into a study of the interactions of college students, children, or military personnel.[17] Or the group studied may be made up of students or children with special characteristics. Thus Polanski, Lippitt, and Redl study influence relationships among emotionally disturbed children.[18] The important point is that the special characteristic of the children, though it may affect the results of the experiment, is not under direct study and is not considered relevant to the experimental design. The particular advantage of using

[16] *Ibid.*, p. 279.

[17] The experiments using college students include those of Bales and his associates (to be discussed in Chapter VI, below), and of Carter and his associates (see Launor Carter, "Some Research on Leadership in Small Groups," in Harold Guetzkow, ed., *Groups, Leadership and Men*, pp. 146-57).

Children's groups were used in the Iowa experiments by Lewin, Lippitt, and White (discussed below in Chapter IX) and by Ferenc Merei, "Group Leadership and Institutionalization," *Hum. Rel.*, 2 (1949), pp. 23-39.

Studies using military personnel include those done at Ohio State University under contract with the Office of Naval Research. See C. L. Shartle and R. M. Stogdill, *Studies in Naval Leadership* (Columbus: Ohio State University Research Foundation, 1952), and numerous studies done at Maxwell Air Force Base.

[18] N. Polanski, R. Lippitt, and F. Redl, "An Investigation of Behavioral Contagion in Groups," *Hum. Rel.*, 3 (1950), pp. 319-48.

students, military personnel, and children as subjects is that their participation over an extended period is easier to arrange and can, in fact, be required. But the particular population from which the subjects are chosen will affect the results of the experiment. Different results have been produced by the same experimental design if high school instead of college students are used, if children of different ages are used, or if families instead of unacquainted college students are used.[19]

Another limitation to the generalizability of experimental results is that most experimental studies of small groups are studies of American subjects. As will be discussed later, certain aspects of leadership behavior in small experimental groups may be traced to the culture of the larger American social system from which the subjects are drawn.

Two other biases that may be introduced by the population of the experimental group must be mentioned, particularly as they have an effect on group leadership—the special interest of the second half of this study. In a large number of experiments, participants tend to be self-selected and/or over-sophisticated. In many cases, participants are chosen from among those members of the class, military unit, or children's group who volunteer to participate in the experiment. When the experiment attempts to study the rates with which individuals initiate influence attempts, as do many of the studies we shall consider later, the fact that all group members are volunteers may introduce a variable neither intended nor controlled by the experimenter.

Similarly, the consciousness that they are subjects of an experiment may lead individuals to behave in ways not expected by the experimenter. Participants may, for instance, behave as they believe the experimenter wants them to behave. This effect was first observed in the Western Electric Haw-

[19] L. Carter, W. Haythorn, and M. Howell, "A Further Investigation of the Criteria of Leadership," *J. Abnorm. Soc. Psych.*, 45 (1950), pp. 350-58, reprinted in Hare, Borgatta and Bales, eds., *Small Groups*, p. 523; R. W. Berenda, *The Influence of the Group on the Judgments of Children* (New York: King's Crown Press, 1950), cited in Asch, *Social Psychology*, pp. 481-83; and Fred Strodtbeck, "Husband-Wife Interaction over Revealed Differences," *Am. Soc. Rev.*, 16 (1954), pp. 468-73, reprinted in Hare, Borgatta, and Bales, eds., *Small Groups*, p. 464.

thorne studies. No matter what changes were made in the physical set-up of the relay-assembly test room, even changes intended to hamper production, production rose. The researchers discovered that the subjects were reacting not to the experimental manipulations of their physical environment, but to what they believed the researchers were interested in—higher production.[20] The more aware the subjects are of the interests of the experimenter, the more likely to contaminate the results is this desire to give the experimenter what he wants. In this connection it is important to note that many experimental subjects have substantial experience with experimental studies. Maier and Solem, for instance, discuss the subjects used in one of their group experiments: "All previously had instruction in group discussion methods and some role-playing experience. They were accustomed to forming small discussion groups. . . ."[21] Gibb reports the results of an experiment on leadership in which the subjects associated leadership with friendship on a post-session questionnaire with greater frequency than had been predicted. According to Gibb, "There is nothing . . . to suggest why this should have occurred," but he goes on to ". . . hazard a guess that participants may have become increasingly aware of the experimental interest in leadership in the study and may have endeavored to make their own records 'look better' by choosing only those whom they expected the observers would also choose on quite different criteria. In other words, there is a possibility that choices became less genuine."[22]

THE OBSERVER EFFECT: The problem of the over-aware subject suggests one of the major problems of social research: the effect upon the subject of the process of being studied. The impact of the observer on the social process he is observing is

[20] See Roethlisberger and Dickson, *Management and the Worker*, pp. 58-59.
[21] N. R. F. Maier and A. R. Solem, "The Contribution of a Discussion Leader to the Quality of Group Thinking," *Hum. Rel.*, 5 (1952), pp. 277-88, reprinted in Cartwright and Zander, eds., *Group Dynamics*, chap. 38.
[22] G. A. Gibb, "The Sociometry of Leadership in Temporary Small Groups," *Sociometry*, 13 (1950), pp. 226-43, reprinted in Hare, Borgatta, and Bales, eds., *Small Groups*, p. 526.

a significant variable in almost all social research, but it has received special attention within the experimental small group studies, possibly because of the greater "presence" of the observer, constantly recording social interaction as it takes place. The role of the observer, as Parsons and Bales suggest, cannot be ignored: "The point of origin for an observer's analysis of a system of action process . . . must be such as to *include himself in the system being analyzed.* This means in social system terms that the *role* of the observer must be explicitly analyzed and treated as part of the system."[23]

The small group experimenters have dealt with the role of the observer largely by trying to limit as much as possible his effect on the experimental process. There are several ways to minimize the observer effect. The behavior of the observer can be standardized for all groups; the subjects can be kept to some extent unaware of the experimental situation; and mechanical means can be used to reduce the "presence" of the observer. Though there are some lapses, standardization of experimental behavior is employed in almost all groups. Edwards stresses the importance of this: "In psychological research, uniformity of the experimental conditions is of particular importance because of the subtleties of the interactions between experimenter and subjects. Subjects may react to the mood, appearance, and behavior of the experimenter as well as to the experimental conditions in which the experimenter is primarily interested. A friendly approach upon the part of the experimenter with some subjects and a more hostile or aggressive approach to others may introduce departures from uniformity which will influence individual performance."[24]

The use of experimental subjects who are to some extent naïve about the experimental situation is another means of lowering the effect of observation. Knowledge, or assumed knowledge, of what the experimenter is seeking, it was pointed out above, will influence the behavior of the group members. So will the very process of being observed. By keeping the

23 Talcott Parsons, Robert F. Bales, and Edward A. Shils, *Working Papers in the Theory of Action* (Glencoe, Ill.: Free Press, 1953), p. 96.
24 Allen L. Edwards, "Experiments: Their Planning and Execution," in Lindzey, ed., *Handbook* . . . , Vol. I, p. 275.

subjects to some extent unaware of the experimental set-up, this effect can be limited. The degree of naïveté of the subjects varies from experiment to experiment. The minimum degree of naïveté exists in those experiments in which the subjects are fully aware that they are being observed, know the observation methods being used, and know generally the aims of the study. Thus in the studies of various communication nets the subjects are told that the experiment is a study of the effectiveness of different communication networks, and the set-up of the experimental situation, as well as their tasks, are explained accurately to them.[25] But, though they are told the study concerns communication, they are not told the precise dependent variables sought and the precise behaviors to be recorded. Many of the studies carried on by Robert Bales and his associates are of this nature.[26] The subjects are observed through a one-way mirror, but they are informed of this. They are told that the experiment is a study of group discussion, but they are told neither the particular recording system used nor that the experimenters may be looking for leadership formation or clique formation. To do so would certainly inhibit spontaneous behavior.

A higher level of naïveté exists in those experiments in which some aspect of the experimental situation, aside from the categories the experimenter uses to record data and the theory guiding his work, is unknown to the experimental subjects. Some mechanical aspect of the study may be presented to the subjects in other than its real form. In Sherif's experiments on group pressures using the auto-kinetic effect, the

[25] See Alex Bavelas, "Communications Patterns in Task-Oriented Groups," *Journal of the Acoustical Society of America*, 22 (1950), pp. 725-30, reprinted in Lerner and Lasswell, eds., *Policy Sciences*; George A. Heise and George Miller, "Problem Solving by Small Groups Using Various Communications Nets," *J. Abnorm. Soc. Psych.*, 46 (1951), pp. 327-35, reprinted in Hare, Borgatta, and Bales, eds., *Small Groups*, p. 353; and H. J. Leavitt, "Some Effects of Certain Communications Patterns on Group Performance," *J. Abnorm. Soc. Psych.*, 46 (1951), pp. 38-50, reprinted in G. E. Swanson, T. M. Newcomb, and E. L. Hartley, eds., *Readings in Social Psychology* (New York: Henry Holt, 1952), pp. 108-25.

[26] See Bales, *Interaction Process Analysis*; Parsons, Bales, and Shils, *Working Papers*; and Bales and Philip E. Slater, "Role Differentiation in Small Decision-Making Groups," in Parsons and Bales, *Family, Socialization and Interaction Process Analysis* (Glencoe, Ill.: Free Press, 1955), chap. 5.

77

subjects were told that a pinpoint of light would move, while it was in fact stationary.[27] Or, in a study of frustration, French gave groups puzzles to solve that were in fact not soluble.[28]

Another device used in many experiments is the employment of stooges. As far as the naïve subjects are concerned, these are experimental subjects. But they have been placed in the group by the experimenter to play a particular role. Stooges are especially effective in developing tension situations. While the naïve subject can maintain a certain emotional detachment vis-à-vis the experimenter because of his expectations from the experimenter role, he expects "normal" behavior from the other experimental subjects. Both Asch, who used groups made up of a number of stooges, and Hemphill, who used one stooge in a group of naïve members, report high levels of tension.[29]

The most extreme level of naïveté occurs when the experimental subjects are not aware that they are being observed, or even of the fact that they are taking part in an experiment. The one-way mirror is now standard equipment in most small group laboratories, and though some researchers make a point of telling subjects that this device is in use, others do not.[30] Such concealment is used to minimize the observer effect. Strodtbeck, who observed husband-wife discussions without their knowledge, reports that "The anticipated experimental difficulties—(a) producing 'polite' interaction because

[27] Sherif, *Arch. Psych.* (1953).

[28] J. R. P. French, Jr., "The Disruption and Cohesion of Groups," *J. Abnorm. Soc. Psych.*, *36* (1941), pp. 361-77, reprinted in Cartwright and Zander, eds., *Group Dynamics*, chap. 10.

[29] Asch, *Social Psychology*, chap. 16; and John K. Hemphill, "Why People Take Leadership," *Adult Leadership*, *5* (1956), pp. 44-46. See also the use of role-playing stooges in the studies of the rejection of deviants by Schachter, *J. Abnorm. Soc. Psych.* (1951); and Schachter, *et al.*, *Hum. Rel.*, *7* (1954).

[30] See, for instance, C. Heinicke and R. F. Bales, "Developmental Trends in the Structure of Small Groups," *Sociometry* (1953); W. Haythorn, *et al.*, "The Behavior of Authoritarian and Equalitarian Personalities in Groups," *Hum. Rel.*, *9* (1956), pp. 57-74; L. Carter and M. Nixon, "Ability, Perception, Personality, and Interest Factors Associated with Different Criteria for Leadership," *Journal of Psychology*, *27* (1949), pp. 377-88; and W. C. Schutz, "What Makes Groups Productive?" *Hum. Rel.*, *8* (1955), pp. 429-66. See especially the discussion by Schutz of the need for such concealment, *ibid.*, p. 462.

of the presence of the experimenter, and (b) structuring the task to such a degree that the mode of interaction would be highly determined—were judged to have been satisfactorily avoided."[31]

One device for reducing the impact of observation on subjects is to have the observer play some participant role that conceals the fact that he is an observer. Lippitt and White, for instance, had "club directors," "visiting adults," and "janitors" as observers in their experiments.[32] And Muzafer Sherif in his study conducted in a children's camp spent the summer posing as a handyman.[33] Sherif takes issue with those small group experimentalists who maintain that the observer effect in laboratory situations does not make a significant difference. If the behavior observed is not to be distorted by the experimental situation, the subjects must be unaware that they are under study.

> To approximate as much as possible the natural process of spontaneous group formation . . . the subjects were kept unaware of the fact that the whole thing was an experiment in group relations. The announced purpose of the study was that it was a study of camping procedures. Contrary to some workers in this area, it is psychologically naïve and unrealistic to have the subjects aware that the process of group formation and their strivings to achieve a status in their group, their hostility expressed in words and deeds, and the like are under study and still to assume that this self-awareness would not come as an important factor in determining their behavior.
>
> It follows that data concerning in-group formation and intergroup functioning should be obtained by participant observers who are perceived as part and parcel of the situation by the subjects. . . . Moreover, the participant observers should not be detected by the participants while recording observations contrary to the natural functions of their announced roles. The argument that subjects cease to be mindful that their words and other behavior are being taken down is contrary to what we have learned concerning the structuring of perception. The presence of a personage, ever observing, ever recording our words and deeds in a situation in which our status and role

[31] Strodtbeck, in Hare, Borgatta, and Bales, eds., *Small Groups*, p. 465.
[32] White and Lippitt, in Cartwright and Zander, eds., *Group Dynamics*.
[33] Muzafer Sherif and Carolyn Sherif, *Groups in Harmony and Tension* (New York: Harper, 1953).

concerns are at stake cannot help coming in as an important anchorage in the frame of reference of behavior in question.[34]

As the earlier quotation from Parsons and Bales suggested, the relationship between observer and observed is one of interaction. We have considered so far the effect of the observer on the observed. But the subjects of the experiment may also have an effect on the observer, causing some systematic bias in his observations. This problem is especially difficult in work with on-going groups in which the sentiments of the observers are likely to be engaged. Polanski, Lippitt, and Redl spent eight weeks studying a summer camp for maladjusted children. The observers were, of course, supposed to be detached and neutral researchers, but eight weeks of close observation of these children made this difficult. The authors admit such an involvement, but are not sure of its effect.[35]

We have shown how the naïveté of the experimental subjects can minimize the interaction between the observer and the observed. Similarly, an enforced observer naïveté can perform the same function. When the researcher uses others (graduate students, paid assistants) as observers in his experimental research, there is some danger that the observers will inadvertently supply the reports that the experimenter seeks by over-recording behaviors that fit the researcher's theory. In a study by John Thibault an attempt was made to meet this problem: "In order to minimize possible bias, they [the observers] were kept totally unaware of the theory guiding the experiment and of the current trends of the results."[36]

The major way in which the effect of observer bias is controlled is the use of systematic observational techniques that reduce the discretion of the observer to a minimum and that attempt to maximize inter-observer reliability. Controlling the observational techniques has become both more significant and more difficult as the experimental studies have turned to

---

[34] *Ibid.*, pp. 304-5.

[35] Polanski, Lippitt, and Redl, *Hum. Rel.*, 2 (1949).

[36] John Thibault, "An Experimental Study of the Cohesiveness of Under-Privileged Groups," *Hum. Rel.*, *3* (1950), pp. 251-78, reprinted in Cartwright and Zander, eds., *Group Dynamics*, chap. 9.

situations in which relatively free interaction is allowed among the experimental subjects and in which interactions are recorded directly by the observer. As the experimentalists tried to increase both the range of material studied and the precision of the observational techniques, new techniques of observation were required.

The earliest studies of experimental groups dealt merely with the result of group interaction and not with the interaction process itself. The question usually asked was, "What change in an individual's normal solitary performance occurs when there are other people present?"[37] Experimenters measured changes in the rate of output, changes in judgment, and changes in attitude, caused by the presence of others. In some studies, the group influence on the individual consisted of reports as to what "experts" or "fellow students" had said on the subject. There was little interaction among the members of the experimental group; and broad studies of group process were left largely to the field research of men like William F. Whyte and Elton Mayo.

Kurt Lewin and his associates at the State University of Iowa first tried to combine experimental controls only possible in groups created by the experimenter with relatively free development of interactions among group members. The work of Lewin, Lippitt, and White is of special interest because of their desire to study actual social problems using the experimental method.

> If one hopes to investigate experimentally such fundamental socio-psychological problems as: group ideology; conflicts between and within groups; types of their spontaneous sub-structuring; the stability of various spontaneous group structures versus structures created by external authority; minority problems; renegade, scapegoat, double loyalty conflicts—one has to create a set-up where group life might be studied under rather free but well defined conditions. Instead of utilizing the groups in schools, clubs, factories, one should create groups experimentally because only in this way the factors influencing group life will not be left to chance but will be in the hands of the experimenter.

[37] G. Allport, "The Historical Background of Modern Social Psychology," in Lindzey, ed., *Handbook* . . . , Vol. I, p. 46.

However, one should break away from the rather narrow aspect of studying the effect of the group influence on the suggestibility of the individual as the main problem; one should consider not only one effect of a given social situation (e.g., the influence on productivity). Rather one should try to approach an experimental procedure: (a) where group life can proceed freely; (b) where the total group behavior, its structure and development can be registered. Any specific problem such as group ideology should be approached in the experimental set-up and in the analysis of the data as a part of this greater whole.[38]

In the earlier experiments where the effect but not the process of interaction was under study, the recording of data was relatively easy: test scores, comparisons of pre- and post-interaction judgments, and the like. But the Lewinian work, in which group members are left relatively free to structure the group as they like and to interact with whomever they want in a variety of ways, demanded new techniques of observation. The complexity of the process of recording data in such free interaction can be appreciated by looking at the types of data recorded in the early Lippitt experiments. There were four observers for each group of five children. A brief description of the data recorded follows:

1. A quantitative running account of the social interaction of the five children and leader, in terms of symbols for ascendant, submissive, and objective (fact-minded) approaches to responses, including a category of purposeful refusal to respond to a social approach.

2. A quantitative group structure analysis minute by minute with running comments to give a record of: activity subgroupings . . . ; the activity goal of each subgroup; whether the subgroup was initiated by the leader or spontaneously formed by the children; and ratings on the degree of interest and unity of each subgroup.

3. Running comments and ratings indicating shifts of interest from minute to minute for each member (from complete involvement in the club activity to "out-of-the-field" preoccupations).

4. A stenographic record of conversations.

[38] Kurt Lewin and Ronald Lippitt, "An Experimental Approach to the Study of Democracy and Autocracy: A Preliminary Note," *Sociometry, 1* (1938), pp. 292-300, reprinted in Hare, Borgatta, and Bales, eds., *Small Groups*, p. 516.

5. To the observers' records outlined above was added a post-meeting write-up by the leader of his impressions gathered from the more intimate contacts with the children.[39]

The purpose of such a large-scale operation was to record as completely as possible total group behavior. The resulting records allow breakdowns into many types of data: individual and group productivity records, rate of sub-group formation, leader-follower relations, and the like. One significant aspect of the technique is that it breaks down individual behavior into discrete acts, recorded at fairly small time intervals in systematic categories. This type of recording allows the computation of rates of behavior of individuals and of the group— rates that can be compared as between groups and between individuals. It allows the presentation of material in a form that lends itself to statistical manipulation, and opens the way for checks on inter-observer reliability.

The most widely used observation technique employing counts of discrete interactions is that developed by Robert Bales. In this scheme interactions are recorded for each individual in twelve categories:[40]

1. *Shows solidarity*: raises other's status, gives help, reward:
2. *Shows tension release*: jokes, laughs, shows satisfaction:
3. *Agrees*: shows passive acceptance, understands, concurs, complies:
4. *Gives suggestion*: direction, implying autonomy for another:
5. *Gives opinion*: evaluation, analysis, expresses feeling, wish:
6. *Gives orientation*: information, repeats, clarifies, confirms:
7. *Asks for orientation*: information, repetition, confirmation:
8. *Asks for opinion*: evaluation, analysis, expression of feeling:
9. *Asks for suggestion*: direction, possible ways of action:
10. *Disagrees*: shows passive rejection, formality, withholds help:
11. *Shows tension*: asks for help, withdraws out of field:
12. *Shows antagonism*: deflates other's stature, defends or asserts self.

[39] *Ibid.*, pp. 518-19.
[40] Bales, *Interaction Process Analysis*, p. 9. The recording scheme developed by Bales is closely connected with his theory of group interaction. This will be discussed more fully in Chapter VI below. The recording technique has, however, gained a wide acceptance among researchers who have used it without the concomitant theoretical system developed by Bales.

Using a scheme of this nature, group roles can be given precise operational definitions in terms of rates of behavior. Thus a non-directive leader as contrasted with a directive leader has a lower rate of activity in categories 4 and 5. Other recording schemes have been developed, some recording all interactions as does the Bales scheme, others recording only some significant interactions. And along with the recording schemes have come mechanical devices to facilitate the observation process.[41]

The use of observational techniques employing interaction counts introduces a high level of precision into the group studies. Tests of inter-observer reliability are possible, and comparisons can be made from group to group on the basis of unambiguous, measurable criteria. But the use of these interaction counts introduces an element of artificiality that seriously limits the relevance of these studies for the study of political affairs. This subject will be discussed much more fully below when the relation between small group studies of leadership and political leadership is considered. Suffice it to mention here that the definition and analysis of group roles in terms of the frequencies of certain acts performed by the group members leave something to be desired. One of the major interests of the small group experimenters— an interest that has led to some of the most politically relevant experiments—is the relationship between leader behavior and the goal attainment of the group. Interaction counts, however, can deal only indirectly with the goal-directed activity of the group. Leaders may be defined by a high rate of activity in the positive task-oriented categories of the Bales scheme (categories 4, 5, and 6), but the rate of suggestion, opinion, and orientation given by the leader tells us nothing of the

41 Hemphill, for instance, uses a scheme that counts only influence attempts (John Hemphill, *et al.*, "The Relation Between the Possession of Task Relevant Information and Attempts to Lead," *Psychological Monographs, No. 414* [1956], entire number). For a longer list of categories than that developed by Bales, see Carter, *et al.*, *Hum. Rel. 4* (1951). Some mechanical devices are described in Bales, *op.cit.*; Carter, *et al.*, *op.cit.*; and E. D. Chappel, "The Interaction Chronograph: Its Evolution and Present Application," *Personnel*, 25 (1949), pp. 295-307.

relative importance of individual acts—some of which may be much more important than others. Cattell and Stice, for instance, distinguish two types of leaders, the "persistent momentary problem solvers" and the "salient leaders."[42] The former type of leader makes consistent contributions to the group process; the latter may influence only one total situation on one occasion, but this single act will have a more significant effect on the group's goal attainment than the more persistent activities of the former type of leader. "Salient leaders," however, could not be found by interaction counts which assume, to some extent, that the person who talks the most is the most useful member of the group—an assumption the unreality of which will be readily apparent to anyone who has ever taken part in group discussion.[43] In fact, any activity in the group that occurs with low frequency—though that activity may be extremely significant in the group process— cannot be handled by the interaction count technique and consequently is usually ignored.[44]

Two other systematic observation techniques are usually employed in small group studies, and these help fill the gaps in the interaction count method. These two techniques are sociometric testing and observer ratings. In the sociometric test, group members are asked to rate their fellows on the basis of some criterion—leadership, liking, substantive contribution to the group. Whereas sociometric choices are made by the group members, ratings are made by the observers. Ratings of the performance of the individual group members or of the group as a whole can be made by the observer after the group session or at stated time intervals during the session. The advantage of this technique is that it is not limited to rates of individual acts, but can take into account

[42] R. B. Cattell and G. F. Stice, "Four Formulae for Selecting Leaders on the Basis of Personality," *Hum. Rel.*, 7 (1954), p. 505.

[43] The assumption is explicitly made by Bernard M. Bass, "An Analysis of Leaderless Group Discussion," *Journal of Applied Psychology, 33* (1949), p. 533. It is implicit in much of the work of Bales and his associates.

[44] See Carter, *et al.*, "The Behavior of Leaders and Other Group Members," *J. Abnorm. Soc. Psych.*, 46 (1951), pp. 589-95, reprinted in Cartwright and Zander, eds., *Group Dynamics*, chap. 37, p. 554.

the relative effectiveness of any single act. The technique lacks, of course, the precision of the interaction count.[45]

THE LABORATORY SETTING: The search for precision in small group studies is one of the causes of the special culture of the experimental group. We have described some aspects of this special culture that derive from the selection of the experimental population and from the observational techniques. But it is perhaps the general setting of the small group experiment that does the most to create the special laboratory culture we are describing. That the experimental situation represents a unique situation as far as the subjects are concerned is clear. The groups are brought together at the behest of the experimenter to perform tasks they would not ordinarily perform. They are assembled in a special room, under controlled circumstances, and they are under observation in ways that are unusual to them. While the experiment is on, all efforts are made to keep the subjects isolated from extraneous pressures and influences. The groups that are formed usually have no past history of relations, and no expectation of future contact after the experiment is over. The effects of the extraneous influences that the subject brings into the experimental situation from everyday life are limited by matching groups in as many relevant characteristics as possible. Consequently, groups tend to be rather homogeneous in composition. Because of the nature of the experimental

[45] Studies of the relationship between the ratings of observers and interaction counts have produced mixed results. Hemphill (*Psych. Monographs*, *No. 414*, p. 7) found a positive but moderate correlation between the leadership ratings given group members by "naïve" observers who made such ratings every five minutes and the leadership scores of the members based on interaction counts. This indicates that leadership as defined by interaction counts is not completely different from leadership as the laymen might define it while watching a group in operation, but the correspondence is not very strong. On the other hand, Carter and Nixon (*J. Psych.* [1949], pp. 251-53) found fairly strong correlations between direct ratings of leadership made after a group session and leadership as defined by interaction counts. Correlations between ratings and interaction counts ranged from .94 to .82 for three different types of tasks.

The difference in the results may be due to several factors. (1) In the Carter and Nixon investigation, the same person did the interaction counting and made the ratings. In the Hemphill work, the raters and the counters differed. And (2) Carter and Nixon dealt with smaller groups. Further discussion of the relationship among various measures of leadership will be found in Chapter V.

situation, the group members are aware of their special and limited commitment to the experiment. They are aware that the situation is artificial, that relations with the other group members will cease at the end of the experiment, and that the roles they play in the group are of limited consequence to them.

This special situation will affect the way in which the experimental group operates. The artificiality of the situation reduces the chances that affect and tension will develop in the group.[46] The lack of past relations among the group members also influences the group behavior. Groups will have to solve a whole series of problems of internal structure that groups with a history will already have solved. The process of group formation will have to take place simultaneously with the solution of the particular problem that the experimenter presents to the group. And the lack of expectations of continuing relationship after the group meetings allows the group members to behave differently from the way in which they would have behaved had they to consider the effects of their behavior on future relationships to which they were committed. This is illustrated in an experiment on three-person families by Strodtbeck—an experiment replicating one by Mills on three-person groups of college students. Strodtbeck found that in the family groups there was less tendency to form coalitions of two members versus the third than there was in the groups of three college students. The author traces this difference to the fact that the family members engaging in the experiment feel a responsibility for the well-being of the other family members. The consequences of their behavior in the experimental situation will carry over into their post-experimental relations in a group from which they can-

---

[46] That the level of affect and tension goes down as the artificiality of the situation increases is seen in a study by Borgatta and Bales. They compared the tension level among group members in situations in which the members were asked to solve a problem with the level in situations in which the members were asked to play roles selected by the group. In the role-playing situation, tension was much lower. As the situation moved away from highly artificial role-playing, tension rose. Edgar Borgatta and Robert Bales, "Interaction of Individuals in Reconstituted Groups," *Sociometry, 16* (1953), pp. 302-20, reprinted in Hare, Borgatta, and Bales, eds., *Small Groups*, p. 389.

not withdraw.[47] Thus, at least to some extent, the internal structuring of the group under experimental conditions is affected by the expectations or lack of expectations of future contact with the other group members. A coalition of two against one would damage the future relations of the group. This was a factor the *ad hoc* groups could ignore, but that the family groups could not.

And lastly, the fact that the experimental situation is one in which the subjects are faced with novel situations they might not expect to meet in ordinary life serves to distort their behavior. Kennedy compared the responses of college students and air force personnel to participation in a mock air-warning system. Among the air force personnel, to whom assignment to such a system was a real possibility, the situation was considered a "real" one and commitment and tension developed. Among the college students, on the other hand, there was less tension and the situation was considered more of a game.[48] This difference between the reactions of the two groups suggests an important variable rarely considered in experimental studies: the experimental subjects' interpretation of the experimental situation. The degree to which the subjects become involved in the experimental task, respect the experimenter, and consider the experimental method a valid means of research will affect their behavior. And these attitudes toward experimentation probably vary quite a bit among groups. One would expect, for instance, that students in the humanities would react quite differently to the experimental situation than do the psychology students used in most experimental studies. Stanley Milgram has found evidence for such group differences in the interpretation of the experimental situation. In a cross-national experimental study of conformity and independence (using a variation of the Asch line experiments), he found that Norwegian students considered

[47] Theodore Mills, "Power Relations in Three-Person Groups," *Am. Soc. Rev.*, *18* (1943), pp. 251-57, reprinted in Cartwright and Zander, eds., *Group Dynamics*, chap. 29; and Strodtbeck, in Hare, Borgatta, and Bales, eds., *Small Groups*, p. 473.

[48] W. C. Biel, *et al.*, "The Systems Research Laboratories Air Defense Experiments," The RAND Corporation, P-1202, October 1957, mimeographed.

the experiment an important endeavor worthy of their respect and serious cooperation, while French students considered the experimental situation a silly example of American empiricism and essentially a waste of time. When the experimental method is interpreted so differently, one cannot be sure that one is measuring real differences in the dependent variable, the rate of conformity. Norwegian students were found to conform to group norms more frequently than French students, but this may be due either to different rates of conformist behavior in the two societies or to the different attitudes toward the experimental situation.[49]

Conclusion

The small group laboratory certainly develops a unique culture. One cannot move from the laboratory to predictions and explanations about phenomena in the "real" world without taking this uniqueness into consideration. The question of how one can "bridge the gap" between the special culture of the laboratory and the real world of social behavior is the subject of the next chapter.

[49] I am indebted to Mr. Stanley Milgram of Harvard University for this material from his as yet unpublished study.

Chapter IV

EXPERIMENTS AND
THE POLITICAL PROCESS
2: BRIDGING THE GAP

Laboratory Culture and Political Behavior:
Some Similarities

BEFORE embarking on a discussion of the ways in which the differences between the laboratory and the political process can be reconciled, it is well to point out that these differences may not be as great as they at first seem. Political situations are many and varied. For some situations, the special characteristics of the experimental group may not represent such an inapt approximation. It was pointed out that emotional commitment is often missing in the small group. Emotional commitment may also be missing in many political activities. The act of voting, for instance, represents an act of relatively little involvement for many people[1]—less perhaps than the involvement in many small group experiments.

A description of a typical experiment should make the similarity between the laboratory and some political situations clear.[2] A group of from three to six previously unacquainted Harvard undergraduates meet for four sessions of forty minutes' duration each. Each meeting is given over to a discussion of a human relations problem in administration. The members are given summaries of the problem which are accurate but incomplete. Different individuals have different relevant bits of information. They are asked to consider themselves an administrative group inquiring into the problem under discussion to see what action can be taken. No leader

---

[1] The Erie County and Elmira studies as well as the nation-wide survey of the 1952 election by the Survey Research Center report that only about one-third of the electorate is greatly interested in the election. The Survey Research Center reports further that only about one-fifth of the electorate thinks it matters a "great deal" who wins the election. Results cited in Berelson, *et al.*, *Voting*, p. 337.

[2] This experiment, typical of many others, is described by Bales, "Equilibrium Problem in Small Groups," in Parsons, Bales, and Shils, *Working Papers*, pp. 113-14.

is appointed. The group must exchange bits of information to get a complete picture of the problem; they must apply several different values to the solution, all of which may not be held as strongly by all the members; and there must be enough influence exerted in the group to achieve a group decision.

This group typifies the characteristics of the experimental group culture. It has no history and must create its structure while dealing with the problem facing it. It is short-lived; there is little affect; and no great commitment. Yet a group of this sort would not be unusual in an administrative situation. New *ad hoc* committees are often set up to deal with relatively unfamiliar tasks, and despite any formal structure that they may be given, they still must solve certain problems of internal structure as they begin to deal with their task. In bureaucratic situations, affective relations among the members of the group are limited. And the group members may have to exchange information and weigh different values. The two situations are, of course, still not the same. The source of motivation will be different, the external roles that affect the behavior in the group situation will be different, and so will a number of other factors. But the artificial situation may not be as different from some real-life situations as one would expect.

Life-like Experiments

SIMULATING REALITY IN THE LABORATORY: Laboratory experiments can be designed to simulate as much as possible the actual, on-going situation to which the researcher wishes to apply his results. An example of such simulation is the mock air-defense system developed at The RAND Corporation.[3] A replica of an air-warning center was manned by airmen assigned to the experiment. The room resembled an actual air-defense center, information came in on mock radar screens,

[3] This project is discussed in John L. Kennedy, "A 'Transition-Model' Laboratory for Research in Cultural Change," *Human Organization*, *14* (1955), pp. 16-18. See also Allan Newell, "Description of the Air Defense Experiments, II: The Task Environment," The RAND Corporation, P-659, 1955; Robert L. Chapman, "Description of the Air Defense Experiments, III: Data Collection and Processing," The RAND Corporation, P-658, 1955; and Biel, *et al.*, RAND P-1202.

and the information fed into the system was carefully designed to simulate actual challenges from various types of flight patterns. The experiment extended over a long period—the airmen worked regular eight-hour shifts for a six-week period—and the group was able to learn and develop. Kennedy suggests that such simulation performs a "wind-tunnel" function for groups—one can observe under controlled conditions how they react to certain stresses and strains.[4] Simulation has also been used in studies of mock juries, and as a combination teaching and research device in studies of international and business situations.[5] The relative effectiveness of simulating limited situations such as air-defense centers and juries, and larger structures such as the international scene or a competitive business situation, will be discussed below.

MOVING THE LABORATORY INTO THE FIELD: A second way to make experiments more "real" is to move the experiment into the field and apply the techniques of a controlled experiment to actual on-going groups. In field experiments, the groups to be studied are not brought together and created by the experimenter. Existing groups, similar in as many respects as possible, undergo different treatments and the resulting effects are compared. In some cases, the experimental variable is introduced by the experimenter. Thus, in a pioneering work on the use of the experimental method in politics, Gosnell chose two voting districts in Chicago as much alike as possible and submitted one to an extensive educational campaign about voting. The two districts thus differed, ideally, only in the receipt or non-receipt of the educational campaign—the experimental variable.[6] Or in an industrial or

---

[4] Kennedy, *op.cit.* Such full-scale simulation is, of course, both expensive and time-consuming. For a discussion of the resources needed (e.g., sixty men, twenty recorders), see Newell, *op.cit.*; and Chapman, *op.cit.*

[5] See Strodtbeck, "The Jury Project" (September 1958); Guetzkow, *Behavioral Sciences* (1959); and G. R. Andlinger, "Business Games, Play One!" *Harvard Business Review, 36* (1958), pp. 115-25.

[6] See Harold F. Gosnell, *Getting out the Vote: An Experiment in the Stimulation of Voting* (Chicago: University of Chicago Press, 1927). See also Greenwood, *Experimental Sociology*, pp. 56-57. On this general subject, see John R. P. French, Jr., "Experiments in Field Settings," in Festinger and Katz, eds., *Research Methods*, chap. 3.

business situation two or more matched work groups or organization sections will be subjected to different forms of supervision. Changes in rate of productivity or worker satisfaction or whatever dependent variable the experimenters are studying can then be traced to the independent variable—the method of supervision.[7] In another form of field experiment, the independent variable is not introduced by the experimenter. Rather he selects two matched units, one of which is scheduled to receive some treatment not scheduled for the other, and compares the two units after the treatment. Thus Dodd selected several similar Syrian villages, one of which was scheduled to be the subject of an hygienic education campaign by an international agency. A few years after the campaign, he compared the hygiene practices in the village that had received the campaign with those in the villages that had not, the difference in the rate of change of hygienic practices being traced to the educational campaign.[8]

The advantages of the field experiment are readily apparent. Though they do not eliminate all possible experimental effects—the subjects may still react to the fact that they are being observed—these effects are not as strong as in the laboratory. What is more important, by investigating behavior in on-going situations, many of the thorny problems of extrapolation from the experimental to the real group are minimized. On the other hand, the use of on-going groups not created by the experimenter increases the possibility that

[7] See, for instance, Lester Coch and John R. P. French, Jr., "Overcoming Resistance to Change," *Hum. Rel.*, *1* (1948), pp. 512-32, reprinted in Cartwright and Zander, eds., *Group Dynamics*, chap. 19; and N. Morse and E. Reimer, "The Experimental Change of a Major Organization Variable," *J. Abnorm. Soc. Psych.*, 52 (1956), pp. 120-29.

[8] Stuart C. Dodd, *A Controlled Experiment in Rural Hygiene in Syria* (Beirut: American Press, 1934).

Logic similar to these field experiments is applied when one attempts to look at the effects of some social action as if it were a "social experiment." Thus one can compare the rate of industrial development and the costs of producing electricity in the area serviced by the TVA with other areas in which this "experimental variable" was not introduced. Or the state of British health after the introduction of the National Health Service can be compared with that of countries that have no such system or with that in Britain before the system was started. Of course the major problem with the analysis of such social experiments is the assumption that everything else is equal, which it never is.

an uncontrolled variable will affect the results. Thus both the industrial and business field experiments cited above attempted to relate a dependent variable (change in productivity) to an independent variable (change in supervisory techniques). But the productivity of the groups under study was affected by conditions uncontrolled by the experimenters, such as a shortage of materials or costs of production in other units of the firm.[9] Dodd reports a similar situation. The village that did not receive the educational campaign on hygienic practices was not completely cut off from contact with the village that did receive the campaign. This contact, he suggests, may have affected the results.[10]

One last problem that the field researcher faces is that, unlike the laboratory experimentalist who is relatively free to present the group with whatever task he wants, the field experimenter must adjust his research to a number of social pressures. His work will have to fit into the goals of the organization with which he is working and he may have to limit his work in other ways.[11]

The line between the natural field experiment and the laboratory experiment is not a sharp one. Just as extraneous variables may get into the field situation, so may they, as we have seen, get into the laboratory situation. On the other hand, controls in field situations can be quite precise. The work of Muzafer Sherif has combined some of the precision of laboratory work with the greater relevance of on-going groups. Using an elaborate set-up in which twenty-four youngsters were brought to an isolated campsite in Connecticut for eighteen days of camping, the author was able to create groups that, to the participants, seemed normal in a camping situation. As Sherif describes the camp conditions: ". . . these experimental conditions and related group goals were not additional topics dragged in for discussion and solution. They

9 Coch and French, *op.cit.*, p. 270; and Morse and Reimer, *op.cit.*, p. 127.
10 Dodd, *op.cit.*, p. xiv.
11 On the social pressures encountered by a field experimenter, see Greenwood, *Experimental Sociology* . . . , pp. 94-97; and Lewin, *Field Theory* . . . , pp. 166-67.

were organic parts of the preoccupations and concerns of the subjects *in the situation*. In short, the experimental conditions were chosen on the basis of studying crucial on-going interests of the subjects in the interaction process."[12]

The Uses of Experimental Studies

TECHNIQUES OF OBSERVATION: Experimental studies are useful to the political scientist only insofar as the knowledge gained can be applied to on-going politically relevant groups and institutions. One rather straightforward use to which small group experiments can be put is the development of techniques for observing and analyzing political behavior. The emphasis in the small group field on precise techniques of observation, on inter-observer reliability, and on the effect that the observer has upon the process he is observing suggests a conscious interest in the processes of observation that would be quite valuable in research. Of particular interest to us here are the techniques for locating those individuals who exercise power and influence in a group and of measuring the amount of power and influence they exercise. Too often political research has assumed that a particular individual, Congressman X, or a particular group, Lobby Y, is influential, without any explicit consideration of what is meant by the concept of influence or of what data are used to establish the degree of influence of the individual or group. Though many of the small group techniques of observation and measurement are not directly applicable to field research in political science, the precision and explicitness of these techniques make the small group studies useful in suggesting new ways of looking at political relationships and in criticizing some of the old ways. As the following chapter will try to demonstrate, the concepts of political science can be sharpened by exploring the operational definition, or the variety of operational definitions, that these concepts have.[13]

[12] Sherif and Sherif, *Groups in Harmony and Tension*, p. 305.
[13] A good example of the analysis of the various operational definitions of a concept is found in March, *Sociometry, 19* (1956). This process of concept-sharpening will be discussed in greater detail in Chapter V.

Some specific techniques of research on on-going groups and organizations that have been taken over from the small group field include sociometric testing and interaction counts. The former has been found useful largely in community studies, where the assumption that the opinions of the individuals in the political system is a useful clue to the influence structure of that system is more likely to be valid than it would be in larger systems.[14] The techniques of interaction recording have been used on on-going small groups in an effort to isolate more precisely some of the processes in those groups.[15]

UNDERSTANDING ON-GOING SMALL GROUPS: Of more interest to this study than the development of specific research techniques that can be applied to political behavior is the development within the small group experimental studies of predictive hypotheses about behavior in non-experimental situations. The closer the small experimental group resembles the real situation to which the predictive hypothesis will be applied, the greater the possibility of "bridging the gap" between the experimental situation and the on-going situation through the use of such an hypothesis. Small group studies can, therefore, more easily be used to predict behavior in real on-going face-to-face groups than in larger organizations. The range of possible applications of small group research to on-

[14] See, for instance, Floyd Hunter, *Community Power Structure* (Chapel Hill, N.C.: University of North Carolina Press, 1953); and Alfred DeGrazia, *Elite Analysis: A Manual of Methods for Discovering the Leadership of a Society and Its Vulnerability to Propaganda* (Stanford, Calif.: Institute for Journalistic Studies, 1955), mimeographed.

[15] See, for instance, the studies of Berkowitz and others at the University of Michigan. Seventy-two meetings of actual decision-making committees in government, business, and industry were observed, and the interactions recorded within a problem-solving set of categories. L. Berkowitz, "Sharing Leadership in Small Decision Making Groups," *J. Abnorm. Soc. Psych.*, 48 (1953), pp. 231-38, reprinted in Hare, Borgatta, and Bales, eds., *Small Groups*, p. 543.

Landsberger applied the Bales categories to recordings of twelve mediation sessions. In this way he was able to locate in these groups certain processes that had been observed in experimental groups using the same observational technique. Henry A. Landsberger, "Interaction Process Analysis of Professional Behavior: A Study of Labor-Mediators in Twelve Labor-Management Disputes," *Am. Soc. Rev.*, 21 (1955), pp. 566-75.

going small groups is suggested by the large number of significant small groups discussed in Chapter II.

Perhaps the largest body of small group literature with the explicit goal of predicting on the basis of laboratory-created situations the behavior of individuals in similar actual situations is the literature on the Leaderless Group Discussion (LGD). Under this technique, a group of previously unacquainted individuals are brought together to discuss a topic or perform a task. No leader is appointed. On the basis of these sessions, the observers attempt to predict the potential leadership ability of the group members. These LGD sessions have been used to select potential leaders in the OSS; in the army, air force, and navy; in the German and British armies; in administrative agencies; and in private businesses.[16] The major advantage to us of the practical orientation of these studies is that they have been followed up by attempts to validate their findings by seeing how predicted leaders actually behaved in later situations assumed to be similar to the experimental situation. The results of attempts to test the validity of predictions have, however, been rather unimpressive. In general the relationship between prediction of future leadership and actual future leadership has been positive but low. The LGD results have been positively correlated with such external criteria as later rank, status, merit ratings, and the like, but these correlations have not been very high. One suggested reason is that the LGD studies have not defined carefully enough the particular situations in which the subjects later find themselves or have been unable to make such a definition because of the variety of possible situations in which the former testees have had to operate. Under the

16 See H. L. Ansbacher, "The History of the Leaderless Group Discussion Technique," *Psychological Bulletin*, 48 (1951), pp. 383-90; Bass, *J. Applied Psych.* (1949); Bernard M. Bass and C. H. Coates, "Forecasting Officer Potential Using the Leaderless Group Discussion," *J. Abnorm. Soc. Psych.*, 47 (1952), pp. 321-25; OSS Staff, *Assessment of Men*; H. Harris, *The Group Approach to Leadership Testing* (London: Routledge and Kegan Paul, 1950); Walter Gelhorn and William Brady, "Selecting Supervisory Mediators by Trial by Combat," *Public Administration Review*, 8 (1948), pp. 259-66; and S. B. Williams and H. J. Leavitt, "Group Opinions as a Predictor of Military Leadership," *Journal of Consulting Psychology*, 11 (1947), pp. 283-91.

different situations, the predictive efficiency of the LGD is seriously limited.[17]

However, if the real situation to which one will apply the small group findings can be precisely defined and reproduced with a high degree of similarity in the experimental laboratory, very useful predictions can be made—though these may be on a low level of generalization. Thus the simulation of an air-defense center or of a jury can produce a series of predictive hypotheses about these structures as they exist in the real world. Some of the ways in which the situation in a real jury or air-defense center is close to that in the simulation follow:[18]

(1) The personnel in the experimental situation are potentially the personnel in the actual situation. The subjects in the jury studies are selected at random from jury panels in the Chicago and St. Louis courts. The personnel in the air-defense system are drawn from air force personnel for whom an assignment to such a system is not unusual.

(2) The information fed to the subjects by the experimenters comes in a form similar to that fed into the analogous real systems. The juries do not watch mock trials, it is true, but they do hear recordings of court cases. (This is to allow the presentation of the same material to several mock juries.) And the air-defense system receives inputs of information in the same symbolic form that a real air-defense system would receive—through radar-scopes and the like.

(3) The situation is such as to induce at least some "suspension of disbelief" among the participants. The jurors in the mock jury, for instance, know that they are not judging a real case, but they are told that their findings and the way in which they reach them will influence the policies toward juries of the bar and the bench. And though the air-defense person-

[17] See, for instance, the work of Carter and his associates, *Hum. Rel.*, 4 (1951) and *J. Psych.* (1949); as well as Bernard M. Bass, "The Leaderless Group Discussion," *Psychological Bulletin*, 51 (1954), pp. 465-92; and OSS Staff, *Assessment of Men*, pp. 392 and 423.

[18] The studies of the mock juries are discussed in Strodtbeck, "The Jury Project" (September 1958). The air-defense studies are discussed in Kennedy, *Hum. Org.* (1955); and in The RAND Corporation papers by Newell; Chapman; and Biel, *et al.*

nel know that the attacks they have to deal with are not real, the fact that they are on an official assignment, the setting of the experimental room, and the length of the sessions produce a similar involvement in the results.

On the basis of these studies, predictions can be made of group performance in the situations that were simulated, though the predictions may be limited to these particular situations. In the jury studies, for instance, one can systematically test the effect of a change in the clarity of the defendant's negligence on the size of the award in negligence cases, or the effect of sex or social status on a juror's influence and decision.[19] Or in the air-defense system, one can study the way in which the group learns to respond to different patterns of challenge from enemy planes.[20]

UNDERSTANDING LARGER SOCIAL SYSTEMS: Though the small group has been shown to be relevant to political science, the political scientist is more interested in the operations of larger social systems—organizations, parties, bureaucracies, pressure groups, and local and national political systems. Can the experimental small group shed light on these larger systems? Can we predict the ways in which organizations and political systems will operate on the basis of the operation of small groups in the laboratory? Or are the systems so different that useful transfer from one level to the other is precluded?

Small group studies are related to organizational behavior on one quite simple level: insofar as small groups have a significant effect upon the operation of the larger systems of which they are part, tools that can tell us something about the operation of these small groups also tell us about the operation of the larger systems. Thus the application of small group experimental work to the understanding of real on-going small groups tells us indirectly about the operations of larger systems.

But just as one cannot understand the operations of a group

[19] Strodtbeck, "The Jury Project"; Strodtbeck, *Sociometry* (1956); and Strodtbeck *et al.*, *Am. Soc. Rev.* (1957).
[20] Newell, RAND Corporation paper (1955).

by describing the behavior of the individual members, so one cannot understand the activities of an organization merely by knowing the behavior of the groups that make it up. Can the results of the experimental method be applied to organizations and other larger systems on the organization or system level? Organizations and political systems are not amenable to experimental manipulation themselves. With rare exceptions we cannot expect larger social systems to interrupt their goal-directed activity to allow the social scientist to introduce his experimental techniques. If the experimental method is to supply useful results for understanding organizations, it will have to be through the transfer of results in experimental small groups to the level of organizational behavior. Though this transfer is fraught with difficulties and is a subject still largely unexplored, there are some encouraging developments in the fields of both organization theory and small group research that hold promise that some such transfer is possible.

We have suggested that the more completely the experimental situation simulates the real situation, the easier it is to bridge the gap between them. As illustrated above, such close simulation is possible if one tries to simulate an on-going unit that is limited as to size and that can be precisely defined. It is a good deal more difficult if one attempts to simulate some much larger system. Thus the attempt to simulate the international system of nations through student role-playing is of necessity highly simplified. The personnel are not the potential role-holders of analogous roles in the on-going system being studied. They all come from one culture; they do not have the training of diplomats. The problems are deliberately simplified. While the mock juror does essentially what the real juror does, the mock statesman does not.[21] Although these strictures are true, the simulation of the international environment may still develop and test a number of useful hypotheses. And if one must simplify to simulate the international environment in the laboratory, the reason for this lies in the inherent complexity of international affairs. Any attempt to describe

[21] See Guetzkow, *Behavioral Sciences* (1959).

these affairs—whether a verbal, a mathematical, or a small group model—is of necessity a simplification. The experimental small group model may be a useful complement to verbal or mathematical models, and may in fact serve to lower the level of abstraction of the latter models. Thus experimental groups can be used to add life to the rationalistic game-theory models of international relations. For instance, though mathematical theories can specify which solution should be rationally favored in a conflict situation, individuals in such situations do not play by the rules of game theory. Decisions are made partially on the basis of intuition and non-logical cues. Group experiments in which there is no obvious rational solution to a problem—as there usually is not in an international conflict situation—may help specify what sorts of non-logical cues are used by decision-makers. Though experimental simulation simplifies situations and eliminates variables, it does not, as do verbal and mathematical models, leave out the element of human variability.[22]

One of the standards by which the applicability of the research in one area to another area can be judged is whether or not the findings in one area confirm general theories developed in the other. Propositions developed on the basis of studies in one field of social research gain greater validity if they can be fitted into systematic theories developed in another field. Some of the most important authors in the field of small group research have believed that such a transfer is possible. Kurt Lewin maintained that through the use of "transposition" one could apply the findings of small group studies to larger systems, transposition being "a change which leaves the essential structural characteristics unaltered." If the patterns of relationships within groups and larger systems are similar, the difference in size is not too great a limitation on applicability. "In view of these considerations," Lewin wrote, "we should be able to investigate the properties of large groups on relatively small scale models."[23] And Bales has suggested that the experimental

---

[22] See Thomas C. Schelling, "Bargaining, Communication and Limited War," *Journal of Conflict Resolution*, *1* (1957), pp. 19-36; and Schelling, "The Strategy of Conflict Resolution: Prospectus for a Reorientation of Game Theory," *ibid.*, *2* (1958), entire number.

[23] Lewin, *Field Theory . . .* , p. 164.

study of small groups be used ". . . as a means of developing a more adequate body of theory relevant to the analysis of full-scale social systems as well as to the analysis of the small groups around which the method is primarily designed."[24]

To transfer from the micro-social system to the larger social system, the two systems must have certain identities in form and structure. And when one compares the literature on the small group with that on the structuring and functioning of larger social units, one finds quite a bit of similarity. Some of this similarity results from a conscious effort by researchers or research teams to apply the same theoretical systems and conceptual schemes to both levels.[25] That such conceptualizations covering both levels can be developed is encouraging. But what is even more encouraging is the convergence of schemes developed by numerous writers working independently either in the field of small group or of organization behavior. To these convergences we now turn.

According to the theory of organization developed by Chester Barnard and Herbert Simon, an organization has several tasks that it must perform if it is to survive.[26] It must satisfy the demands of three types of participants upon whom it depends. The three types of participants are labeled customers, entrepreneurs, and employees. A "customer" of an organization is a term ". . . used in a generic sense . . . to refer to any individual . . . for whom the organization objective has personal value." Thus one group of participants is interested in the instrumental task of the group. For a second group, the "entrepreneurs," the satisfaction of their personal goals derives from the internal operation of the organization—". . . the size and growth of the organization."[27] Rather than deriving their

---

[24] Bales, *Interaction Process Analysis*, p. iii.

[25] One of the most conspicuous efforts to deal with both the small group and the larger social system within the same conceptual scheme and theoretical system is found in the collaborative work of Parsons and Bales. See Parsons, Bales, and Shils, *Working Papers* . . . , chap. 1; and Parsons and Bales, *Family, Socialization.* . . . These studies will be discussed more fully in Chapters VI and VII, below.

[26] See Chester I. Barnard, *The Functions of the Executive* (Cambridge, Mass.: Harvard University Press, 1938), chaps. 11 and 16; and Herbert Simon, *Administrative Behavior*, 2nd ed. (New York: Macmillan, 1957), chap. 6.

[27] *Ibid.*, pp. 114-17.

personal satisfactions from the achievement of the external goal of the organization, they concentrate on the way in which the organization operates internally. And lastly, the "employees" participate because they satisfy certain personal goals, not directly related to the internal or external operations of the organization. Thus they participate in order to receive wages or other perquisites.

Several comments on this distinction are in order. Though the distinction is drawn in terms of the types of satisfactions that the various participants receive from their association with the organization, it also characterizes the various tasks that the organization must perform, since the continued association of the several types of individuals is necessary for the organization's survival. Secondly, the distinction among the three types of participants is an analytic distinction, not a concrete one. Any single individual may associate with the organization because of satisfactions received from more than one area—he may receive satisfaction, for instance, both from the internal operation of the organization and from its external objective.

Studies of small groups have used a conceptualization that is strikingly similar to that developed by Barnard and Simon. In a survey of the categories used to describe behavior in numerous small group works, Launor Carter indicates that these behaviors can be grouped into three basic dimensions:

1. *Individual Prominence and Achievement*: These are behaviors of the individual related to his efforts to stand out from others and individually achieve various personal goals.
2. *Aiding Attainment by the Group*: These are behaviors of the individual related to his efforts to assist the group in achieving goals towards which the group is oriented.
3. *Sociability*: These are behaviors of the individual related to efforts to establish and maintain cordial and socially satisfying relations with other group members.[28]

These three dimensions, or quite similar ones, emerged on the basis of factor analysis applied to individual behaviors in small groups, in studies conducted independently by eight different

[28] Adapted from Launor Carter, "Recording and Evaluating the Performance of Individuals as Members of Small Groups," *Personnel Psychology*, 7 (1954), pp. 477-84, reprinted in Hare, Borgatta, and Bales, eds., *Small Groups*, p. 496.

researchers, and with groups of different size and composition.[29] These three factors are clearly quite similar in content to the three dimensions of group tasks suggested by Barnard and Simon. The factors, however, describe the behaviors of individuals as these behaviors were observed by researchers, rather than certain functions that groups must perform. But the fact that these three dimensions emerged in all the various groups whose description is summarized by Carter suggests that the tasks in small groups can be conceptualized in ways quite similar to the tasks in organizations. Benne and Sheats, for instance, found that there were three functional roles performed in small discussion groups: a role having to do with group locomotion toward the group goal; a group-maintenance role centered around supporting and positively affective relations in the group; and the individually oriented roles of the group participants, centered around such activities as personal recognition and aggression.[30] It is clear that these three roles, or the three types of behavior described in the dimensions located by Carter, would produce the three outputs Barnard and Simon suggest an organization must produce: satisfactions deriving from the external goal activities of the group, satisfactions deriving from the internal group processes, and individual satisfactions.

Of particular use in connecting the studies of small groups and of organizations is the emphasis in both types of study on the internal and external tasks of the group or organization. In the work cited above, the internal group task consists of the maintenance of an effective and satisfying internal organization in order that it may direct energy toward the external task facing it. In a factor analysis of group dimensions, Raymond B.

[29] *Ibid.*; see especially Table I, p. 444.

[30] K. D. Benne and P. Sheats, "Functional Roles of Group Members," *Journal of Social Issues*, 4 (1948), pp. 41-49. These three dimensions of group activity, though found through factor analysis, have a high degree of common sense validity. It is interesting to note that in a study of small political units—local political clubs—Roy Peel suggests that political clubs may be evaluated by the same three criteria: "1) To what extent and in what manner is group cohesion for political purposes affected? 2) To what extent and in what manner are the social needs of the community met by group activities? 3) To what extent and in what manner are the needs of the individual satisfied?" Peel, *Political Clubs of New York*, p. 134.

Cattell divides group "synergy" (defined as ". . . the total indi-vidual energy taken into the group—absorbed by its activities . . .") into effective synergy and intrinsic or group-maintenance synergy. The former is the ". . . energy expressed in gaining outside goals for which the group has come together," and the latter is the energy absorbed in ". . . internal friction and in maintaining the cohesion of the group." Whereas the externally directed effective synergy is instrumentally oriented energy, the internal group-maintenance synergy is largely absorbed in affectively oriented activities within the group. Group-mainte-nance synergy "absorbs not only selfish, anti-social and aggres-sive motivations . . . , but also the self-submissive and self-assertive satisfactions of leader-follower activity and the needs of the gregarious drive."[31] The distinction of the two forms of synergy accords quite well with the distinction by Barnard between the efficiency and the effectiveness of organizations— the former having to do with the extent to which organiza-tions can satisfy the needs of the organization members, and the latter with the extent to which the organization can achieve its external instrumental goal.[32] And Homans distinguishes the internal and external systems of groups in a similar way: "We shall not go far wrong if, for the moment, we think of the external system as group behavior that enables the group to survive in its environment and think of the internal system as group behavior that is an expression of the sentiments towards one another developed by the members of the group in the course of their life together."[33]

[31] Cattell, in Hare, Borgatta, and Bales, eds., *Small Groups*, pp. 116-17. The concept of "synergy"—i.e., "energy taken into the group"—leaves out by definition the individualistic dimension of group behavior cited by Simon; Barnard; Carter; and Benne and Sheats.

[32] Barnard, *Functions* . . . , pp. 55-59 and *passim*.

[33] Homans, *Human Group*, pp. 109-10. Similar distinctions have been drawn in studies of leader behavior. Thus Kahn and Katz found that suc-cessful supervisors had to have "technical know-how" as well as "human relations skill." Robert L. Kahn and Daniel Katz, "Leadership Practices in Relation to Productivity and Morale," in Cartwright and Zander, eds., *Group Dynamics*, chap. 41. And Hemphill, on the basis of a factor analysis of the responses to a "Leader Behavior Description Questionnaire," found that items describing leader behavior could be grouped into two main factors, Consideration and Initiating Structure. "Consideration refers to leader behavior that is characterized by warm friendly relations with

This distinction between the external task-oriented aspect of group behavior and the internal affectively oriented aspect represents perhaps the single most significant convergence in the study of small groups and larger social systems. Though there are many differences between small groups and organizations, the fact that they both have instrumental and expressive tasks to perform opens the way to a wide range of studies that can relate the two systems. The convergence of the work of Parsons and Bales, for instance, has centered around the need in both small groups and larger social systems of roles that can deal with the instrumental and the affective aspects of group behavior.[34]

The internal and external tasks of groups and organizations are interrelated; both must be carried on at once, and the internal and external tasks mutually affect each other. Both the small group literature and the literature on organizations have described this interrelationship in terms of equilibrium analysis. The use of equilibrium analysis of behavior on the level of organizations as well as on the level of the small group is another significant point of convergence in the studies.[35] Lewin,

group members and concern with group member welfare. . . . Initiating Structure refers to leader activities that introduce organization, new ways of doing things, and new procedures for solving group problems, etc." John Hemphill, "Leadership Behavior Associated with the Administrative Reputation of College Departments," *Journal of Educational Psychology*, 46 (1955), p. 388.

[34] See Parsons, Bales, and Shils, *Working Papers . . .* ; and Parsons and Bales, *Family, Socialization. . . .* The subject of role differentiation in small groups and larger systems will be discussed more fully in Chapter VII, below.

[35] For a general discussion of the use of equilibrium analysis for the comparison of systems on different levels, see Alfred E. Emerson, "Homeostatis and the Comparison of Systems" in Grinker, ed. *Toward a Unified Theory . . .* , chap. 12.

David Easton, in "Limits of the Equilibrium Model in Social Research," *Behavioral Sciences*, 1 (1956) pp. 96-104, criticizes the application of equilibrium analysis to political affairs. He maintains that it is a useful approach for the study of economics or of small groups, but that it is still of doubtful utility in political analysis because the variables used in political analysis (power and influence) cannot be quantified (pp. 101-4). But this argument could be applied to all political analysis, not only that using an equilibrium model. Until the major political variables can be quantified, analysis will have to be less precise. And as Easton himself points out, useful results can be obtained from equilibrium analysis even if the existence of equilibrium is ascertained by inspection rather than by exact measurement (pp. 102-3).

A more serious criticism of equilibrium analysis is its alleged inability to deal with the problem of change. See, for instance, the exchange between

for instance, describes groups as being in a state of "quasi-stationary equilibrium" such that attempts to move the group to a new level of activity will induce pressures directed toward returning the group to its former level. This creates special problems for group leadership if it attempts to induce change in the group. Attempts to control the behavior of group members in the direction of the attainment of some external goal will lead to negative reactions within the internal system of the group that will hinder the achievement of the external goal. The task of leadership under such an equilibrium situation is to maintain a balance between the satisfactions of the group members and the goal-oriented activity of the group.[36]

A similar equilibrium problem has been found by Bales and his associates in their studies of group interaction.[37] Attempts to deal with the instrumental task of the group disturb the group equilibrium, and this is brought back into balance by activities of an expressive nature. The fact that control attempts aimed at the accomplishment of the group's instrumental task are likely to be followed by negative affective reactions places special pressure upon the group's leadership structure to maintain the instrumental activities of the group without the damaging impact of negative affect.[38] The task of the leader or the leaders of small groups is then the task of Barnard's executive in the large organization; he must maintain an equilibrium between effectiveness and efficiency—between the desires of the individual members and the instrumental task of the organization.[39]

Emerson and Karl Deutsch in Grinker, ed., *op.cit.*, pp. 161-62. In Chapters VI-X, we shall deal with the problem of certain types of equilibrium as discussed in small group literature and the problem of change in on-going social systems. The general nature of equilibrium analysis as applied in small group situations, and the way in which this analysis relates to social problems in on-going social systems, will be considered more fully. In this chapter we are interested more in specifying certain convergences without exhaustively defining them and without considering some of the limitations on convergence.

[36] See Lewin, *Field Theory . . .* , pp. 202-7.

[37] See Bales, "The Equilibrium Problem . . . ," in Parsons, Bales, and Shils, *Working Papers . . .* , chap. 4.

[38] For a fuller discussion, see Chapter VI below. The ways in which this problem is solved in experimental small groups and in on-going social systems will be compared in Chapter VII.

[39] Barnard, *Functions . . .* , chap. 16.

That certain equivalent functions have been found on the small group and the organizational levels does not mean that these systems are identical. The relationship between the two levels is a relationship between analogous, not homologous, mechanisms.[40] The processes on the small group and organization levels may be similar in function, but they are not necessarily similar in structure or in origin. As Simon has put it, "Functional equivalence does not imply structural equivalence."[41] That both the small experimental group and the on-going social system are faced with the problem of maintaining an equilibrium between internal and external demands does not mean that they will solve these problems in a similar fashion. As will be suggested in Chapter VII, the solution of this problem in small experimental groups by a process of role differentiation into an instrumental and an expressive leader does not necessarily hold for on-going groups. That the small group and the larger social system share certain problems, then, does not allow us to predict behavior in one system from knowledge of the other system. But the similar problems they must solve does allow us to use studies in one field to develop hypotheses about the way in which these problems can be solved. The testing of these hypotheses on other levels will shed light upon the way in which that other level operates, whether or not the hypothesis is confirmed. If the mechanism for dealing with the equilibrium problem on the organizational level or on the level of the political system differs from the mechanism on the small group level, the nature of these differences will be useful in understanding behavior

40 Though there is some criticism of the use of analogy as a technique of comparison between systems, this critique is more properly applied to what might be called "analogous determinism" (because x exists in system y, x′ will exist in system y′). The question of whether or not there are analogues of one system in another is for us an empirical question to be answered on the basis of research.

At the present level of knowledge, comparisons between systems on different levels will have to deal with analogous comparisons. As Alfred Emerson has put it: "We certainly have to consider analogies if we are to integrate various sciences because we have to deal with different mechanisms of organization in the systems with which we are concerned." Emerson, in Grinker, ed., *Toward a Unified Theory . . .* , p. 150.

41 Herbert Simon, "Comments on the Theory of Organization," *Am. Pol. Sci. Rev.*, *46* (1952), p. 1137.

on the organization or political system level. That the same questions can be asked about small group behavior and about organizational behavior indicates that the study of the former can be useful for the latter. It does not mean the answers will be the same.

Conclusion

This analysis of the relation between small group experimental studies and behavior in actual on-going situations suggests that if the small group studies are to be useful for the analysis of political behavior, they cannot remain in the isolation of the laboratory. The hypotheses they suggest must constantly be tested in field situations, and the field study must also return to the laboratory at times to test new relationships. The experimental study must be part of a chain of studies. The successful use of the experimental technique does not mean that political science will become a laboratory science. More traditional methods—field studies, surveys, and historical studies—will still provide the bulk of political science research. But experiments, used in conjunction with other methods, not in the vacuum of the laboratory, will be a valuable adjunct.

The relations between the small group and the larger social system have been described in rather general terms. The problems of applying small group research to political behavior have been dealt with by implication, but no attempt has been made to consider specific political problems. This is our next task—to deal with the relevance of small group experiments to political science by taking a more limited area of small group research and attempting to trace its connections to political affairs. This area is the study of leadership, a major topic of small group study and a major interest in political affairs.

Chapter V

THE CONCEPT OF LEADERSHIP

THE STUDY of leadership has been chosen as the means of illustrating more specifically the relevance of small group analysis to political science. There are several reasons why leadership was selected as the unifying concept for the remainder of this work. Leadership has long been a central concern in the study of politics. From the search in classical political thought for the ideal leader to current attempts to map the elite structure of a modern community or nation, the problem of identifying leaders and describing their characteristics has been at the core of political analysis. Leadership has also been a center of attention for small group researchers. There is a vast literature on the development of leadership in small groups, on the problems of measurement and observation of leadership, and on the relations between leaders and followers under various conditions. This parallel interest gives us a large body of material to use in assessing the relevance of small group analysis to political analysis.

But it is more than the mere fact that both political and small group researchers have dealt with the concept of leadership that led to the concentration on leadership studies. It is the general argument of this book that small group studies have dealt with social processes of high political relevance. And this is especially the case with studies of leadership. Because of the isolation of the small group laboratory and because many workers in small groups have been interested in the study of uniformities of behavior within the laboratory without consideration of the relation between the laboratory and the realm of on-going social institutions, the relevance of these small group studies has rarely been made explicit. Nevertheless I shall try to show how the methods for identifying and measuring leadership and the theories of the relations between leaders and followers are useful models for the study of political leadership.

Leadership in small groups is, of course, something quite different from the leadership studied in politics. The situations and the methods of analysis are not the same. Yet the two have a common focus: in both politics and small group analysis, the study of leadership deals in some rough way (I shall try to be more precise about the concept of leadership soon) with the relation between the more and the less powerful, between those who make decisions and those who are the subjects of decisions. It is this combination of similarity and difference that allows small group analyses to make a unique contribution to political analysis. By focusing on a social relationship of great political significance and at the same time approaching the study of that relationship with entirely new tools, small group analysis is able to suggest new modes of thinking about politics. If the study of leadership in small groups can add something to our observational and theoretical vocabulary for the study of leadership in general, it will have made a significant contribution indeed.

This chapter will deal with problems in the measurement and identification of leaders. The small group literature on leadership and leadership identification is useful in this connection. Unlike many of the political studies of leadership, small group studies have used criteria for leadership selection that are both precise and, what may be more important, explicit. In studies of political leadership, inferences are often made on the basis of observations of political events without a clear and conscious consideration of the sources of these inferences. Researchers may describe an individual as an "influential Congressman" or a "powerful labor leader," without specifying what behavioral cues were read in order to arrive at this description. Is it the deference accorded the individual; the large number of activities in which he is engaged; the fact that decisions tend to be those he favors; or the fact that those "in the know" in Washington report that he is influential or powerful? In the midst of a research project concerned with an on-going agency or organization, it is sometimes difficult for the researcher to stand back and ask himself what in fact he is taking for his evidence. In the small group situation, on the other hand, where the behaviors to be recorded must be consciously and precisely defined and the observer's conduct can be carefully controlled, such questions can be dealt with more adequately.

Furthermore, one can observe leadership in actual operation within the small group—something that, because of limited access, complexity of the leader-follower relationships, geographical extension, and so forth, is barred in much political research. This allows greater direct study of the functions of leaders in the small group than is possible in most political situations. And lastly, leaders in small groups can be observed in interaction with their followers. One does not have to infer the behavior of followers from the behavior of leaders. The reactions of followers to leaders—so important in understanding how leaders operate—can be directly observed.

This chapter, which will deal with the concept of leadership, will be followed by several chapters which deal with specific problems faced by leaders—problems in the leader-follower relationship confronting leaders both in small groups and in political situations. Again the small group studies of these leadership problems will be useful because of the ability in small group work to be precise and to observe the actual leader-follower interaction.

What goes on in the laboratory will not be directly transferable to the political sphere. Not all the techniques of measurement and observation developed in small group research can be applied to political research—though some, as will be pointed out below, could be and have been used for the observation of on-going social and political processes. In general, however, political groups—Congressional Committees, the Supreme Court—are not going to be lured into a group dynamics laboratory to expose their interactions to the eye of the ubiquitous one-way mirror. What a consideration of the measurement techniques in small groups can contribute to political analysis is a chance for students of political leadership to enrich their observational vocabulary, and to make it more precise and explicit. And the theories of leader-follower relationships developed in small group work will, it is hoped, aid our theoretical approaches to political leadership.

The Political Study of Leadership

The traditional approach to political leadership has often been a normative one. Political philosophers have dealt with the question of who should lead: what qualities the leader should bring with him to his office, from what social group he should come, how widely dispersed leadership should be, and so forth. Similarly, much attention has been paid to the question of how the leader should lead: how the leader should behave, what values or whose values he should serve, and what his relation with his followers should be. In many instances, the term "leader" itself implies a value orientation that differentiates it from other forms of power relationship. Leadership is distinguished on the one hand from domination, in which one individual controls the behavior of another or the behavior of a group by force or by emotional appeal, and on the other hand from what we might call administrative control, in which one individual controls the behavior of others solely on the basis of his position in some administrative or organizational hierarchy. Under this concept, leadership exists only when followers make free and rational choices to follow.

The normative approach to the study of leadership has been characteristic not only of traditional political theory, but of many modern studies interested in improving the quality of the public service. From the rather low intellectual level of the campaign biography up to the sophisticated studies of public administration, we find a wealth of propositions about the training, the skills, the qualities, and the performances expected from leaders.

Our approach to leadership will be descriptive-analytic rather than normative. We are interested in who in fact leads, not who should lead; how leaders in fact behave, not how they should behave. This approach, though quite different from the normative approach, is not in conflict with it, but rather complements it. On the one hand, the normative approach inspires the descriptive-analytic approach. If leadership were not important and worth knowing about, there would be little reason to study it objectively. On the other hand, the descriptive-analytic approach should serve normative purposes. For instance, one often hears that there is a great demand for "creative" leadership, which means roughly that we need leaders who can innovate when faced with new situations. Our study will deal with the problem of creative leadership in terms of certain inherent characteristics of the leader-follower relationship that inhibit innovation on the part of the leader (see below, Chapter VIII) and the ways in which these inhibitions can be overcome. Information of this sort should make demands for certain types of leadership better informed as to what sorts of creativity we can expect from what sorts of leaders.

The small group approach is especially relevant to the descriptive-analytic study of political leadership because of a gap in our theories and methods of analysis of such leadership. Though leaders and elites are of interest in the study of politics because of the functions they perform in the political system, there is little explicit theory on those functions and the way in which they perform them, and few adequate methods to observe the performance. Political scientists, concerned with the distribution of power in a social unit—be it group, organization, or nation—naturally turn to study the leaders of that unit who are, as Lasswell and Kaplan define them, "its most active power holders, effectively and in the perspectives of the group."[1] Others have stressed this central functional role of leaders. Leaders and elites have come under intensive study by students of political affairs because they perform those social functions "related to power";[2] because "they are in positions to make decisions having major consequences";[3] and because power in organizations inevitably tends to gravitate into their hands.[4] But though leaders and leadership groups are of interest because of their functions as "power-holders" or as "decision-makers," this interest has not

---

[1] Harold D. Lasswell and Abraham Kaplan, *Power and Society: A Framework for Political Enquiry* (New Haven: Yale University Press, 1950), p. 152.

[2] Hunter, *Community Power Structure*, p. 2.

[3] C. Wright Mills, *The Power Elite* (New York: Oxford University Press, 1956), p. 4.

[4] Michels, *Political Parties, passim.*

been followed up by direct analysis of the leadership function. And though rough approximations tell us that Committee Chairman X or Comrade Y is a major leader, we lack adequate measurement techniques to locate and weigh the power of leaders and elite groups.

Though leaders are studied because of the functions they perform, most studies of political elites neither begin nor end with a direct consideration of the functions performed by elites. Leaders are defined and located not by the functions they perform in a group or organization, but by their structural position in the group. The most usual structural definition of leadership is the holding of high organizational office. Leaders hold high institutional positions in the executive, legislature, or judiciary, or in important private institutions.[5] This method of defining and locating leadership is by far the easiest and most convenient. And for many purposes it is perfectly adequate. But structural position tells us little of what leaders actually do.

Another technique of locating the leaders of a group is to ask some or all of the group members to identify them. Variations of the sociometric technique developed largely in small group studies have been used to locate community leaders, and opinion leaders to whom individuals go for advice and, recently, in an attempt to locate the major national decision-makers.[6] Again, we have leaders defined by a structural definition—within what might be called the structure of perceived power—but their functions are not directly considered.

Both of these definitions of leadership—in terms of organizational position and in terms of the reports of respondents—are reasonable, operationally clear, and unambiguous. But an operational definition of leadership is useful only if it can be related to other concepts within a systematic theory. What is of particular interest to us here is the way in which the concept of leadership as defined in structural terms relates to

[5] See, for instance, the RADIR studies by the Hoover Institute at Stanford, described in Lasswell, Lerner, and Rothwell, *The Comparative Study of Elites* (Stanford, Calif.: Stanford University Press, 1952).

[6] See Hunter, *op.cit.*; Katz and Lazarsfeld, *Personal Influence*; and Hunter, *Top Leadership: USA* (Chapel Hill: University of North Carolina Press, 1959).

the functional concept of leadership in terms of influence or decision-making. The authors using the structural definition are in fact interested in the leadership function—for many of them, the structural definition is merely a convenient place to begin. As Lasswell writes: "Since the true decision-makers are not necessarily known at the beginning of research the investigator can select government in the conventional sense as the convenient starting point."[7] Similarly, the definition of the elite in terms of a sociometric test should not be considered the end of research on the topic. One must study how those to whom influence or power is ascribed behave in fact. Commenting on the Rovere study, which used a sociometric technique to trace interpersonal influence, Merton writes: ". . . interpersonal influence is here regarded as not simply a matter of evaluation, but as a matter of fact. Whether the *judgments* of informants and the *objective observation* would lead to the same results remains an open question. . . . A full-fledged study would utilize observations as well as interviews to ascertain the actual degree of interpersonal influence and the spheres in which this is exercised."[8]

But most studies of elites do not go from the structural definition of leadership to consider the ways in which the leaders thus selected function. Rather they usually turn to an analysis of the social background or the personal characteristics of the leaders. Thus one can demonstrate that those selected as leaders on the basis of a sociometric test come largely from particular occupational or social strata; or that holders of high office are likely to have a certain social background or personality characteristic. These studies of the social and personal traits of leaders deal more with the reasons why certain individuals assume leadership roles than with the way in which they function in that role. The assumption (and it is a reasonable assumption) is that the personality and social background characteristics of political elites will influence their leadership behavior. But without consideration of the way in which leaders function in groups—of their

[7] Lasswell, Lerner, and Rothwell, *op.cit.*, p. 8.
[8] Robert K. Merton, *Social Theory and Social Structure* (Glencoe, Ill.: Free Press, 1957), p. 410, n. 15.

relations with the group followers and with the external environment of the group—it is hard to specify the way in which personal or social characteristics interact with the group situation to influence leader behavior.

Leadership as a Group Function

Studies of leadership within small groups have, in contrast to the studies of political leadership cited above, been able to consider the functioning of leaders in groups as well as the particular characteristics that they bring with them into these groups. Earlier social-psychological studies of leadership had been quite similar to the political studies cited above.[9] But the relative fruitlessness of the search for traits of leadership led students of the subject to consider leadership as a functional relationship within groups. The use of small group analysis is especially fruitful for the analysis of leadership functions because of the ability of the researcher to observe the group in operation. One does not have to use the "convenient" methods of structural position or sociometric choice to select leaders who are assumed to perform certain functions. One can select leaders directly on the basis of their activities in groups. Of course, sociometric choice and structural position are still significant measures in small group studies of leadership, but they can be related to actual leader functioning. It is because of the emphasis of small group studies upon leadership as a functional role in the group and because of the possibility, through the use of small groups, of relating this functional role to other definitions of leadership that we believe a study of the concept of leadership as

[9] It is interesting to note that the political science approach to the study of leadership is essentially that employed by most earlier psychological studies of leadership. Stogdill, in a survey of literature on the traits of leadership, found that the two most frequent definitions of leadership were the holding of high office and selection on a sociometric test. These leaders were then compared with non-leaders to see in what way their traits—intelligence, height, appearance, personality, etc.—differentiated them from non-leaders. How the leader actually functioned in the group and how the group situation interplayed with the traits of the leaders were not considered. See R. M. Stogdill, "Personal Factors Associated with Leadership: A Survey of the Literature," *J. Psych.*, 25 (1948), pp. 35-71; and Gibb, in Hare, Borgatta, and Bales, eds., *Small Groups*, pp. 87-94.

used in small group analysis will sharpen the use of that concept in political research.

One of the first writers to consider leadership as a process or function was Pigors: "Leadership is a process of mutual stimulation which, by the successful interplay of relevant individual differences, controls human energy in pursuit of a common cause. Any person may be called a leader during the time when, and in so far as, his will, feeling, and insight direct and control others in the pursuit of a cause which he represents."[10] This definition is stressed because of its usefulness and its wide influence on later writings. Leadership, according to this definition, requires a group with a common goal and a differentiation in the tasks performed by the group members such that one or more members may "direct and control" others in the pursuit of the goal. The major point to be noticed in this definition is that leadership is not a trait possessed by an individual but a group process related to the functioning of the group. Even in relation to a single group, an individual is not necessarily a leader or a non-leader. He may at times perform the leadership function; at times he may not. More than one person may perform the leadership function. That an individual performs such functions in one group does not necessarily mean that he will perform them in other groups. It becomes an empirical question whether or not individuals who perform these functions in one group are more likely to perform them in other groups; whether groups will have one, two, or more leaders; and whether these different leaders (if there are different leaders) will be specific to particular group enterprises or whether several leaders will operate at once on the same task.

INTERPERSONAL INFLUENCE: Leaders, in Pigors' definition, influence other group members in pursuit of a common cause. The notion that leaders exert interpersonal influence is central to the definition of leadership throughout the small group literature. A technical expert who performs a task by himself is not considered a leader. If in an experimental group an

[10] P. Pigors, *Leadership or Domination* (Boston: Houghton-Mifflin, 1935).

individual working alone accomplishes the task set for the group, he has furthered the group's goal-oriented activity, but not through the act of leadership. As Campbell, for instance, defines leadership, it is "the contribution of a given individual to group effectiveness, mediated through the direct efforts of others rather than himself."[11]

GOAL ORIENTATION: Pigors emphasizes the goal-oriented activities of the leader—he leads the group in pursuit of a "common cause." For our purposes, this aspect of the definition is not too useful. To consider as leadership only goal-directed activities would involve us in the thorny problem of the definition of the goal for any particular group. There may at times be several group goals (achievement of an external task as well as maintenance of internal harmony, for instance). Acts that further one goal may damage another. Furthermore, we shall be interested also in influential group members whose influence directs the group away from its goal. It would be unfortunate if the concept of leadership did not let us consider under it those leaders whose specialty is thwarting the group. Whether or not a leader's activities effectively move the group toward its goal shall be an empirical question.

LEADERSHIP VS. HEADSHIP: The stress on interpersonal influence in the definition of leadership points up the significance of the leader-follower relationship. The statement that leaders direct implies that followers comply. The small group researchers have stressed, with such writers on larger social systems as Weber and Barnard, that the authority of the leader depends upon the acceptance of his directives by the other group members. Gibb suggests a distinction between leadership and headship based upon the consent of the followers. Leadership exists when the consent of the followers is given "spontaneously" because of a recognition of the leader's contribution to the group goal; headship exists when followers obey because of the organizational position of the headman or for any other reason but the spontaneous recogni-

11 Donald Campbell, *A Study of Naval Leadership* (Columbus: Ohio State University, Personnel Research Board, 1953), p. 6.

tion of the authority of the leader for the particular task at hand.[12] This distinction is too sharp. On the one hand, even authoritarian systems depend in part on consent; the purely coercive system is probably unstable. The directives of those in formal hierarchies can be rejected (or sabotaged). On the other hand, the unstructured situation in which consent of followers is spontaneously accorded or withdrawn, depending upon the perceived contribution of the leader to the group goal, is also a limiting case. Even in short-lived leaderless experimental groups there soon develops, as we shall see, a rather stable leadership structure. Furthermore, the status an individual receives for his instrumental achievement at one point in time develops into a general status not specific to any task and not dependent upon consistent performance. Thus we cannot expect to find systems in which consent has no significance or systems in which consent is spontaneously accorded an individual on a momentary basis. Our interest will be both in leadership supported by a formal structure and leadership without this support. The reason why leadership directives are accepted is a question left open for further study.

The Behaviors of Leaders

The statement that the leader exerts interpersonal influence in the pursuit of a group goal does not tell us what behaviors we can expect from leaders. What sorts of activities will leaders engage in while performing their leadership function? The specification of leader behaviors is difficult because, though the leadership role is specialized, it is ". . . paradoxically a specialization in generality. The leader is a person who is recognized as specializing in doing whatever has to be done."[13] Specific leadership behaviors, therefore, vary from situation to situation. Different groups with different tasks will require different leadership functions. And insofar as any single group has a variety of tasks or goals, there will be a variety of leadership functions. As Lasswell has put it: "There are as many elites as there are values. Besides the

[12] Gibb, in Hare, Borgatta, and Bales, eds., *Small Groups*, p. 94.
[13] *Ibid.*, p. 347.

elite of power (the political elite) there are elites of wealth, respect and knowledge (to name but a few)."[14] It is, however, important to note that since leadership is a group role and not an individual trait, the fact that there may be several leadership roles in a group associated with various group tasks does not necessarily mean that different individuals will occupy those roles. One individual may occupy several or all leadership roles; or leadership may be divided among several group members. In the next chapter we shall consider some aspects of the differentiation of the leadership role.

If the definition of leadership on the basis of functions performed in the group rather than on the basis of structural position is to be useful, leadership functions have to be specified precisely enough so that they can be recognized. A statement that the leadership function consists of contributing to group-goal achievement through interpersonal influence gives little indication as to what behavior cues a researcher must seek as evidence that such a function is being performed. Yet leadership functions should not be so specifically defined that they are relevant to only one group or one type of task. Too specific a definition of the functions of the leader of a particular group would preclude useful comparisons of leadership in that situation with leadership in other situations. Several techniques have been used to specify the types of behavior that leaders engage in while carrying out the leadership function. One technique directly records the behaviors of individuals in groups who have been selected by observers as having contributed the most to the group process or who have been designated leaders by the researcher before the group session.[15] Other studies using on-going groups have attempted to specify the behaviors of those who contribute most to the group process. One technique is to match on-going groups on all characteristics but productivity and supervisor behavior. The groups are then divided into those with high and those with low productivity in an attempt to see how the

---

[14] Lasswell, Lerner, and Rothwell, *Comparative Study* . . . , p. 7.
[15] Both of these techniques have been used in the University of Rochester studies by Carter and his associates. See Carter, in Hare, Borgatta, and Bales, eds., *Small Groups*.

supervisory behavior differs for the two types of groups.[16] Another technique for discovering leadership behaviors is the questionnaire method. Respondents are asked to designate the behaviors concentrated upon by the leaders of the groups to which the respondents belong.[17] What is significant is that these various studies, using different techniques, produce similar results.

The particular types of behavior on which leaders concentrate are quite significant in connection with the relation between leadership and the functioning of the group. On the basis of a factor analysis of questionnaire returns, Halpin and Winer found that leader behavior could be described as falling within four dimensions:[18]

I. *Consideration* (49.6%): This dimension is probably best defined as the extent to which the leader, while carrying out his leader functions, is considerate of the men who are his followers. There is no implication, however, of laxity in the performance of duty, in this consideration. Individual items indicate that the positive pole of this factor is characterized by warmth of personal relations, readiness to explain actions, and by willingness to listen to subordinates.

II. *Initiating Structure* (33.6%): This dimension represents the extent to which the leader organizes and defines the relation between himself and his subordinates or fellow group members. . . .

III. *Production Emphasis* (9.8%): This represents a cluster of behaviors by which the leader stresses getting the job done. It is probably best described as a way of motivating the group or organization members by emphasizing the job to be done, or the group goal. . . .

IV. *Sensitivity* (*Social Awareness*) (7.0%): The leader characterized by this factor stresses being a socially acceptable individual in his interactions with other group members. . . .

[16] This technique is employed by Kahn and Katz, in Cartwright and Zander, eds., *Group Dynamics.*

[17] This technique was used extensively in the Ohio State Leadership Studies. See J. K. Hemphill, *Leader Behavior Description* (Columbus: Ohio State University, Personnel Research Board, 1950); Halpin and Winer, *The Leadership Behavior* . . . ; and R. M. Stogdill and A. E. Coons, *Leader Behavior: Its Description and Measurement* (Columbus: Ohio State University, Bureau of Business Research, 1957).

[18] Halpin and Winer, *op.cit.* The paraphrase quoted here is from Gibb, "Leadership," in Lindzey, ed., *Handbook* . . . , pp. 891-92.

The dimensions and the variations due to each factor are interesting. Though leadership is basically conceptualized as directing the group toward some external goal, a large part of leader behavior is directed toward the internal situation of the group—toward maintaining a proper affective tone and social relationship within the group (Consideration and Sensitivity); and toward maintaining an effective group structure (Initiating Structure). Only category III, which accounts for a small part of the variance, represents activity directly connected with the external task—though of course the internal group tasks affect the performance of the external task. This may be due in part to the fact that the groups studied by Halpin and Winer were air crews, for whom the nature of the external problem and the methods of dealing with it were rather rigidly defined. But the heavy emphasis on the internal group tasks—both the expressive and the instrumental—suggests that leaders, in order to further a group's external task, will have to concentrate much effort on maintaining a satisfactory affective tone and an effective group structure within the group.

It is significant that these behaviors of leaders parallel the general group tasks that were spelled out in the previous chapter. The leader, it seems, must deal with both the external and the internal, the socio-emotional and the instrumental aspects of the group activity. Gibb identifies some of the factors found in several studies of leadership behavior as (1) an emphasis on behaviors directly connected with the achievement of the external group goal; (2) behaviors that maintain satisfactory internal relations of the group through leader sociability and the like; and (3) behaviors that tend to promote the individual prominence of the leader.[19] That leader-

[19] Gibb, *op.cit.*, p. 892. There are several aspects of leader behavior that these descriptions of its dimensions do not cover. Since these aspects of behavior will be useful later on, it is well to mention them here in the discussion of leader behavior. One such aspect deals with whether or not the leadership behaviors were intended by the leader. Another aspect deals with whether or not attempted leadership acts are, in fact, followed; and a third with whether or not, if followed, they direct the group in the direction anticipated by the leader. Hemphill suggests several categories of leadership acts that allow us to deal with these aspects. "Attempted" leadership acts are those acts connected with a conscious intent of the leader to direct the

ship is a "specialization in generality" is clearly supported by this finding that leaders deal with those tasks with which it was found all groups must deal. The several tasks that leaders must perform suggest a number of significant questions about leadership: How is an equilibrium maintained between the various group tasks? Under what circumstances are the various leadership tasks likely to be performed by one leader? Under what circumstances will separate leaders specializing in the internal or the external, the expressive or the instrumental tasks arise?

The Origins of Leadership

THE DEMANDS OF THE TASK: As the parallel between the group tasks and the tasks performed by leaders indicates, functional leadership arises in response to the demands of the group task. It is possible, of course, for groups to deal with task demands without developing a structure of role differentiation such that one or a few group members assume special responsibility for dealing with those demands. But there is evidence that this is rare. Groups that do not achieve at least the minimal stage of internal organization associated with role differentiation of leaders and non-leaders are likely to be short-lived.[20] On the other hand, groups with a high level of consensus as to who exercised the most influence or who was the most effective leader have been found to be more productive and more satisfactory for the group members.[21] Furthermore, studies of experimental small groups, with no previous contact among the members and no structure supplied by the experimenter, indicate that role differentiation in response to the demands of the task develops rapidly; evidence

group. "Successful" leadership acts are those directive attempts that are accepted and followed by the group members. And "effective" leadership acts are those "successful" acts that contribute to the group goal. All effective acts are necessarily successful. Not all successful acts are effective. J. K. Hemphill, *A Proposed Theory of Leadership in Small Groups* (Columbus: Ohio State University, Personnel Research Board, 1954), p. A-18.

[20] See R. M. Stogdill, "Leadership and Morale in Organized Groups," in J. E. Hulett, Jr., and Ross Stagner, eds., *Problems in Social Psychology* (Urbana, Ill.: University of Illinois Press, 1952), p. 141.

[21] Heinicke and Bales, *Sociometry, 16* (1953).

has been found of considerable agreement among group members as to who is the group leader and who contributes the most to the group within fifteen minutes of the beginning of interaction in groups that had had no previous contact.[22]

Evidence that leadership role differentiation develops in response to the group task is found in studies of groups with clear tasks in which those expected to assume the leadership role do not assume that role. The non-performance of those group members who, because of their formal position, are expected to take on the leadership role leads to the assumption of that function by another emergent leader. The appearance of emergent leaders to fill the gap left by the non-performing expected leaders has been observed in both experimental groups and in on-going groups in business and government.[23]

GENERALIZED LEADERSHIP: That leadership arises in response to the demands of the group task suggests the importance of the situation in determining leadership. As the failure of the trait approach to the study of leadership indicated, leadership can be understood only in relation to the situation in which it arises. But the situationist approach to leadership should not imply that leadership is necessarily specific to situations; that the knowledge that an individual is performing a leadership role in one situation is useless in predicting the probability that he will assume such a role in another situation. Several experimental studies have demon-

[22] The evidence for this rapid development of role differentiation is presented by R. R. Blake, J. S. Mouton, and B. Fruchter, "The Consistency in Interpersonal Behavior Judgments Made on the Basis of Short-Term Interactions in Three-Man Groups," *J. Abnorm. Soc. Psych.*, 49 (1954), pp. 573-78. Shaw and Gilchrist found that experimental subjects in a highly structured task situation quickly became aware of the need for coordination on the task they were given. After a few interactions they achieved a high level of agreement as to who the coordinator ought to be. This individual then began to perform differentiated functions—initiating suggestions and the like. M. E. Shaw and J. E. Gilchrist, "Inter-group Communication and Leader Choice," *J. Soc. Psych.* 43 (1956), pp. 133-38.

[23] For a discussion of this emergent leadership in experimental groups, see R. W. Heyns, "Effects of Variation in Leadership on Participant Behavior in Discussion Groups" (Unpublished Ph.D. dissertation, University of Michigan, 1948); and Berkowitz, in Hare, Borgatta, and Bales, eds., *Small Groups.* For a discussion of the same process in on-going groups, see W. H. Crockett, "Emergent Leadership in Small Decision-Making Groups," *J. Abnorm. Soc. Psych.*, 51 (1955), pp. 378-83.

strated that leadership roles are to some extent transferable. Bell and French have shown evidence of this consistency when the group situation is changed by changing the membership of the group. They correlated the score an individual received on a sociometric test in one group with his average score received in five other groups of different membership, the degree of correlation being assumed to be a measure of the degree to which one could predict an individual's leadership status in groups of novel membership on the basis of his previous performance in a group. On the basis of an average correlation of .75 for all the individuals studied, they conclude that there is a high consistency of leadership status. Work by Carter and his associates suggests that leadership is not necessarily specific to a particular task. They studied the consistency of leadership performance as the group task was varied. They found that, though there was some variability, the leader on one task had a higher probability of being the leader on another task than did other group members. In particular, consistency in leadership tended to cluster around clerical tasks on the one hand and mechanical tasks on the other.[24]

That leadership performance is consistent from group task to group task does not necessarily mean that it is a trait inherent in individuals. It is rather that the status an individual achieves in one situation by his task performance carries over to other tasks. Parsons, Bales, and Shils describe the process whereby status accorded an individual on the basis of task achievement will develop into a generalized ascribed status, transferable to other situations: "Insofar as a given person 'gets on the right track' and receives Positive Reactions from other members, he will be reinforced in his direction of movement, and will tend to keep on talking. He will 'generalize' from the premises, logical and emotional, which underlay his original successful attempt. . . . And, reciprocally, the

[24] See Bell and French, in Hare, Borgatta, and Bales, eds., *Small Groups*; Carter, in Guetzkow, ed., *Groups, Leadership and Men*, pp. 152-53; Carter, in Hare, Borgatta, and Bales, eds., *Small Groups*; and Carter, in Cartwright and Zander, eds., *Group Dynamics*.

other members will 'generalize' from his earlier attempts, gratifying in some sense to them, to an expectation of further effective behavior on his part. The member begins to build a 'specialized role.' Insofar as the activity he performs is felt to be effective in terms of the functional problems of the group, its goals and value norms, the 'status' of the member will begin to rise. There will be a 'generalization' from the specific *performance* of the person to a *qualitatively ascribed* 'position' in the group which bears a rank relation to other positions similarly developed."[25]

The validity of this description of the development of generalized ascribed leadership status is supported by the fact that in groups with a longer life and in which commitment is more total than in ordinary experimental groups, such a generalized leadership structure is likely to appear. In groups where relationships are more diffuse and affective, leadership is less likely to be specific to a particular task. Thus, in a study of leadership in a summer camp, Lippitt comments: "Our data leads us to believe that in these cabin groups, where group life approaches total 24-hour living, attributed power tends to be undifferentiated as to situation and activity. This is to say, the actor's power may have initially derived from pre-eminence in some particular type of activity or characteristic, e.g., fighting, sports, camp-craft, disobeying adults, strength or size, but fellow members tend to generalize this pre-eminence to the general range of group situations and activities."[26]

The maintenance of this ascribed leadership from situation to situation is supported by the ability of the generalized leader to delegate his leadership in situations in which he is not equipped to give adequate task direction. In a camp situation similar to that studied by Lippitt and his associates, Sherif describes such delegation: ". . . when the groups were brought together in a tournament of competitive games, the leader of each group delegated authority to another high-

[25] Parsons, Bales, and Shils, *Working Papers* . . . , p. 133.
[26] Lippitt, *et al.*, "The Dynamics of Power," *Hum. Rel.*, 5 (1952), pp. 37-64, reprinted in Cartwright and Zander, eds., *Group Dynamics*, chap. 31, p. 480.

status member to act as the athletic 'captain.' But, while the tournament progressed, the leader did not drop out of the picture. The athletic director directed team activities with the leader's approval."[27]

That leadership cannot be predicted or explained solely upon the basis of the situation in which it appears suggests the important research task of looking for those variables that affect the probability that a particular individual will assume a leadership role in a particular situation. In this respect a study of the traits of leadership—i.e., those personal or social characteristics that an individual brings with him into a situation—might be useful. Though the group task leads to the development of role differentiation and leadership structure, individuals are not necessarily selected for leadership roles on the basis of their abilities for the group task. Personality traits affect the probability that an individual will assume a leadership role. So do certain characteristics of the group structure. Some of the factors that influence the probabilities that an individual will assume a leadership role may be briefly discussed. These are (1) an individual's structural position in the group; (2) his status in the cultural environment external to the group; (3) his personality traits; and (4) his motivation to assume the leadership role.

STRUCTURAL POSITION IN THE GROUP: The influence of one person over the behavior and opinions of another can be exerted only through communication. Furthermore, any technical information that is needed to aid the group in the achievement of its instrumental goal must be communicated to be effective. A central position in the communication network of a group, therefore, will have a significant effect upon the probability that an individual will assume a leadership role. This has been shown in experimental studies of highly structured communication nets, as well as in studies of on-going groups.[28] The relationship between a central communication

---

[27] Muzafer Sherif and Carolyn Sherif, *An Outline of Social Psychology* (New York: Harper, 1956), p. 214.

[28] See the experimental work of Bavelas, in Lerner and Lasswell, eds., *Policy Sciences*; Leavitt, in Swanson, Newcomb, and Hartley, eds., *Readings . . .* ; Heise and Miller, in Hare, Borgatta, and Bales, eds., *Small*

position and leadership is, furthermore, reciprocal. Just as the central position in a communication net increases the chances that an individual will assume a leadership role, so does the assumption of such a role increase the probability that an individual will become a central communication figure.[29] This latter tendency for communications to be channeled through the group leader after he has assumed that role is one reason why leadership achieved in one task tends to become generalized for other tasks and situations.

Status in the External Culture of the Group: The generalized status that an individual brings with him into a group situation affects the probability that he will assume a leadership role. Thus, in new groups assembled to deal with a specific task and without a formal structure of leadership, it has been found that status factors irrelevant to the task at hand—such as male sex, high occupational status, and high rank in a company—had a definite effect on the amount of influence asserted by the group members and on the extent to which group members were chosen as leaders.[30] This variable may interact with the previous one of structural position. Individuals who because of their position in the communication net transmit a large amount of communications may not assume a leadership role if their generalized status is too low. Thus Sayles and Strauss point out that cleaning personnel in a factory have a high rate of communication transmission because of their mobility, but their low status keeps them from exercising the influence associated with leadership.[31]

Personality Traits: The trait theory has gone into disrepute largely on the basis of studies that have shown a lack

---

Groups; and M. E. Shaw, "A Comparison of Two Types of Leadership in Various Communications Nets," *J. Abnorm. Soc. Psych., 50* (1955), pp. 127-34. Festinger, Schachter, and Back found that in a housing project those who lived in the center of a court were more likely to be opinion leaders than those on the periphery. *Social Pressures . . . ,* pp. 157-58.

[29] See Homans, *The Human Group*, p. 182, and chap. 16.

[30] Strodtbeck, *Sociometry, 19* (1956); Strodtbeck, *et al., Am. Soc. Rev.* (1957); and B. M. Bass and C. Wurster, "Effects of Company Rank on LGD Performance of Oil Refinery Supervisors," *J. Abnorm. Soc. Psych., 37* (1953), pp. 100-4.

[31] Leonard R. Sayles and George Strauss, *The Local Union: Its Place in the Industrial Plant* (New York: Harper, 1953), p. 149.

of agreement on the personality traits of successful leaders. This rejection of a trait-deterministic theory of leadership ought not to blind us to the possibility that certain characteristics influence the probability that a particular individual will assume a leadership role in a particular situation. Certainly such traits as intelligence or particular skill increase leadership potential in some situations. The important point to be remembered about leadership traits is that "Leadership is both a function of the social situation and a function of personality, but it is a function of these two in interaction. . . ."[32] One study of the relationship between personality traits and the structure of the group indicates that in highly structured groups, a central communication position is a better predictor of leadership than personality test score or previous leadership behavior.[33] Much useful work remains to be done on the relationship between personality and other variables and between specific personality traits and specific group situations.

MOTIVATION TO ASSUME A LEADERSHIP ROLE: Motivation to perform leadership acts may derive from two sources: the individual needs that can be satisfied by assumption of the leadership role, and the cognitive expectation that one's leader-

[32] Gibb, in Hare, Borgatta, and Bales, eds., *Small Groups*, p. 89.
[33] See Leonard Berkowitz, "Personality and Group Position," *Sociometry*, *19* (1956), pp. 210-22. Berkowitz divided his experimental subjects into high, medium, and low ascendents based upon a combination of personality test scores, amount of interactions initiated in a previous group session, and leadership rating received from the other group members in the previous session. He then created four-man groups consisting of one high, two medium, and one low ascendent. The groups were given a task to perform using the "wheel" communication net (i.e., all communications go through one central figure). In half the groups, high ascendents were placed in the central communication position; in half, low ascendents were so placed. Thus the relative effect of personal characteristics (measured in terms of personality tests and previous performance) and communication position could be tested. The results are interesting. On the first group trial, personality types played an important role. Low ascendents in central positions were much more passive than high ascendents in central positions. Furthermore, on the first trial, low ascendents in central positions were more passive than the high ascendents in their groups who held a peripheral position in the communication net. But by the third group trial, low ascendents in central positions were performing leadership acts on about the same level as the high ascendents in central positions. Furthermore, they were more active than the high ascendents on the periphery of their own groups. Thus over time the communication net of the group had a greater effect on leadership performance than personal characteristics.

ship acts will be successful and effective. The needs to be satisfied by performance of leadership acts may be those connected with the acts themselves—for instance, the compensation for feelings of inadequacy that lead some men to seek power positions—or needs connected with the achievement of the group goal. There is evidence that the more satisfaction an individual derives from the achievement of the external goal of the group, the more willing he will be to take on an instrumental leadership role.[34] There is little information on the influence of the expectation of the success and effectiveness of one's leadership acts on the assumption of the leadership role. A study by Hemphill suggests that "in and of itself" such expectation "does not affect attempted leadership scores."[35] But one would assume that insofar as an individual expects his attempted leadership acts to be rewarded by being accepted by the group, and by helping move the group toward its goal, he will be more likely to engage in such acts.

Observation and Measurement of Leadership

Some aspects of the functional concept of leadership have now been indicated. How do the various techniques for locating and identifying leaders relate to this concept and how do they relate to each other? Four techniques of locating leaders will be discussed: the leader as the most active group member, the leader so designated by the group, the leader as holder of high office, and the leader as the individual favored by the group decisions. Each one of these measures has a high degree of face validity as a measure of functional leadership. The most active group member, it is reasonable to assume, will exercise the most interpersonal influence on the decision. Leadership acts, it was pointed out, must be communicated to be effective; and leaders tend to be in the center of communication nets. Similarly, the leader so designated by the group on a sociometric test, it is reasonable to assume, will exercise the most interpersonal influence. This

---

[34] See Bales, "Equilibrium Problem . . . ," in Parsons, Bales, and Shils, *Working Papers* . . . , pp. 160-61.
[35] Hemphill, *et al.*, *Psych. Monographs* (1956), p. 17.

accords well with the assumption made by several investigators that leadership is accompanied by high prestige and deference from the group members. The holding of high office is also a reasonable clue to existence of functional leadership. High office gives the office-holder both the legitimate use of power and control over the group's communication network and bureaucratic structure. And lastly, since leading a group involves both directing the group toward a goal and to some extent setting that goal, one can assume that the member whose personal goal is most similar to the group goal will be the leader. We will now turn to a consideration of these various measures.[36]

THE LEADER AS THE MOST ACTIVE GROUP MEMBER: Within the small experimental group it is possible to observe directly the interpersonal contacts of the members. As was pointed out in the previous chapter, techniques have been devised to reduce these contacts to standard types and to develop indices based upon their frequencies. It is a significant finding that even in groups with no formal leader and no structure of role differentiation introduced by the experimenter, a clear differential in the rates of performing certain activities soon appears among the group members. Bales, for instance, found that in his initially leaderless groups striking differences in the rates of activity of the individual members soon develop. The individual who talks the most also received the most communications. And there are significant characteristics of the interactions flowing to and from this most active member. He tends to direct a larger proportion of his statements

---

[36] Three of these measures have been discussed by James March in a significant experimental study of influence relationships, *Sociometry*, **19** (1956). Though our emphasis is on the leadership role rather than on influence as a function, the two concepts are closely related. Perhaps one advantage of dealing with the concept of leadership rather than with that of influence is that an analysis of the several functions that the leader—the most influential person in a group—must handle will allow us to shed some light upon the reasons why several measures of leadership and influence do not correlate highly. The correlation among the various leadership measures will be discussed at the end of this chapter, and an analysis of why certain of these measures do not correlate will be attempted in the next chapter. Because of the straightforwardness of the office-holding criterion of leadership, we shall not discuss it in the following section, while we consider the technical problems associated with other measures.

to the group rather than to individual members, and he tends to have more interactions in the positive task-oriented categories—giving suggestions, information, and opinions.[37] Thus, on the basis of systematic counts of what the group members say, one can discover a clear functional differentiation among them.

Since the groups studied by Bales and his associates are discussion groups where the only significant form of behavior is verbal, it is reasonable to assume that the individual who makes the most suggestions or gives the most opinions has the greatest effect upon the group. But to link the amount of interaction initiated with the amount of influence over the group product is tantamount to equating talking the most with contributing the most to the group—an obviously invalid equation. Before one can move from a knowledge of the interaction rates of an individual to the influence that an individual exerts within a group, one would have to know if the interactions in which the individual attempts to direct the group were successful and effective. Homans' comment on this problem is apt: "The leader is at the center of the web of interaction; much interaction flows toward him and away from him. But it is impossible to define the leader merely by saying that he is the person who most often initiates interaction for the other members of the group. We must also know the content of his orders and the degree to which they are obeyed. A member of a group may make a suggestion to the rest, and they will greet it with scornful laughter. *He has originated interaction to which the others have responded, but the response is not the one he wished and he is obviously not a leader.*"[38]

[37] Bales, in Parsons, Bales, and Shils, *Working Papers.* . . . See also the more detailed discussion of this body of material in the next chapter.

[38] Homans, *op.cit.*, p. 418. There are ways to consider the response to an interaction in the interaction count. A preliminary attempt is suggested by Bales' "index of control," in Parsons, Bales, and Shils, *Working Papers.* . . . This is a measure that compares the amount of response received by an individual in the category of agreement with that received in the category of disagreement. Though this measure does not trace the reactions to any particular event, it does give an indication of the general response to an individual's statements. A more elaborate technique for considering influence chains—A's influence on C through B—is suggested by Godfrey Gardner in "Functional Leadership and Popularity in Small Groups," *Hum. Rel.,* 9 (1956), pp. 491-509.

A further problem is that the observer using a system of interaction counting may miss the "sense" of the discussion. He will be so busy counting individual actions that he will not be able to estimate the overall impact of an individual on the group. Those who use the interaction count technique would maintain that the rates of interaction give a more precise and accurate estimation of this impact. But, as was mentioned above, a single significant act may have more impact than a large number of trivial suggestions. The leader chosen by interaction counts may not be the leader that another observer would have found. Hemphill found that a "naïve" observer who rated the group members on leadership every five minutes was in only slight agreement with an observer using a system of interaction counting.[39] The positive but low correlation indicates that leadership as defined by interaction counting is not entirely different from leadership as a layman might define it, but is certainly not the same. This in itself does not mean that interaction counting is an inadequate technique, but it does suggest that the relation between leadership as defined by rates of interaction and other measures of leadership must be carefully considered.

THE LEADER SO DESIGNATED BY THE GROUP: Several aspects of the functional role of leaders suggest that a designation of leaders by the group members would accurately select those group members who perform the leadership role. Leaders are active in interpersonal influence and depend upon the acceptance of their acts by the group members. Furthermore it is assumed that they are prestigeful individuals. If these are leadership characteristics, it is certainly reasonable to expect that members can identify the leaders.

The importance of the group members' perception of the leadership structure of their group—whether or not the perception accords with "objective" reality—as well as the convenience of the method for groups that the researcher cannot observe directly, has led to the wide use of the sociometric technique in leadership studies. A number of problems exist

[39] Hemphill, *et al.*, *Psych. Monographs* (1956), p. 7.

in the use of a sociometric test for the selection of leaders. One problem is associated with the large number of different criteria used in sociometric studies of leadership. Some typical criteria are: the person one would most like to live with, the person who exercised the most leadership, contributed the best idea, or best guidance to the group, the person who was best liked, the person who had the best "all-around ability as a combat officer," and the person with whom one spent the most time "getting things done."[40] Clearly these varied criteria do not measure the same thing. Some sociometric questions ask about actual behavior (With whom do you spend the most time getting things done?); some ask about perceptions of actual behavior (Who contributed the most to the group?); and some ask about personal preferences (Whom would you choose as a friend?). Leadership functions are quite varied— they may be directed toward the external task, toward the internal group organization, or toward maintaining the affective tone of the group. The various criteria may, therefore, measure different forms of leadership. The relative validity of the various criteria and whether or not they measure the same aspects of leadership are still open questions. We shall return to this in a later chapter.

Another difficulty in using a sociometric test for leadership lies in the question of the meaning of the number of choices. Is anyone who is mentioned on a sociometric test for leadership assumed to be a leader, or only those who receive more than a certain minimum of votes? Most studies limit leadership to those individuals who receive more than a minimum number of votes, or to the most highly chosen individual or individuals. But insofar as leadership is a function that may be shared by many, sociometric tests that limit the respondent to one (or two or three) choices, and then define leaders as those receiving more than a designated amount of votes might tend to find a much more centralized leadership structure

[40] See H. H. Jennings, "Structure of Leadership Development and Sphere of Influence," *Sociometry,* 1 (1938), pp. 99-153; Bales and Slater, in Parsons and Bales, *Family, Socialization* . . . ; Williams and Leavitt, *J. Consulting Psychology* (1947); and R. M. Stogdill, "The Sociometry of Working Relations in Formal Organizations," *Sociometry,* 12 (1949), pp. 276-86.

than actually exists. Furthermore, the number of votes received may not represent the amount of actual influence as accurately as would the quality of the votes received. Several studies have pointed out that a few strategic connections in a group or organization may be more significant than a larger number of votes.[41] And lastly, there is the possibility that the group members will be mistaken; that the ones they select as leaders will not be the ones who exercise the most interpersonal influence on the group. Whether the group members or an external observer would have more accurate knowledge of the power structure of a group depends upon the nature of the group. It is important to note, however, that even if the group members are "mistaken"—that is, select someone who by other criteria would not be considered a leader—we cannot dismiss the group selection as merely the opinion of the group on leadership structure. Since leadership depends upon the acceptance by the group of the leader's directive, the perceptions of the group members as to who is the leader is a significant factor.

SIMILARITY BETWEEN PERSONAL AND GROUP OPINION: This technique compares the opinions of the various group members before a group meeting with the opinions expressed by the group after a meeting. It is assumed that the individual whose pre-test opinion is closest to the post-test opinion of the group exerted the most influence on the group. This "pre-test, interaction, post-test" method is one of the most widely used and oldest methods in research on opinion formation. In a study by Moore in 1921, for instance, the pre-test opinions of individuals on certain questions of musical taste, grammar, and morals were compared with the post-test opinions of these individuals on the same questions after they had been told what the "expert" or "majority" opinion was on the subject.[42] The change of opinion between the two tests was as-

---

[41] See F. S. Chapin, "Sociometric Stars as Isolates," *Am. J. Soc.*, *56* (1950), pp. 263-67; and J. L. Moreno, "A Note on Cohesion in Small Groups," *Sociometry*, *13* (1950), p. 176.

[42] H. T. Moore, "The Comparative Influence of Majority and Expert Opinion," *American Journal of Psychology* (1921), pp. 16-20. This is a typical early experiment in which there was no interaction among the participants. Interpersonal influence was exerted through reports of what participants were alleged to have said.

sumed to be due to the "expert" or "majority" opinion. Numerous more recent small group studies have used the pre-post-test method to evaluate the influence of the various group members.[43] This technique is also used implicitly in studies of actual political events; it is essentially the technique used in estimating the influence of the face-to-face group in panel studies of voting decisions. The voting intention of the respondent is discovered at an early interview (the pre-test), as is the voting preference of the members of the face-to-face groups with whom he interacts. At a later interview his voting intention is again recorded (post-test). Changes in intention from the pre-test to the post-test are assumed to have been caused by interaction with the face-to-face group between the tests. Thus the findings of the voting studies show that those respondents who belong to face-to-face groups with opinions compatible with their original voting intention rarely change their intentions between the two interviews, while the rate of change to the opposite party or to non-voting is greater among those with incompatible face-to-face groups or with little or no face-to-face contact.[44]

The pre-post-test method, however, is effective only when there is a clear opinion conflict in the pre-test. If all group members have the same opinion, there is of course no way of measuring the relative influence on the change of opinion that takes place during the group interaction. What is more important, the same limitation holds true if two or more members hold opinions that represent the direction in which the group moves. If the group opinion moves in a direction favored by more than one member, one cannot tell which of these members has the greatest influence, even if one member held that opinion more strongly. If a highly influential group member has a "disciple" who always agrees with him, this technique could not differentiate between the two members.

[43] See, for instance, Mills, in Cartwright and Zander, eds., *Group Dynamics*; Strodtbeck, in Hare, Borgatta, and Bales, eds., *Small Groups*; A. P. Hare, "Small Group Discussions with Participatory and Supervisory Leadership," *J. Abnorm. Soc. Psych.*, 48 (1953), pp. 273-75.
[44] Berelson, *et al.*, *Voting*, p. 120.

RELATIONSHIP AMONG THE TECHNIQUES: The methods of discovering group leadership that have just been discussed have a high degree of face validity and have been widely used. They are also the methods implicitly used in ordinary political discourse. One can easily think of situations in which the attribution of leadership in government is based on the reports of qualified informants, on the amount of activity carried on by an individual, or on the congruence between the decision reached by a governmental body and the desires of an interested party. But the various techniques have a number of weaknesses. Furthermore we are not sure to what extent they tap the same group dimension—whether those selected as leaders by one criterion would be so selected by another.

Studies of the correlations among the several measures report a wide variety of results. In one of the fullest studies of the relationship among these measures, James March compared the intercorrelations among eight measures of influence in a group. Three were sociometric measures of attributed influence (one a measure taken before the group meeting, and two taken after the group meeting asking about the influence of a group member on the respondent and on the group). Three measures were forms of a pre-post-test measure of opinion change, while the final two measures were of amount of interactions initiated (total number of interactions, and specific influence attempts). In each experimental group, the group members were ranked on all eight measures, the rankings were paired, and the mean for all ten groups of the correlation of each pair of rankings was calculated. The correlations between the rankings were positive but usually low. Half of the correlations were below .30 and only two pairs were over .60. Every subject was ranked either most or least influential by at least one measure, and nineteen out of fifty subjects were ranked most influential by one measure and least influential on another. The only strong correlations were between the two post-interaction measures of attributed influence (.76 between attribution of influence on the respondent and on the group) and between the two interaction counts (.81).

138

Opinion change correlated the least with the other measures. March concludes that ". . . common measures of influence do not yield identical results consistently and that in some cases the intercorrelations between rankings of individuals generated by the different measures tend to be quite low. In particular, opinion change measures are substantially independent of the other two types of measure."[45] Other studies have also reported low correlations among the various measures.[46]

A number of studies, on the other hand, have found close relationships among the various measures of leadership. Lippitt *et al.*, in their study of influence relationships among boys in a summer camp, found that there was a close relationship between attribution of influence by other boys and number of influence attempts.[47] Strodtbeck found a closer relationship between amount of interactions initiated and opinion change measures than was found by March, who found that opinion change was very slightly related to other measures.[48] And Bass found a correlation of .93 between an interaction count meas-

---

[45] March, *Sociometry, 19* (1956).

[46] Carter and his associates (Carter, *et al.*, *J. Psych.* [1949]; and Carter, *et al.*, in Hare, Borgatta, and Bales, eds., *Small Groups*) found low correlations among several measures used in experimental groups (leadership attribution, interaction counts, and observer ratings) and even lower correlations between these measures and extra-experimental measures of leadership (ratings by friends and faculty and participation in extra-curricular activities).
It has been noted that those leaders selected by the group on a sociometric test were no more able to influence the group's choice of a new activity than were the other group members. Katz, *et al.* "Leadership Stability and Social Change: An Experiment with Small Groups," *Sociometry, 20* (1957), pp. 36-50.
Bales and his associates (see, for instance, Slater and Bales, in Parsons and Bales, *Family, Socialization* . . .) and Gibb (in Hare, Borgatta, and Bales, eds., *Small Groups*) found a low correlation between sociometric choice by a personal affective criterion and both interaction counts and sociometric choice by other criteria. These studies will be considered more fully in the next chapter.

[47] Lippitt, *et al.*, in Cartwright and Zander, eds., *Group Dynamics*, chap. 31.

[48] Strodtbeck, *et al.*, *Am. Soc. Rev.* (1957); and Strodtbeck, in Hare, Borgatta, and Bales, eds., *Small Groups*. In this latter article, Strodtbeck concludes that the ultimate decision of the group "could most accurately be predicted by simply weighting the privately pre-determined opinion of each participant by the total time he had spoken during the experimental interaction."

ure of leadership and the number of attributions of leadership that an individual receives on a sociometric test.[49]

Clearly there is much work to be done on the relationship among various leadership measures. The absence of clear connections among the several measures suggests that one must be cautious in inferring the equivalence of two leadership measures. The sociometric technique, for instance, while of great use in studies of leadership groups, is not sufficient by itself as a measure of leadership. Individuals selected as leaders on a sociometric basis may not be leaders by other criteria, such as participation in major decisions or holding high office in government or private organizations.[50]

There is much research to be done on this subject. It is not enough to state that certain measures of leadership select different leaders. We must ask why certain measures will produce the same set of leaders and others will not. Under what circumstances, for instance, will the group members select as leader the member who contributes the most to the group? In what situations will they be unaware of the actual leadership structure in the group as defined by the functions the leader performs? Under what conditions will the opinions of the most active member be accepted, and under what conditions will they be rejected? The relations among the measures vary and no attempt will be made here to explain all of these variations. We shall, however, in the next chapter explore more fully the

[49] Bass, *J. Appl. Psych.* (1949). Strodtbeck, *et al., Am. Soc. Rev.* (1957), found a correlation of .69 between amount of participation in a group and number of choices received from group members for contributing the most.

[50] In a study of a small community (*Social Forces*, 1956), Fanelli compared the rankings of individuals on sociometric tests using a "community leadership" criterion with the amount of actual participation in community affairs. He found three different patterns. He located active influentials, who were both highly chosen as influential and were in fact influential in community affairs; prestige influentials, who were highly chosen but actually took little part; and active sub-influentials, who took an active part but received few choices. The data of this study are little more than suggestive, but they do suggest the range of possible relationships between the sociometric and actual behavior criteria. Schulze and Blumberg found that there was a great difference between the leaders of a small community selected by a panel of judges (a variation of the sociometric technique) and those who held high office in the local political and economic structure. R. O. Schulze and L. A. Blumberg, "The Determination of Local Power Elites," *Am. J. Soc.*, 63 (1957), pp. 290-96.

relations between amount of activity in the group and leadership selection by the group. It will be suggested that one reason for the divergence of measures of attributed leadership and measures of amount of activity is that leaders perform several functions at once. In some situations leadership will tend to be split among several leaders, each of whom performs one of the leadership functions. The different measures, it will be suggested, locate these different aspects of leadership.

Chapter VI
LEADERSHIP: AFFECTIVE AND INSTRUMENTAL

1

THE PURPOSE of this chapter is to explore one aspect of the leader-follower relationship as it is found in both small experimental groups and on-going social systems. This aspect is the dual function that the leadership structure of a group must perform if the group is successfully to reach the goal that brought it together. In attempting to achieve its goal, a group must, as was pointed out above, direct activities both toward the instrumental task it faces and toward the maintenance of the internal structure of the group. The group's internal maintenance function must be performed in such a way that the individual members find their participation in the group at least satisfactory enough to keep them from leaving the group. And, as was suggested in the previous chapter, it is the function of the group leadership to operate in both these areas—the instrumental and the internal group maintenance.

The importance of the affective tone and emotional aspects of the leader-follower relationship in political and other social situations has long been recognized. Individuals do not give their allegiance to a state or their support to a political leader solely because of the material benefits they receive in return. The decision on the part of a follower to accept the directive of a leader is based on more than a rational calculus of the advantages to be gained from that acceptance. Loyalty to a state, for instance, usually has an emotional component, reinforced by more or less elaborate systems of symbols and rituals. Though there has been much analysis of these nonrational aspects of politics insofar as they affect the individual political participant, there has been little systematic consideration of the dynamic interaction between emotional attachment and material outputs within the leader-follower relationship.

This chapter will attempt to shed some light on the relationship between instrumental and affective leadership through the use of small group studies. The relationship within the small group will be used as a model of that in actual social and political situations. This chapter will, thus, attempt both to learn about the substantive question of affective and instrumental leadership as it applies to political affairs, and to assess the strengths and weaknesses of small group analysis for the analysis of political affairs.

Small Group Analysis as a Tool

Leader-follower relations in small experimental groups and in on-going groups and organizations share certain significant characteristics. These similarities make it possible to use knowledge of leader-follower relationships in small groups for an understanding of those relations in on-going social systems. However, owing to some equally significant differences between the small group situation and the situation in on-going social systems, one cannot predict behavior in on-going systems directly from knowledge of behavior in the experimental system. The differences are in some ways as useful as the similarities. The specification of the differences between the experimental and non-experimental situation will highlight some of the limitations of the use of small group work for political analysis, but the very specification of these differences will also increase our understanding of behavior in on-going groups.

The question of whether or not the processes observed in the small group actually have analogues or homologues in on-going groups and organizations is an open one to be answered empirically. Thus, in this chapter we shall discuss one of the major findings of small group research: the development in small experimental groups of two leaders, one specializing in the socio-emotional aspect of leadership and one in the instrumental aspect. The existence of such a bifurcation of the leadership role in small experimental groups leads one to ask whether such a bifurcation can be observed in on-going groups and organizations. If such a bifurcation exists in on-going

143

social systems and the discovery of it in experimental groups led us to seek it in on-going systems, then the small group literature will certainly have increased our knowledge of on-going organizations and groups. If, on the other hand, this pattern of leadership splitting is not discovered in on-going social systems, the question can then be posed: what differences between the two systems account for the differences in the observed leadership pattern? If leadership bifurcation is found to develop in experimental groups in response to certain pressures, one can ask if such pressures exist in on-going situations. If so, how does the on-going group or organization deal with these pressures? Thus the specification of the ways in which leader-follower relationships develop in small experimental groups is used as a model with which we can compare the operations of larger, more permanent units. The ways in which the patterns of behavior in on-going social systems are similar to those in small groups as well as the ways in which they fall off from the patterns described by the small group model will lead, it is hoped, to greater understanding of the on-going social system.

The Dual Leadership Task in Small Groups

In the previous chapter, it was pointed out that leaders are responsible for the performance of several tasks. These are the external and internal group tasks—those directly connected with the goal-oriented activities of the group, and those associated with the maintenance of the internal structure of the group and the satisfaction of the needs of the individual members. A similar conceptualization of the leader's tasks would differentiate these into the affective and the instrumental—those tasks related to maintaining the satisfactions of the group members by the creation of a satisfactory affective tone for group interaction and those tasks directly connected with the group's external task. This is essentially the distinction that Barnard makes between effectiveness (achievement of the group purpose) and efficiency (satisfaction of the individual members).[1] Several studies indicate that those leadership structures are most effective that manage to deal with both aspects of the leader-follower relationship. This has been found to be the case in studies of air crews, naval crews, and college departments.[2] In the study of college departments, Hemphill found that those departments with the best reputation for administration are led by chairmen who ". . . concern themselves with (1) organizing departmental activities and initiating new ways of solving departmental problems, and at the same time with (2) developing warm considerate relations with the members of the department."[3] The requirement that the leader perform in both these areas is enforced by the expectations of followers that both will be considered. Commenting on the results of a poll on the ideal image of leadership, Shartle states: "There are stereotypes of ideal leader behavior in organizational settings as perceived by the group or staff members. The dimensions suggest that the ideal leader in most instances is one who places few demands upon the person he leads, he does not interfere with their freedom, and he is a group member and 'one of the boys.' However, at the same time, he is perceived as ideally not a part of the group, as one who can do things for the group that the group cannot do, and as one who gets things done. There seems to be a basic conflict in our ideologies of leaders. We want persons in leadership roles and yet we do not want to place limitations upon ourselves to submit to leadership."[4]

The difficulties of the leadership position derive not merely from the fact that the leader must be active in both the instrumental and affective group tasks, but from the fact that these two tasks are closely related. The way in which the group

[1] Barnard, *Functions* . . . , pp. 55-59. The distinction between the affective and instrumental aspects of leadership ought not to be taken to imply that leadership acts are necessarily either affective or instrumental in content. Many acts will have both aspects.

[2] A. W. Halpin, "The Leadership Behavior and Combat Performance of Airplane Commanders," *J. Abnorm. Soc. Psych.*, 49 (1954), pp. 19-22; Carroll Shartle and Ralph M. Stogdill, "Studies in Naval Leadership," in Guetzkow, ed., *Groups, Leadership* . . . , pp. 119-45; and Hemphill, *J. Educ. Psych.*, (1955).

[3] *Ibid.*, p. 395.

[4] Shartle and Stogdill, *op.cit.*, p. 130.

functions in one area will influence functioning in the other. If group members have a satisfactory affective relationship with the leader, they will be more likely to accept his instrumental directives.[5] On the other hand, if the level of member satisfaction with group leadership is low, members may withdraw from the group, reject the group leader, or reject the group leader's instrumental directives.[6] All these activities lower the instrumental effectiveness of the group. Conversely, the success or failure of the instrumental activity of the group will influence the affective rewards to the members. Group members may derive satisfaction directly from the successful completion of the instrumental task of the group or from certain other rewards that are the bi-product of that task completion. Insofar as the group cannot achieve its instrumental goal, satisfactions will be lowered. Maintaining a balance between the satisfactions of the group members and the task achievement of the group may well be the most important task of the group leader.

EQUILIBRIUM PROBLEM: Maintaining the balance between affective satisfactions and instrumental performance is, however, a difficult and delicate task. Several studies of group process have suggested that attempts to direct the group toward the accomplishment of its instrumental task may be greeted by negative affective reactions on the part of group members. The theoretical and experimental work of Kurt Lewin and his associates first pinpointed the problem within small groups. In Lewin's theoretical formulation, attempts to direct the group toward the group goal disturb the equilibrium of the group by restricting the freedom of the members. This in turn causes a negative reaction that can take two forms: it may take the form of a rejection of the instrumental directive,

[5] See M. W. Horowitz, J. Lyons, and H. V. Perlmutter, "Induction of Forces in Discussion Groups," *Hum. Rel.*, 4 (1951), pp. 58-76; Back, *J. Abnorm. Soc. Psych.* (1951); and John R. P. French and Richard Snyder, "Leadership and Interpersonal Power," in Dorwin Cartwright, ed., *Studies in Social Power* (Ann Arbor, Mich.: Institute for Social Research, 1959).

[6] See Elihu Katz, *et al.*, "Leadership Stability and Social Change: An Experiment with Small Groups," *Sociometry*, 20 (1957), pp. 36-50; and John W. Thibault and Harold H. Kelley, *The Social Psychology of Groups* (New York: John Wiley, 1959), chap. 2.

in which case equilibrium is restored by negating the directive's effect; or the reaction may be an acceptance of the directive accompanied by increased hostility toward the leader. In the latter case, equilibrium is restored but at a higher level of tension between leader and follower.[7]

Examples of this process of negative reaction to directive leadership can be found in the classic experimental work of Lippitt and White carried out under Lewin's direction. In these experiments with democratic and authoritarian group climates, it was noted that directives from an authoritarian leader, though followed, were accompanied by negative affective reactions on the part of the group members, expressed in hostility toward the leader, a scapegoat, or other groups. Furthermore, the acceptance of the leader's directives in the authoritarian situation was external rather than internal. When the leader left the room and the external pressure was removed, the group members ceased complying with the instrumental directive.[8] Experimental work in field situations produced similar results; attempts to direct change in a group led to negative affective reactions on the part of the group members that in turn limited the effectiveness of the instrumental directive. Coch and French, for instance, found that an attempt by management to direct certain changes in the work process ". . . had the effect for the members of setting up management as a hostile power field. They rejected the forces induced by this hostile power field, and group standards to restrict production developed within the group in opposition to management."[9] The problem of leadership is clearly presented by these examples. The achievement of the group's instrumental goal must proceed along with the continuing satisfaction of the individual needs of the group members, but frequently the attempts themselves to achieve the instrumental

[7] For a discussion of the Lewinian equilibrium, see Kurt Lewin, *Field Theory in the Social Sciences* (New York: Harper, 1951). See below, Chapters IX-X, for a more complete discussion of the work of Lewin and his followers.

[8] See White and Lippitt, in Cartwright and Zander, eds., *Group Dynamics.*

[9] See Coch and French, *ibid.;* Kahn and Katz, *ibid.;* and Lewin, *ibid.*

goal lower the level of affective satisfaction of the group members. This lowering will in turn feed back upon the instrumental achievement and hamper it. Thus the several tasks of the leader may not all be consistent with one another.

The treatment of the problem of control and instrumental achievement in the work of Lewin and his associates bears a significant resemblance to the treatment of the problem in the work of Robert F. Bales and his associates at the Harvard Laboratory of Social Relations. In the small experimental groups used by Bales in the formulation of his theoretical system, the formation of the group takes place around the instrumental task presented to the group by the experimenter.[10] The initial differentiation among the group members evolves in response to the demands of this task. Certain members tend to become more active in directing the group toward the completion of its instrumental task. But attempts to control the group in relation to the instrumental task disturb the equilibrium of the group and cause tensions in the expressive integrative area of the group's activities. These negative reactions to control attempts may, like the negative reactions found in the work of Lewin and his associates, be directed at the leader or at a group scapegoat.

Evidence for the negative reaction received by the group member who attempts to lead the group in the direction of instrumental task achievement is derived from six measures taken by Bales during the group experiments. Two measures are based on interaction counts using the Bales scheme; these are simply measures of the amount of interactions initiated and the amount received. After each group session the members are asked to rate all members on a sociometric test using three criteria: the member who contributed the best ideas to the group, the member who contributed the best guidance and the member who was best liked. And after all four group

---

[10] These tasks include discussing an administrative problem and playing a game against the experimenter. The work of Bales and his associates is discussed in Bales, *Interaction Process Analysis*; Bales, in Parsons, Bales and Shils, *Working Papers* . . . ; Bales and Slater, in Parsons and Bales *Family, Socialization* . . . ; and Slater, "Role Differentiation in Small Groups," *Am. Soc. Rev.*, 20 (1955), pp. 300-10, reprinted in Hare, Borgatta, and Bales, eds., *Small Groups*, p. 498.

sessions the members are asked to select the one who contributed the best leadership. The percentage of times the same group member occupies the highest position by more than one measure is calculated. Thus on one batch of experimental groups, Slater calculated the percentage of times that the individual selected as the best leader was highest by another criterion. The results follow:

The "best leader" was also ranked highest on guidance 80 percent of the time; on receiving, 65 per cent; on ideas, 59 per cent; on talking, 55 per cent; and on liking, 25 per cent. Clearly, the member who is best liked is rarely associated in the minds of the group members with the individual who is the best leader. Furthermore, Slater found that "liking" was not associated with any of the other measurements of leadership. The individual chosen highest by the socio-emotional criterion of best-liked was three times as likely to hold the highest position by that measure alone than were those who were most highly chosen by any other measure. Thus, those group members who are active in directing the group, or who are selected by the group members as having contributed to the instrumental task of the group, are not likely to receive choices on a sociometric test using an expressive criterion.[11] The results clearly indicate that the individual who attempts to control the instrumental activities of the group lowers his chances to be highly thought of by the group according to an affective criterion.

EXTERNAL RELATIONS OF THE LEADER: The conflict between directing the group and maintaining one's acceptance by the group would seem to be the unique problem of the group leader. This conflict is heightened in the groups discussed above by the fact that the task toward which the in-

[11] *Ibid.* See also the data in Bales, in Parsons, Bales, and Shils, *Working Papers* . . . , p. 152, table 5; p. 153, table 6; and p. 154, table 7 and chart 4.
That the member who receives the affective choices of the group is not engaged in instrumental activities is further reflected in the interaction "profiles" of this member and the other members. Thus the "Best Idea" man tends to concentrate his activity in those areas directed toward the instrumental task, while the "Best Liked" man concentrates more on socio-emotional interactions; Slater, *op.cit.*, p. 507.

strumental leader directs the group is set for the group externally by the experimenter. Insofar as the task is set for the group externally rather than chosen by the group, attempts at instrumental control are more likely to engender negative reactions. This proposition is supported in an experimental study by Katz *et al.* of a number of four-man groups. After the performance of one task, the groups were asked to select a leader for a second task. In some cases, the task was one that the group had chosen; in others, it was imposed by the experimenter. The results support the proposition that when the task is imposed upon the group externally, the negative reaction against the leader who attempts to direct the task activity will be greater. In those cases where the group performed a second task that it had selected for itself, all those who had been chosen as leaders after the first task were again so chosen at the end of the second. On the other hand, when the group was assigned a task that it had not selected, only one-third of those who had been chosen as leaders after the first task retained that position after the second.[12]

The Dual Leadership Task in On-going Systems

We have now located one major conflict faced by leaders in small experimental groups—the conflict between maintaining both instrumental effectiveness and a satisfactory affective tone in the group. If such a conflict can be located in on-going social systems, we will then be in a position to compare and contrast the ways in which the conflict is resolved in the two systems. Such a comparison should increase our understanding of both systems and also allow us to make some evaluation of the usefulness of small group analysis for the understanding of behavior in other situations.

EXTERNAL RELATIONS OF THE LEADER: In trying to isolate the relationship between leadership control and leadership acceptance in on-going social systems, it may be well to start with the relationship between the group leader and the external setting of the group. In experimental groups the

[12] Katz, *et al.*, *Sociometry*, 20 (1957), p. 49.

relationship between the group and the external world, represented by the external task set for it by the experimenter, is a major source of the conflict between instrumental control and affective acceptance. To see the significance of this for leaders of actual groups, we must look at the special position the leader of a group or organization has in relation to the external environment of the group. Writing in 1950, Robert Merton complained of the assumption found in much of the small group literature that ". . . a Chinese wall shuts off the group from the world around it . . . , with the result that there has been little systematic analysis of the interconnections between the internal organizations of groups and their social surroundings."[13] This has been true of many studies of leadership in small groups. They have considered leadership to be a relationship within the group, not related to the external environment of the group. But small groups—whether experimental or non-experimental—are parts of larger social systems. Non-experimental small groups are sub-systems of larger social systems—communities, organizations, nations. Furthermore, in Western industrialized societies where groups tend to be relatively functionally specific, the external relations of small groups probably assume greater significance. In dealing with group leadership, we must consider the external relations of the group.

Many studies of on-going groups and organizations have found that the group leader is more active in contacts with the external environment of the group than are the other group members. This higher degree of external relationship seems, furthermore, to be independent of the technique of measurement used. Horsfall and Arensberg, for instance, found that those group members in an industrial situation who had the highest rates of interaction within the group also had the highest rates of interaction with non-members of the group.[14] Or, using sociometric tests, Festinger, Schachter, and Back in a study of a housing project found that those highly chosen

---

[13] Robert K. Merton, Introduction to Homans, *The Human Group*, pp. xx.
[14] A. B. Horsfall and C. M. Arensberg, "Teamwork and Productivity in a Shoe Factory," *Hum. Org.*, 8 (1949), pp. 13-25.

within a small face-to-face group tended to be highly chosen by those outside the group as well.[15] William Whyte, in his classic study of a street gang, comments: "The leader is better known and respected outside his group than are any of his followers. His capacity for social movement is greater. One of the most important functions he performs is that of relating his group to other groups in the district. Whether the relationship is one of conflict, competition or cooperation, he is expected to represent the interests of his followers. The politician and the racketeer must win support of the leader in order to win support of his followers. The leader's reputation outside the group tends to support his standing within the group, and his position in the group supports his reputation among outsiders."[16]

Whyte emphasizes the important point that the leader's external relations not only result from his leadership position within the group, but that this external position in turn increases his leadership ability within the group. The ability of the leader to relate the group to the external environment and manipulate that environment for the benefit of the group increases his acceptance and interpersonal influence.[17] Communications from the external environment to the group and

[15] Festinger, Schachter, and Back, *Social Pressures*, chap. 5; and Helen Jennings, *Leadership and Isolation* (New York: Longman's Green, 1950), pp. 76-77.

[16] Whyte, *Street Corner Society*, pp. 256-57; see also Homans, *op.cit.*, p. 186.

[17] D. C. Pelz, in a study of small work groups, found that the amount of acceptance group leaders received from the group members depended in part upon their degree of influence in the external environment of the group. Those leaders who had high influence within the larger organization were able to support the needs of the group members by obtaining promotions and the like for them. Those influential leaders who attempted to support the needs of the group members, therefore, received high acceptance ratings from the members. On the other hand, those group leaders with little influence in the larger organization did not receive high acceptance ratings even if they were sympathetic with the needs of their followers. "Leadership Within a Hierarchical Organization," *J. Soc. Issues*, 7 (1951), pp. 49-55.

Lerner, in a study of the modernization of the Middle East, supports this proposition. As the external environment of the traditional village becomes more significant to the village during the process of modernization, those traditional village leaders who have no connections with that environment will tend to be replaced by a new set of younger group leaders who, because of their contact with the mass media and greater "empathy," are in closer connection with the newly significant external world. Daniel Lerner, *The Passing of Traditional Society* (Glencoe, Ill.: Free Press, 1958), pp. 185-96.

from the group to the external environment will tend to go through the group leader, who becomes in this way an opinion leader or "gate-keeper."[18]

CONFLICTING EXPECTATIONS: The position as communicator between the group and the external environment places special burdens upon the leader and is the source in on-going groups of a conflict between instrumental control and acceptance similar to that found in small experimental groups. The demands made upon the group by the external situation, expressed in the group's instrumental task, as well as the demands of the group members for an emotionally satisfying relationship within the group, will all be centered on the leader. Caught between the expectations of those outside of the group and the demands of the group members, he truly becomes the "man in the middle."[19]

It is significant that the conflict experienced by the group leader is not a conflict between two roles that he holds simultaneously, such as a role in the family and a role in the work group, it is rather a conflict caused by incompatible expectations placed upon the leader in his leadership role. In describing the position of the non-commissioned officer, Stouffer presents a clear example of such a conflict situation faced by the leader of a group that is part of a larger organization; "On the one hand, the non-com had the role of agent of the command and in case the orders from above conflicted with what his men thought were right and necessary he was expected by his superiors to carry out the orders. But he also was an enlisted man, sharing enlisted men's attitudes, often hostile attitudes, toward the commissioned ranks. Consequently, the system of informal controls was such as to reward him for siding with the men in a conflict situation and punish him if he did not. There was some evidence that unless his men had confidence that he could see their point of view, he was an

---

[18] For a discussion of the "opinion leader" or "gate-keeper" position of leaders, see Katz and Lazarsfeld, *Personal Influence*, part I.

[19] The classic case of the "man in the middle"—the foreman—is discussed in W. F. Whyte and B. B. Gardner, "The Man in the Middle," *Applied Anthropology*, 4 (1945), pp. 1-28.

ineffective leader; on the other hand, open and flagrant disobedience by him of an order from above could not be tolerated by the command."[20]

The conflicting expectations[21] that the group members and those in the external system have of the leader can vary in content. Members of an organizational hierarchy may expect the group leader to be oriented toward advancement in that hierarchy, while the group members may expect the leader to remain as similar as possible to them. Of particular interest to us here is the potential conflict between the leader's socioemotional tasks and his instrumental tasks. Several studies of the expectations that organizational superiors and group members have of leaders indicate that while the organizational superiors expect the leader to be oriented to the instrumental task, the group members expect the leader to be more active in the affective sphere. In a study of eighty-seven air crews, Halpin compared the leadership rating given air-crew commanders by crew members and superiors. It was found that while ". . . squadron and wing superiors . . . rate favorably the performance of those commanders who show high Initiating Structure behaviors . . . , crews will prefer as aircraft commanders those leaders who are high on Consideration behavior."[22] This finding is supported in other studies of military situations, as well as industrial situations.[23] On the one

[20] Samuel A. Stouffer, "An Analysis of Conflicting Social Norms," *Am. Soc. Rev.*, *14* (1949), p. 707.

[21] By "expectations" as to the leader's behavior, we mean evaluative standards, not predictions. Thus when we say that followers have certain expectations as to the leader's behavior, we mean that followers believe that the leader *should* behave in a certain way, not necessarily that he *will* behave in a certain way. Cf. Neal Gross, *et al.*, *Explorations in Role Analysis* (New York: John Wiley, 1958), pp. 58-59.

[22] Andrew W. Halpin, "The Leader Behavior and Effectiveness of Airplane Commanders," in Stogdill and Coons, eds., *Leader Behavior: Its Description and Measurement* (Columbus: Ohio State University, Bureau of Business Research, 1957), chap. 4, p. 53.

[23] Ralph M. Stogdill and K. Koehler, *Measurements of Leadership Structure and Organization Change* (Columbus: Ohio State University Research Foundation, 1952), and E. L. Scott, *Perceptions of Organization and Leadership Behavior* (Columbus: Ohio State University Research Foundation, 1952), found a similar pattern for middle-rank leaders in naval crews. Similar results are reported in Samuel Stouffer, *et al.*, *The American Soldier*, Vol. I (Princeton: Princeton University Press, 1949), chap. 8. See also Whyte and Gardner, *op.cit.*

hand, leaders are expected to be formal, avoidant, task-oriented instrumental leaders. On the other, they are expected to be more affectively oriented, indulgent, informal, and companionable group members. This conflict is perhaps exaggerated by examples from military and industrial situations in which the demands of the organizational hierarchy may not coincide with the needs and desires of the group members. But such a conflict can be observed in other contexts. Eisenstadt discusses the conflicting situation of immigrant groups in Israel, caught between the demands of the new external environment and their traditional patterns of life. This conflict is felt especially by the group leader who must mediate between the demands of the external situation and the demands of the traditional group. If the leader conforms to the new demands of the external environment, he risks rejection by the group. If, on the other hand, he rejects adjustment to the new external system, he may cease to be an effective leader in terms of his ability to satisfy the economic and political needs of his group.[24]

Conflicting Expectations: Their Effect on the Group

LEADER MOTIVATION: Leaders in experimental and on-going groups are both faced with the same dilemma, a dilemma that derives from the seeming incompatibility between maintaining the acceptance of the group members and directing the group toward the achievement of its instrumental goal. Before turning to ways in which this dilemma is dealt with in experimental and non-experimental situations, we must deal with one other aspect of the conflict of expectations—the effect of the negative affective reaction that may be associated with instrumental leadership upon the leader's willingness to assume the role of instrumental leader. If the socio-emotional relations within the group, particularly between the leader and his followers, are unsatisfactory, this results in negative reactions on the part of the followers. These negative reactions in turn feed back upon the instrumental task and make its

[24] S. N. Eisenstadt, "Patterns of Leadership and Homogeneity in Israel," *International Social Science Bulletin*, 8 (1956), pp. 36-54.

accomplishment more difficult because of the possibility that the leader's directives or the leader himself will be rejected or simply because of the increased tension in the group. But the lack of satisfactory affective relations will have an effect upon the willingness of the leader to lead, just as it has an effect upon the willingness of the followers to follow. Acceptance by the followers may be looked at as a reward for the leader. If this is the case, the motivation of the leader to assume an instrumental leadership role will be lowered if he is greeted by negative affective reactions to his leadership attempts. The motivation to lead, furthermore, will be lowered even if the attempt at instrumental leadership has been both successful (i.e., the group members have followed the directive) and effective (i.e., it has brought the group closer to the instrumental goal).

An interesting experiment by John Hemphill is relevant to this hypothesis. A number of four-man groups were brought together, made up of two "stooges" and two naïve subjects. In all the groups the naïve subjects were highly motivated by the offer of a reward to accomplish the task set for the group by the experimenter. And they were given enough technical competence during some pre-training to direct the group effectively to the accomplishment of that task. The experimental variable was the reaction of the stooges to the leadership attempts of the naïve subjects. In half the groups the stooges were instructed to (1) express interest in the accomplishment of the group task, (2) follow the instrumental directives of the naïve subjects, and (3) praise the naïve subjects for directing the group. In these groups the naïve subjects were very active as leaders. In the remaining groups the stooges were instructed, as were the stooges in the other groups, (1) to express interest in the successful completion of the task, and (2) to follow the instrumental directives of the naïve subjects. But, unlike the stooges in the first batch of groups, the stooges in the second batch were instructed to show disapproval of the directive attempts of the naïve subjects. Thus, though they followed his directions, they were instructed to make remarks about not liking "bossy people" or people who told them what to do. In these groups leadership activity came to a virtual standstill. At times, Hemphill reports, fifteen to twenty minutes would pass with the naïve subjects saying nothing, even though they had the motivation and the skills to direct the group. Needless to say, tension ran high.[25]

The results are clear. Negative affective reactions lowered the willingness of the naïve subjects to assume the instrumental directive role, which in turn lowered the degree of task accomplishment of the group. Similar findings are presented by Bales, who reports that his experimental subjects, when faced with a choice, preferred the affective acceptance of the group to the assumption of the lead in the instrumental area of the group's activities; and by French and Snyder, who found that the amount of influence attempted by the group leader varied with the degree to which the leader was accepted by the group members.[26] Though negative affective reactions may not have the dramatic effect observed in the Hemphill experiments—i.e., they may not stop control attempts completely—one can certainly argue that such negative reactions, especially in face-to-face situations, will lower the disposition of the individual to assume an instrumental directive role. Bales suggests that the ability of an individual to lead the group in its instrumental task requires a certain degree of immunity to hostile reactions. Insofar as the individual's personality needs are for group acceptance, he will tend to abandon the instrumental direction of the group.[27] In a percep-

[25] Hemphill, *Adult Leadership* (1956).
[26] Bales, in Parsons, Bales, and Shils, *Working Papers* . . . , pp. 160-61; and French and Snyder in Cartwright, ed., *Studies in Social Power*.
[27] *Ibid.*, p. 161; and Bales and Slater, in Parsons and Bales, eds., *Family, Socialization* . . . , p. 295.
It is difficult to evaluate the extent to which the lack of willingness to accept negative reactions as the price of instrumental accomplishment is due to the particular culture of the groups under discussion. Both Bales and Hemphill used groups of college students. One may suggest that this reluctance to experience rejection as the price of instrumental performance may be a general trait in our culture (particularly as found in college communities). Recent literature has suggested a tendency to value acceptance by one's fellows more highly than unique achievements. See David Reisman, *The Lonely Crowd* (New York: Doubleday, 1954); and William H. Whyte, *Organization Man* (New York: Doubleday, 1956). It would be interesting to

tive study of courageously "maverick" senators, Senator John Kennedy suggests a similar point. Those senators who were highly motivated toward a particular goal and wanted to lead the rest of the Senate in that direction despite strong opposition had to have a certain immunity from the pressures to "get along" with and obtain the "comradeship and approval" of the other members of the Senate.[28]

GROUP ACCOMPLISHMENT: The dilemma faced by the leader in reconciling the demands for satisfactory affective relations within the group and effective instrumental activity can, as has been shown, hinder the effective operation of the group. Insofar as the negative reactions of the followers reduce the extent to which they accept the instrumental directives of the leader or the extent to which the leader is motivated to undertake such instrumental directives, the leader will be forced to concentrate more and more on the socio-emotional aspect of group interaction and ignore the instrumental. This will be especially the case in those groups—such as the experimental groups with no previous experience together—in which the leader has not built up enough general prestige to allow him to survive some negative reactions without being rejected as leader. Though the long-run satisfactions of the group members may be greater if the instrumental task of the group is accomplished, the uncertain leader may not be able to ask the group members to delay their satisfactions until that later time. Until a stable leadership structure able to survive some negative affective reactions is developed, group task accomplishment will lag. This viewpoint is supported by several experimental studies comparing groups that have evolved

---

perform experiments of the type described above on groups in other cultures to see the extent to which the results are culture-bound.

[28] John Kennedy, *Profiles in Courage* (New York: Harper, 1956), p. 4. Similarly, such political innovators must be to some extent immune from the affective responses of their constituents if they are to carry on activities which they feel will have instrumental significance. Kennedy quotes Daniel Webster's speech to his constituents after he had supported the compromise of 1850—an unpopular act in New England: "Necessity compels me to speak true, rather than pleasing things. . . . I should indeed like to please you, but I prefer to save you, whatever be your attitude toward me." *Ibid.*, p. 74.

stable leadership patterns with those that have not. Heinicke and Bales compared groups which had evolved a stable pattern of leadership and a high degree of group consensus as to who was the group leader with groups in which there was greater fluctuation of leadership and less agreement as to who was the most influential in the group. They found that in the stable, high-consensus groups there was greater speed and accuracy in the solution of the problem presented to the group as well as greater member satisfaction. The unstable, low-consensus groups had to spend time on solving the problem of leadership that was used by the stable group for task accomplishment. Experimental work by March and Borg also found that groups with a stable pattern of leadership performed more effectively and spent less time in resolving internal group conflicts.[29]

A stable leadership structure is important if the group is to accomplish its instrumental task. But such stability is difficult to achieve because of the conflicting demands for task accomplishment and affective satisfactions. Insofar as the group can achieve some satisfactory balance between the instrumental and the affective aspects of its interaction and a stable leadership structure is developed, the group will be effective and contribute to the satisfactions of its members. Insofar as such a balance cannot be reached and such a structure is not developed, groups will either fall apart or continue operating at high levels of tension. This problem, we can assume, is faced not only by small groups, but by larger organizations and political systems as well. Unless the unlikely prospect of a state totally run by coercion is to be considered, some minimum of acceptance of the system by the participants must be maintained at the same time that the organization or political system carries on instrumental activities that inhibit freedom and, presumably, lower the satisfactions of the members. The importance of affective relations in political systems and of the acceptance by the followers of

---

[29] Heinicke and Bales, *Sociometry*, *16* (1953); March, *Sociometry*, *19* (1956), p. 270; and Walter S. Borg, "The Behavior of Emergent and Designated Leaders in Situational Tests," *ibid.*, *20* (1957), pp. 95-104.

the leader's directives has long been recognized in political science. As Merriam has written: "No power could stand if it relied upon violence alone, for force is not strong enough to maintain itself against the accidents of rivalry and discontent. The might that makes right must be a different might from that of the right arm. It must be a right deep-rooted in emotion, embedded in feelings and aspirations. . . ."[30] The question must then be asked: how do social systems—whether small experimental groups, on-going groups, organizations or political systems—maintain a satisfactory level of affective integration at the same time that they carry on instrumental activities whose tendency may be to lower the degree of affective satisfaction of the participants?

[30] Charles E. Merriam, *Political Power* (New York: McGraw-Hill, 1934), p. 102.

Chapter VII

LEADERSHIP: AFFECTIVE AND INSTRUMENTAL

2

Conflicting Expectations: Their Resolution in Small Groups

THE TWO LEADERS: To shed some light upon the way in which the conflict between instrumental and affective leadership is resolved, we turn first to the small group experimental literature. The resolution of the conflict in these small groups will then be compared with the resolution in larger, on-going social systems. In the small groups studied by Bales and his associates, the conflict between instrumental and affective leadership is resolved by a differentiation within the leadership role. In these groups different individuals tend to specialize in the instrumental leadership role and in the socio-emotional leadership role. The evidence for this role differentiation is found in the material cited above: those members highly selected by the group by an affective criterion were not likely to be selected by the group as having contributed to the instrumental task, nor were they likely to be active in giving the group direction toward the accomplishment of that task. On the other hand, the individual selected by the group as contributing the most to the external task (Best Ideas) was also highly selected as contributing most to the instrumental aspect of the internal group task (Best Guidance). High choice by one criterion was closely correlated with high choice by the other, and the individual rated lowest by one was likely to be lowest by the other. The findings by Bales and his associates that the leadership role tends to be split between a task-oriented instrumental leader and a "sociometric star" is supported by small group studies of other authors. Both Gibb and Olmstead found that affective choice did not correlate highly with choice by an instrumental criterion. And Cattell and Stice in a factor analysis of leader characteristics found that different characteristics are associated with leadership defined in "syntality" terms (i.e., in terms of contribution to changes in group productivity) and leadership defined by an affective sociometric criterion.[1]

ACTIVITIES OF THE TWO LEADERS: The fact that group leadership tends to be split between two individuals is reflected not only in the fact that group members choose different individuals by socio-emotional and instrumental criteria, but also in the fact that the behavior patterns of the individuals thus selected differ. When one looks at the interaction rates of the group members most highly selected on the basis of the socio-emotional and the instrumental (Best Ideas) criteria, one finds significant differences. The socio-emotional leader tends to initiate and receive more interactions in the socio-emotional categories of interaction than does the task specialist. He gives and receives more solidarity and tension-release interactions. The task specialist, on the other hand, is more active in giving opinions and suggestions; and he receives larger amounts of agreement, questions, and negative reactions. The difference between the behavior of the two leaders is best described by Slater: "The most salient general difference between the rates of interaction of the two types of leaders is the tendency for the Idea man to initiate interactions more heavily in Area B (Problem Solving Attempts) and the Best-liked man in Area A (Positive reactions). . . . On the Receiving end, the

[1] Bales, in Parsons, Bales, and Shils, *Working Papers* . . . , p. 147; Michael S. Olmstead, "Orientation and Role in the Small Group," *Am. Soc. Rev.*, 19 (1959), pp. 741-51; and Cattell and Stice, *Hum. Rel.*, 7 (1954). It should be pointed out that role differentiation of this sort is a tendency in small groups, not something that happens in every small group—even in experimental situations. See Robert F. Bales and Philip E. Slater, "Notes on 'Role Differentiation in Small Experimental Groups': Reply to Dr. Wheeler," *Sociometry*, 20 (1957), pp. 152-55. However, Parsons and Bales (*Family, Socialization* . . . , chap. 7) suggest that this role differentiation has a high level of generality. Morris Zelditch (*ibid.*, chap. 6) presents evidence for such a role differentiation within the nuclear family between the father (the instrumental leader) and the mother (the affective leader). We shall, however, look at the development of leadership bifurcation as an hypothesis to be tested in different situations. As we shall see, in some social situations there are mechanisms that lower the level of functional necessity of this role differentiation.

situation is largely reversed, with the Idea man receiving more agreement, questions and negative reactions, while the Best-liked man receives more problem solving attempts, and more solidarity and tension release. The general picture is thus one of specialization and complementarity, with the Idea man concentrating on the task and playing a more aggressive role, while the Best-liked man concentrates more on social emotional problems, giving rewards, and playing a more passive role."[2] The qualitative ratings given the two leaders by the group members are thus reflected in their quantitative interaction rates.

The difference between the two specialists extends to the attitudes of these two group members. Not only do they specialize in certain areas of the group activity, but they receive their satisfactions from those areas. The instrumental leader, it has already been suggested, is relatively less motivated to receive positive affective responses from the group. His personal satisfactions derive not from the affective responses of the group members, but from the instrumental task directly. For the "sociometric star," on the other hand, ". . . *primary* satisfaction derives from his success in his role as promoter of solidarity and provider of opportunities for tension release. . . ."[3] The socio-emotional leader also tends to be more accepting of the other group members, while the task specialist differentiates among the other members in the degree to

[2] Slater, in Hare, Borgatta, and Bales, eds., *Small Groups*, p. 507. See Bales and Slater, in Parsons and Bales, *Family, Socialization . . .* , p. 279, table 6, for the rates of interaction of the two specialists; and *ibid.*, pp. 280-83, for the tests of significance that have been applied to the data.

[3] Bales, in Parsons, Bales, and Shils, *Working Papers . . .* , p. 250. The distinction between the two types of leaders based upon the source of their satisfaction from participation in the group is similar to the distinction between various organizational clientele made by Barnard and Simon. See above, Chapter IV.

It bears a close resemblance as well to the distinction drawn by Harold Lasswell (based on quite different psychological evidence) between the two political types—administrator and agitator. "The essential mark of the agitator is the high value he places upon the emotional response of the public" (*Psychopathology and Politics*, p. 78). Administrators, on the other hand, ". . . are distinguished by the values they place upon coordinated effort in continuing activity." Whereas agitators are emotionally involved with the people with whom they deal politically, the administrators ". . . display an impersonal interest in the task of the organization itself. . . ." (*ibid.*, p. 263).

163

which he accepts them. On the sociometric question in which the group members were asked to rate the other members on the degree to which they liked them, 42 per cent of the socio-emotional leaders did not differentiate among the members (they said, in effect, "I like everybody") while only 20 per cent of the task leaders did not so differentiate.[4]

RELATIONS BETWEEN THE TWO LEADERS: The balance between affective tone and instrumental accomplishment is maintained in these groups, then, by the development of two leaders. The disturbance in the expressive area caused by the instrumental directives of the task leader is countered by positive affective reactions from the socio-emotional leader. In understanding this process, it is important to note the relations between the two leaders. Bales and Slater found that the two had close relations, one with the other. The task and socio-emotional leaders tended to interact more frequently with each other than did any other pair of members; and, what is equally significant, tended to agree more frequently with each other.[5] In this way, it may be suggested, the task leader receives indirectly through the socio-emotional leader the expressive support that he could not directly obtain because of his instrumental role. That such a coalition between the two group leaders is important for the effective functioning of the group is suggested by a comparison made by Bales and Slater between High Status Consensus groups and Low Status Consensus groups.[6] In the former type of group—in which, as was pointed out earlier, task accomplishment and member satisfaction are both higher—the relationships between the two leaders are statistically significant. In the Low Consensus groups, though there is a tendency for the two leaders to interact with each other, the pattern is neither as consistent nor as strong.[7]

---

[4] Bales and Slater, *op.cit.*, p. 294. The difference is significant at the .06 level using a Chi square test.

[5] *Ibid.*, pp. 282-84.

[6] For a definition of these two types of groups, see *ibid.*, pp. 274-77.

[7] *Ibid.*, pp. 283-84. The discovery of the dual functions of leaders and the fact that these functions tend to be split between two different group members suggest one reason why low correlations have been found between

Conflicting Expectations:
Their Resolution in On-going Systems

The conflict in expectations placed upon leaders has now been spelled out. In small experimental groups we have found that this conflict is resolved by the development of two leaders —an affective and a task leader—accompanied by an implicit coalition between the two men. On-going social systems, including political systems, must also deal with instrumental and affective relationships. Political systems, as well as small groups, depend upon inputs from their members of both instrumental activities (contributions of resources, services, etc.) and affect (loyalty, respect, etc.). And these systems maintain the adherence of their members by outputs in both these areas: specific services as well as affective rewards for participation in the system.[8] The model suggested by the studies of experimental groups suggests that the conflict between the affective and the instrumental aspects might best be resolved by a bifurcation of the leadership function. Faced with this conflict, does the on-going social system develop such a differentiated leadership structure, or are other mechanisms available to it to resolve this conflict? Clearly we can give no final answer to such a broad question. But a preliminary attempt to explore the resolution of this conflict in on-going social systems will be rewarding both in heightening our understanding of these systems and, what is more important in terms of this present

---

various measures of influence. We may define influence, as does March, in terms of its effect on the recipient of the influence attempt—i.e., ". . . if the individual deviates from the predicted path of behavior, influence has occurred. . . ." (J. G. March, "An Introduction to the Theory and Measurement of Influence," *Am. Pol. Sci. Rev.*, 49 [1955], p. 435.) Under this definition, influence may have a single result: changing the behavior of the recipient of the influence attempt. But several behaviors may be required of the influential to accomplish this. An influence act may, for instance, have an instrumental and affective component. And, as the studies cited in the text indicate, the two components of such an act may be divided between two individuals. Studies that find a low correlation among measures of influence may not be demonstrating the weakness of these measures, but may reflect the complexity of the influence act and the fact that a single influence act may be performed by several influentials at once.

[8] This analysis of political systems is suggested by David Easton, "An Approach to the Analysis of Political Systems," *World Politics*, 9 (1957), pp. 383-400.

study, in helping us to specify some of the differences between processes in experimental and non-experimental systems. An understanding of these differences is essential if we are to attempt to apply the results of experimental studies to non-experimental systems.

SPECIAL CHARACTERISTICS OF SMALL GROUP LEADERSHIP: When one attempts to compare the way in which the conflict between the two group tasks is handled in experimental and non-experimental systems, one is struck by certain special characteristics of the culture of the experimental laboratory—characteristics that tend systematically to affect the nature of the relations between the two tasks. The situation in the experimental groups is such as to raise the level of conflict between instrumental control and affective acceptance above that which one would expect in non-experimental situations. This heightened conflict derives from the external culture of these groups as well as from the internal structure.

The experimental groups discussed by Bales and his associates and by Gibb commence their interaction with a leaderless internal structure. No leader has been appointed or sanctioned by the experimenter. The object of these experiments is to see the way in which leadership structures develop in response to the group task. But the behavior of the leader with no external support who must emerge from a group differs significantly from the behavior of a leader who has some external sanction for his leadership position. In a series of experiments, Launor Carter found that group leaders who had been appointed by the experimenter were less active in expressing opinions, in arguing, and in defending their positions from attack than were group leaders who emerged on their own. "It appears that in the appointed situation, the leader may conceive of his role as that of a coordinator of activity or as an agent through which the group can accomplish its goal. In the emergent group, on the other hand, the person who becomes the leader may take over the leadership by energetic action and by trying to get the other members to accept his leadership."[9] The em-

---

[9] Carter, *et al.*, in Cartwright and Zander, eds., *Group Dynamics*, p. 557.

ergent leader, it would seem, is engaged in a struggle for power in the group. His directive acts are not supported by the sanction of the experimenter's appointment and are not expected by the group members. If his directives are to be accepted he must exert his direction more vigorously than must an appointed leader. And increased vigor leads to increased resistance.

This position is supported by studies of leaders who have developed high status in a group over time. As their status becomes more secure, they can afford to "let up" and lower their amount of directive acts without risking their position. Thus Heinicke and Bales found that in later meetings of a group in which a high-status individual had emerged, the high-status person performed fewer directive acts than he had performed in the group meetings that preceded his achievement of high status.[10] March suggests a similar tendency for leaders, selected as such on a post-session sociometric test, to reduce their overt attempts to influence other group members in those cases where such overt behavior does not seem to be necessary.[11] Moreover, leaders in on-going groups with diffuse and long-term relations are able to delegate their leadership in particular instrumental areas without risking their overall position. Whyte's description of the street corner gang leader is instructive in this connection: "It is my observation that interaction can be patterned and still have no resemblance to the stereotype of autocratic leadership. Take for example, Doc in the Nortons gang as described in my *Street Corner Society*. Doc gave the impression of being very unaggressive in that he did not often come out with ideas for action for the group. On the contrary there were many occasions when members of the group would suggest actions that the group subsequently carried out. But note this important point. The suggestions were always made to Doc and were not acted upon positively unless Doc gave at least his acquiescence. I observed that activity involving the whole group would be initiated

[10] Heinicke and Bales, *Sociometry, 16* (1953), pp. 35-37.
[11] March, *Sociometry, 19* (1956).

either through the acceptance by Doc of suggestions presented by others or by proposals directed from Doc to the group."[12]

This description of leadership in an on-going group with a history of interactions suggests that experimental groups with no previous experience together differ in a systematic way from such systems. Insofar as members are similar in age, insofar as they are similar in status in the external culture of the group, and insofar as the experimenter supplies no sanction for any particular leadership structure, any directive attempt by a group member will be looked upon as a challenge to the other members. With no status consensus among the group members at the beginning of interaction and no status guides, would-be leaders in the new experimental groups are placed in a clear power struggle. The increased vigor necessary to control the group increases the negative reaction to the leader and heightens the conflict between acceptance and instrumental control.

The nature of the task in the small experimental groups

[12] W. F. Whyte, unpublished paper, quoted in Heinicke and Bales, *op.cit.*, p. 36.

That longer-lived groups are not beset by such a sharp split between instrumental and affective aspects of leadership suggests that, as experimental groups continue their interaction over time, the division between the two leaders should diminish. One would expect that the split between the two forms of leadership would be quite sharp during the first few group sessions before any leadership structure had been developed, but that as a consistent leader emerged whose control attempts came to be expected by the members, the negative affect in response to his control attempts would diminish. The experimental evidence on this point is mixed. Slater found that as the meetings of his experimental groups progressed, the percentage of times in which the same member held the highest position on Best Ideas and Best-liked fell considerably—from 56.6 per cent of the time in the first meeting to 8.8 per cent of the time in the fourth. (Significant by Chi square at the .01 level. See Slater in Hare, Borgatta, and Bales, eds., *Small Groups*, p. 504, table 4.) Gibb, on the other hand, reports a tendency for the split between affective choice and instrumental leadership to diminish over time (*ibid.*, p. 536, table 3). It is in any case doubtful whether the groups used by Slater or by Gibb had sufficient time together to test the hypothesis that the leadership split will diminish over time. (There were four sessions in the Slater experiment, and three in the experiment by Gibb.)

Furthermore, our hypothesis states that as the group progresses over time, instrumental controls will receive less negative affect. This does not mean they will necessarily receive positive affect. As a stable group structure develops, group members may begin to differentiate themselves more from the group leader and direct their positive affect toward peers in the group rather than toward the higher-status leader.

also tends to heighten the conflict between the affective and instrumental aspects of the leadership function. Insofar as the accomplishment of the group task is important to the group members, those leaders who contribute to the accomplishment of that task will be rewarded with positive affect from the group members. But in the experimental groups considered above, the group task is assigned to the group by the experimenter and is not one toward which the members are highly motivated. The members may recognize that a particular individual contributed more to the accomplishment of the task, but they will not like that group member any more because of this.[13] Furthermore the use of college students of similar age may well create groups that negatively value the exertion of direct interpersonal influence. The evidence from the experiment by Hemphill cited above suggests a reluctance to use interpersonal influence in these groups. Similarly, Beatrice Shriver found that there were definite cultural limits beyond which group members selected as leaders by the experimenter would not go in exerting influence in the group. Thus the group leaders balked at selecting certain group members to receive higher rewards for their participation in the group. When it was suggested that they give bonuses to the most effective group members, the leaders either refused to make such a selection or did so by some random means (flipping coins, throwing darts).[14]

In the experiments, therefore, individuals who do not value highly interpersonal control by others are brought together in groups where the exercise of such control has no external backing from some extra-group hierarchy. The members are unknown to each other and have no apparent status differences

[13] In a replication of the Bales experiment, Philp and Dunphy increased the motivation of the experimental subjects to accomplish the task set for them. The subjects were told that group performance would be taken into consideration in deciding upon class grades. Under this situation of heightened motivation to accomplish the task, affective-instrumental conflict was not as strong as in the work of Bales. See Hugh Philp and Dexter Dunphy, "Developmental Trends in Small Groups," *Sociometry, 22* (1959), pp. 162-74. A similar finding is reported by March, *ibid., 19* (1956), pp. 260-61.

[14] B. Shriver, unpublished Ph.D. dissertation, cited in Launor Carter, *Annual Status Report*, Office of Naval Research, Contract Nbonr-241, Task Order V, Feb. 1, 1952.

such that one member would be expected to exert more influence in the group than another. Under these circumstances it is no wonder that the most active group member, even if he contributes the most to group performance, will tend to be rejected by the group on socio-emotional criteria. His control attempts are viewed as arbitrary and as direct personal challenges. And such directives are likely to arouse negative reactions. As Frank has put it, "Resistance to an activity is readily aroused if it involves submitting to an arbitrary personal demand of someone else, and it is thereby equivalent to a personal defeat."[15]

LEGITIMATE LEADERSHIP: Such arbitrary interpersonal influence exists when the recipient of the influence attempt does not consider that attempt legitimate—i.e., when the recipient does not feel that the leader *should* perform the acts he does perform. In cases where there is a non-legitimate use of interpersonal influence, followers may accept the directives of leaders because the leader controls certain sanctions or because of a desire to see the group task accomplished, but such influence relationships are likely to cause resistance and to be unstable. On the other hand, if the recipient of the directive believes that directive to be right and proper, resistance will not develop. Where, as in the experimental work by Carter described above, the appointed leader had his position legitimized by the experimenter, he was not rejected by the group nor did he have to engage in as much overt influence. A more striking example of the difference between legitimate leadership that is expected and non-legitimate leadership is found in the contrasting reaction to the directives of the emergent leader and the directives of the experimenter himself. One often forgets that there is an authority figure in the leaderless experimental groups—the experimenter. He is usually older and of higher status. Above all, by entering the experimental situation the group members expect his directives and accept them as legitimate. Consequently, unlike their rejection of the emergent

---

[15] J. D. Frank, "Experimental Studies of Personal Pressure and Resistance," *J. General Psychology, 30* (1944), pp. 23-56.

leader, experimental subjects follow the directives of the experimenter without complaint or resistance. In fact, Frank reports the failure of an experiment to measure resistance to unpleasant tasks because subjects could not be induced to resist any task assigned them by the experimenter.[16]

In on-going groups and organizations, it is the development of a *legitimate* leadership structure rather than the development of a dual leadership structure that constitutes the major way in which the conflict between affective and instrumental leadership is resolved. In a study of 72 on-going chaired committees in business and government, Berkowitz found that when the chairman who was expected to control the group did so, the satisfaction of the group members increased. Negative reactions developed only when he failed to perform as expected. Furthermore, and this is significant, when the chairman performed as expected and controlled the group, control attempts initiated by other group members led to the rejection of those members by the group—just as the control attempts of the non-legitimized leaders in the experimental groups led to negative reactions. But where the chairman did not perform as expected, the group member who attempted to fill the gap was not rejected by the group.[17] In

---

[16] *Ibid.*

[17] Berkowitz, *J. Abnorm. Soc. Psych.* (1953). Several other studies support this point. Heyns compared two sets of experimental groups. In one set a high-status leader performed the leadership acts expected of him. In the other set of groups, the leader did not so perform. In the first case, where the control of the leader was expected and the leader did in fact exercise such control, attempts to lead the group by other members resulted in their rejection on a sociometric test after the group session. In the groups where the leader did not perform as expected, control attempts by other members resulted in their receiving higher rankings on a post-session sociometric test. (R. W. Heyns, "Effects of Variations in Leadership on Participant Behavior in Discussion Groups," unpublished Ph.D. dissertation, University of Michigan, 1948.) Similar findings are reported by Crockett, *J. Abnorm. Soc. Psych.* (1955).

That the group member from whom the other group members expect control attempts will be rejected not for these attempts but for violating the group's expectation that he will exercise such control is supported by a finding in the classic Lippitt and White experiments. They found that of the three leader styles they used—the democratic, the authoritarian, and the laissez-faire—the style least liked by the children in the groups was the laissez-faire. Since the group leaders were adults appointed as leaders of the children's clubs, it is likely that the rejection of the laissez-faire leader, whose instructions were to keep his activity down to a minimum, resulted from his

groups in which there is an expected leadership pattern, negative affect will be engendered not by the control attempts of the legitimate leader, but by a failure of that leader to perform as expected; or if he performs as expected, by individuals who challenge his leadership.

The negative reactions to leader non-performance suggest that the model developed by Bales and his associates must be modified when the instrumental control attempts come from a legitimate leader. When control attempts are initiated by someone who is expected to initiate them, the disequilibrating force is not the control attempt, but any opposition that may develop to that control. Violation of the directive, not the directive itself, disturbs the smooth functioning of the group. In this case, the equilibrating mechanism is the sanction that the leader or the other group members employ to enforce acceptance of the directive.

Role of Norms in Follower Compliance: One of the most effective ways in which the instrumental directives of a group leader acquire legitimacy and avoid being received as personal, arbitrary challenges to the group members is for the leader to be perceived as acting not as an individual but as the agent of some impersonal force, such as the "demands of the situation" or the group traditions and norms. The invocation of some external authority by the group leader relieves the follower of the burden of accepting the control of another individual. Thibault and Kelley, in a study of power relations in the dyad, conclude that group norms have the effect of reducing the tension between the more powerful and the less powerful member of the group. The impersonalization of expectations of behavior through the adoption of norms makes the influence relationship between the more and the less powerful

---

violations of the children's expectations that he would lead. See White and Lippitt, in Cartwright and Zander, eds. *Group Dynamics.*

Informal leadership, it would seem, arises in general as a gap-filler when formal leadership does not perform as expected. Kahn and Katz, for instance, point out that in production groups led by supervisors who did not perform differentiated leadership functions, an informal leader who spoke for the group was more likely to arise than in those groups where the supervisor performed the differentiated leadership functions expected of him. Kahn and Katz, in *ibid.*

group member more stable and palatable for both of them. For the less powerful member, the use of controls without a normative base would make those controls arbitrary and unpredictable, and lead to resistance on his part. For the more powerful member of a dyad, the use of purely personal power would also be unpleasant. He must either reduce his attempted control (and thereby perhaps endanger the accomplishment of the group goal) or risk the negative reactions of the other member. Thus the exercise of control in the name of a set of norms that legitimizes the control is to the advantage of both leader and follower. Alvin Gouldner makes a similar point in relation to bureaucratic organizations. The advantage of impersonal rules in a bureaucratic situation is not that these rules completely replace interpersonal influence, but that they make that influence less visible. In a society that stresses equalitarian norms, this reduction in the visibility of control increases legitimacy and reduces tensions.[18]

Impersonalization of control has been noted to be an effective means of social control in a number of contexts. Mannheim maintains that a key transition point in the development of human societies occurs when regulation of conduct ceases to be carried on in the name of an individual and begins to be exercised in the name of the needs of the group. Primitive groups, he points out, develop social functions that must be performed if the group is to survive. "Provision for such necessary functions is the external source and motivation of regulation in contrast to mere person-to-person relationships. The collective responsibility calls for recurrent and lasting functions, including that of leadership. The leader may give orders to the subordinate members of his team and on occasion use physical or psychological pressures. In so doing, he links his personal, physical and mental strength to an objective function. . . . In this situation a strange metamorphosis occurs: the 'archaic' experience of purely personal power is linked to and, so to speak, transfused into the social function. . . . The

---

[18] Thibault and Kelley, *The Social Psychology of Groups*, chap. 8; and A. W. Gouldner, *Patterns of Industrial Bureaucracy* (Glencoe, Ill.: Free Press, 1954). See also March and Simon, *Organizations*, p. 44.

metamorphosis is also significant because it demarcates the beginning of the process that substitutes the control of man by institutions and organizations for that of man by man. . . ."[19]

Mary Parker Follett has emphasized the greater effectiveness of impersonal control in industrial situations. If industrial managers are to receive acceptance for their directives, she suggests, they must phrase those directives as coming from the "demands of the situation."[20] Blau gives an example of the way in which the introduction of statistical records of performance in a bureaucratic situation reduced negative reactions to criticism by supervisors. Rather than the subordinate receiving criticism from the superior as an individual, the subordinate perceived the criticism as engendered by the objective records, which were allowed to "speak for themselves."[21] The impersonalization of control is an especially useful technique in situations where individual autonomy is highly valued and in which challenges to that autonomy are likely to lead to strong negative reactions. Micaud and Crozier, writing of controls in French administration, suggest that it is the depersonalization of the control of subordinates by superiors in the name of traditional rules of conduct that allows the inferior personnel to accept the directives and maintain their dignity.[22] And impersonalization has been found to be an effective technique in that bastion of individuality, the French Chamber of Deputies. Melnick and Leites discuss the tendency of members of the Chamber jealously to guard their independence when it is challenged by personal persuasion. On the other hand, they will bow to constraint when it comes in the guise of the "force of events." "Before the first ballot [for President of the Republic] no power of human persuasion could convince an important majority of the URAS to support an outside candidate. But . . . face to face with the figures they . . . readily accept this policy. Submission to the dictates of the event is not regarded as in-

19 Mannheim, *Freedom, Power* . . . , pp. 51-52.
20 Mary Parker Follett, *Freedom and Coordination* (London: Management Publications Trust, 1949), p. 22.
21 Blau, *Dynamics of Bureaucracy*, p. 40.
22 Micaud, manuscript, chap. 2, p. 7; Crozier, *Esprit* (1957); and Crozier, *Rev. Française de Sci. Pol.* (1956).

compatible with freedom of movement. On the contrary, the individual seems to feel that in heeding the lesson derived from the facts he is making full use of his freedom, while he would feel very differently about accepting the opinion of a colleague or leader. . . . He does not chafe at the constraint [the events] impose on him, for it is impersonal. . . ."[23]

ROLE OF NORMS IN LEADER MOTIVATION: The introduction of norms in on-going situations is a technique for mitigating the negative affect of the followers and for increasing the probability that they will comply with the directives of the leadership structure. Norms also operate upon the group leader. By insulating him from the negative affective reactions of followers, they make it easier for him to engage in task-oriented activities. The particular norm that operates to insulate the leader from the affective response of his followers is the norm of social distance. Studies cited above have shown that instrumental leaders tend to cut themselves off from satisfactory affective relationships with other group members and that leaders must to some extent be willing to accept this lack of affective support. The isolation of group leaders has been noted in many contexts. In a review of group studies, Chapin notes that individuals highly chosen by the group on various sociometric criteria rarely reciprocate choices they receive. Their highly chosen position sets them apart from the other group members.[24] Riecken and Homans emphasize the tendency of the group leader—especially in highly structured groups—to be cut off from his followers. "A ship captain at sea is socially the most isolated man in the world. Ashore, he drinks—with other captains."[25] The distance between the leader and his followers, enforced in on-going structured groups and organizations by social distance norms, allows the leader to perform more adequately as an instrumental leader

[23] Constantin Melnick and Nathan Leites, *House Without Windows: France Selects a President* (Evanston, Ill.: Row, Peterson, 1958), p. 34.

[24] Chapin, *Am. Soc. Rev.* (1950).

[25] Riecken and Homans, in Lindzey, ed., *Handbook* . . . , p. 825. Harry Truman has written that "To be President of the United States is to be lonely, very lonely at times of great decisions." *Year of Decisions: The Truman Memoirs*, Vol. I (New York: Doubleday, 1956), p. ix.

by lowering his susceptibility to the affective reactions of the group. This hypothesis is supported by Fiedler in a study of on-going groups in military and business organizations. Those groups were more effective whose leaders were avoidant and distant from the followers.[26] Similar findings are reported in studies of air crews.[27] And Blau, in his study of a bureaucratic organization, suggests that bureaucratic authority cannot be as effectively exercised by supervisors having close informal ties with their subordinates as it can by more distant supervisors.[28]

When the leader does not have close personal ties with his followers, he can make decisions on instrumental grounds, rather than on particularistic personal grounds. Just as the development of norms in the group allows the leader to carry on instrumental activities without the negative affective reactions that might lower his instrumental effectiveness, so the development of norms leading to social distance enables him to function effectively in the instrumental area without being dependent upon the affective responses of his followers.

THE PROCESS OF LEGITIMATION: The development of the type of leadership found in experimental groups (leadership perceived by followers to be arbitrary and personal) into the type found in most on-going systems (leadership perceived to be impersonal and proper)—i.e., the process of legitimation of leadership—is probably one of the most important processes in political affairs. How does leadership that is seized by an individual with no sanction from the group become leadership that is accepted and expected by the group? Laboratory studies of groups with no expectations of leadership might be an ex-

---

[26] See Fred L. Fiedler, "A Note on Leadership Theory: The Effect of Social Barriers on Leaders and Followers," *Sociometry, 20* (1957), pp. 87-94.

[27] Halpin found a negative relationship between a crew's rating of the "consideration" of the aircraft commander and that commander's effectiveness as rated by his superiors. *J. Abnorm. Soc. Psych.* (1954). Fruchter, Blake, and Mouton report that ". . . the crews that rated aircraft commanders highest for making crew membership more enjoyable, accepting responsibility, etc., were least effective in terms of the performance criterion." Benjamin Fruchter, Robert R. Blake, and Jane S. Mouton, "Some Dimensions of Interpersonal Relations in Three-Man Crews," *Psychological Monographs, 71* (1957), no. 448.

[28] Blau, *op.cit.*, pp. 162 and 167-71.

cellent place to study this question. Do the laboratory studies thus far shed light upon this process of the legitimization of leadership? Unfortunately, at this time the answer is probably no.

The development of a legitimate leadership structure out of the leaderless group structure found at the beginning of the experimental studies would have to move through three stages. In the first place, certain members of the group must, in response to the group task, begin to differentiate their activities from those of the other group members. Secondly, the other group members must perceive the difference in the behavior of the group member or members who devote themselves more directly to the group task. And, lastly, the group members must come to regard this differentiated activity as right and proper. The first stage is reached in almost all experimental groups studied. Behavior counts show that significant differences in the behavior of the various members can be found in the first meetings of the new groups. The second stage, the recognition of the differing activity patterns, is also reached in many small group studies. But it is difficult to say if the third and crucial stage is reached—the stage at which the group members come to consider the differentiated activity of the group leader or leaders right and proper. The problem is that the small groups cited above do not deal with expectations of leadership. This can be seen in the conception of role used in these studies. Role as defined by Slater is ". . . a more or less coherent and unified system of items of interpersonal behavior."[29] A group role is thus defined by the particular behaviors (as measured by interaction counts) in which a member engages. This definition does not take into account the expectations others may hold about the role performer.[30] The

[29] Slater, in Hare, Borgatta, and Bales, eds., *Small Groups*, p. 498.

[30] A more usual definition of role would be in terms of the expected proper behavior for the occupant of a particular status. Thus Hartley and Hartley define social role as ". . . an organized pattern of expectancies that relate to the tasks, demeanors, attitudes, values, and reciprocal relationships to be maintained by persons occupying specific membership positions and fulfilling definable functions in any group. The emphasis here is on expectancies rather than on behavior because the role is defined by what others expect of the person filling it." (Eugene L. Hartley and Ruth E. Hartley, *Fundamentals of Social Psychology* [New York: Knopf, 1952], p. 486.)

existence of expectations as to the leader's behavior is not observed directly in these studies, but is ". . . inferred from consistencies in overt behavior, consensus on ratings, and congruence between behavior and received ratings."[31] This inference is not necessarily valid. That a group member behaves in a certain consistent way and that the other group members agree that he is so behaving do not necessarily imply that the other group members sanction this behavior. The assumption that they do not sanction the leader's behavior is supported by the evidence that he receives negative affect for his instrumental control. In view of the absence of direct measures of expectation, we must agree with the cautious comment of Bales and Slater that "The degree to which differentiated roles in the fully structural sense appear in these small decision-making groups is perhaps a moot point."[32]

Since expectations of behavior are so significant for ongoing groups, it is to be hoped that small group researchers will begin to deal with them directly. One problem is that even those studies that do deal with legitimacy deal with it as an independent variable—i.e., legitimacy is introduced by the experimenter to see how it affects some dependent variable such as productivity or acceptance.[33] But if we wish to study the development of legitimate leadership, we must hope for studies of legitimacy as a dependent variable. What group structures, for instance, are conducive to the development of leadership that is accepted by the group? What sort of behavior on the part of an emergent leader indicates to group members that they ought to accord legitimacy to this individ-

---

This is not to argue that the definition of role in the work of Bales, Slater, and their associates is a "wrong" definition. Role has been defined in many ways; at times, as a set of behaviors. (See Gross, *et al.*, *Explorations in Role Analysis*, p. 14.) The definition of role used in these studies has been emphasized because it sheds light upon the types of relationships studied in these experiments.

[31] Bales and Slater, in Parsons and Bales, eds., *Family, Socialization . . .*, p. 260.

[32] *Ibid.*

[33] See Bertram H. Raven and J. R. P. French, "Legitimate Power, Coercive Power and Observability in Social Influence," *Sociometry, 21* (1958), pp. 83-97; and J. R. P. French, H. William Morrison, and George Levinger, "Coercive Power and Forces Affecting Conformity" (forthcoming).

ual? What type of task encourages the growth of legitimate leadership? These are some of the questions the answers to which would greatly increase our knowledge of political behavior. The small leaderless experimental groups may differ from on-going groups in that they have no pattern of expectations of differentiated leadership behavior. In some ways this limits the usefulness of these small groups for analysis of on-going social systems. But it also presents the possibility of studying in these small groups the process by which such expectations develop.

Experimental Groups and On-going Social Systems Compared

Experimental groups and on-going systems resolve the problem of conflict within the leadership role in different ways. The existence of these differences, however, does not imply that experimental studies are useless in understanding behavior in on-going social systems. It is to be hoped in fact that the very process of specifying some of the differences between experimental groups and on-going groups has added somewhat to our understanding of the processes in the latter. In any case, such specification of the differences between the two systems is necessary if studies relating the two levels are to be attempted.

SOME SIMILARITIES BETWEEN THE TWO SYSTEMS: It should be pointed out that the differences between the two systems may not be as great as would first seem. The balance between instrumental control and affect is achieved in experimental groups by role differentiation within the leadership role. In on-going groups the balance may be achieved by the development of a leadership structure in which the instrumental control attempts are not identified with the personal arbitrary will of the leader. In both cases, the effects of negative affect in response to instrumental control attempts are mitigated by separating the responsibility for the instrumental directive. In the experimental group, this is accomplished by the development of two leaders. In the on-going situation, the responsibility for instrumental acts is projected on to the demands of the situation or the group norms.

LEADERSHIP ROLE DIFFERENTIATION IN ON-GOING SYSTEMS: Furthermore, the need for instrumental achievement as well as for affective satisfactions may, even in on-going groups, best be met by the development of a dual leadership structure. We have emphasized above that instrumental leadership in on-going groups may be insulated from negative reactions by a normative pattern that legitimizes the instrumental control. But this does not mean that instrumental leadership in an on-going social system is the best source of positive affective outputs to the groups members. It may well be that under certain circumstances the need for positive affective outputs is best satisfied by the development of a dual leadership structure.[34]

There are certainly situations in which a separation of the instrumental and affective aspects of group leadership plays an important part in the functioning of the system. Argyris, for instance, points out some of the difficulties that prevent formal organizations from satisfying the affective need of participants. In response to these needs a separate informal organization and leadership structure develops, better able to deal with the expressive aspects of the participation in the organization.[35] Similarly, Barnard points out that the informal organization is largely concerned with "feeling in the ranks."[36] And it is useful in this connection to remember Bagehot's classic distinction between the efficient and the dignified parts of the British Constitution—a distinction similar to that between instrumental and affective leadership. The two parts of the British Constitution perform different functions: ". . . first, those which excite and preserve the reverence of the population—the *dignified* parts . . . ; and, next, the *efficient* parts—those by which it, in fact, works and rules." The important point is

---

[34] Parsons maintains that the role differentiation observed in the small experimental group is a general pattern of group structuring to deal with the affective and instrumental aspects of group interaction. He bases this largely on certain similarities between patterns in the experimental groups and in the nuclear family. See Parsons and Bales, *op.cit.*, p. 381.

[35] Chris Argyris, *Personality and Organization*, chap. 4.

[36] Barnard, *Functions . . .* , p. 169.

that though the efficient parts perform the actual instrumental functions, the dignified parts motivate individuals to participate in the system. "The dignified parts of the government are those which bring it force—which attract its motive power. The efficient parts only employ that power."[37]

There are probably many other situations in on-going groups where a division of the leadership function operates to increase the group effectiveness. But if we wish to test the proposition that it is the absence of normative expectations in experimental groups that leads to the tension between affective and instrumental leadership, it may be better to look at the structure of leadership in on-going social systems where the actions of the leader are not sanctioned by his followers. One situation in which leaders are forced to engage in such unsanctioned activities arises when a group is faced with a new challenge and demand for change from the external environment. If, because of training or values, the traditional group leader is unable to deal with the new group problems, he may be replaced by a new leadership structure that does not have the fund of acceptance of the traditional leader. In situations of this nature, if the system is to remain stable, a bifurcation of leadership would be a way of balancing the new instrumental demands and the affective needs of the members. Eisenstadt points out that such a division of labor into an instrumental and a socio-emotional leadership is one of the most effective means by which immigrant groups in Israel can adjust to their new environment. "If the principal economic and political positions which are directly related to the institutional framework of the absorbing society are successfully performed by the new elite, and if the old elite is satisfied with performing more 'private' expressive functions (religious, ritual, etc.) there exists at least the possibility of a positive group transformation."[38]

Functional differentiation is, therefore, a means of solving the conflict caused by new demands upon group leaders. In a

[37] Walter Bagehot, *The English Constitution* (London: D. Appleton, 1920), pp. 72-76.
[38] Eisenstadt, *Int. Soc. Sci. Bull.* (1956).

book on the problems facing professional "change agents" in group and community work, Lippitt, Watson, and Westley suggest that this division of labor can be consciously used in attempts to change communities and groups. They discuss the negative affective reactions that can arise in response to attempts to change a community. The "change agent," while avoiding too close a relationship with the client, must keep this negative affect to a minimum and must try if possible to develop positive affect with the group he is trying to change. One technique that has been tried by community workers is the use of teams of workers, some of whom are oriented solely toward the task at hand and some of whom are oriented toward a sympathetic emotional relationship with the client.[39]

A division of the leadership function may also be a useful technique when an instrumental act is likely to result in a sharp negative reaction. It is a common political practice for leaders to delegate control functions to a "scapegoat" leader when those controls are ones of which the followers are not likely to approve. Thus informal leaders—a Colonel House or a Harry Hopkins—may be used by the President to expedite unpopular changes. Or unpopular policies may be associated with a subordinate leader rather than with the President himself. The delegation of unpopular control acts to a "scapegoat" leader as a means of protecting the group leader from negative affect may be especially useful when the leader leads several groups at once. In these cases an act satisfying one group may not satisfy another. Machiavelli writes of the technique employed by the kings of France when faced with conflicting demands from the nobles and the masses. The king wished to relieve himself ". . . of the dissatisfaction that he might incur among the nobles by favoring the people, and among the people by favoring the nobles. He therefore established a third judge that, without direct charge of the king, kept in check the great and favored the lesser people. . . . From which another notable rule can be drawn, that princes should

[39] Ronald Lippitt, Jeanne Watson, and Bruce Westley, *The Dynamics of Planned Change* (New York: Harcourt, Brace, 1958).

let the carrying out of unpopular duties devolve on others, and bestow favors themselves."[40]

Conclusion

This chapter has explored an aspect of the leader-follower relationship found to be significant in both small experimental groups and in on-going social systems. The use of a leadership problem common to both levels has given us a frame of reference within which the two systems can be compared. Though there are significant similarities between the ways in which this problem is resolved in the two systems, there are also significant differences. The latter have been traced largely to the special culture of the experimental situation.

The differences between the two levels do not destroy the usefulness of studies on one level for understanding relations on the other. Rather, *if these differences are known*, the small experimental group can be used as a model of relations in on-going situations. Both the ways in which the on-going system accords with and the ways in which it differs from the experimental model will increase our knowledge of on-going social systems. Further, it has been suggested that certain significant social processes in on-going situations—in particular, normative expectations of the followers—might fruitfully be built into the experimental studies. That connections between the experimental and the on-going situations cannot be made on a one-to-one basis does not imply that all such connections are useless. Cautious and continuing attempts to relate the two systems show promise of increasing our fund of knowledge of social and political processes.

The relationship between instrumental and affective aspects of social systems is highly significant for the understanding of political behavior. Political systems must provide their members with both types of outputs—the instrumental and the affective. In what ways can actual political systems provide both at once? Is it possible for an elite group of a society to perform both instrumental and affective leadership functions?

[40] Niccolo Machiavelli, *The Prince* (New York: Modern Library, 1940), pp. 69-70.

Or do most systems have separate elites for this? Can the individual member of a political system receive affective outputs from non-political relationships—the family, for instance —that lower the pressure on the political system to provide them?

These questions and many others are suggested by the analysis of leadership problems in this chapter. The student of political systems and organizations would do well to consider the often neglected relationship between affective and instrumental outputs of these systems and organizations. In particular, the attachment to political symbols and the effect of this attachment on instrumental effectiveness deserve study. Is low or negative affect always associated with low instrumental output? Was pre-Gaullist France such a system? Or can low affect be combined with high instrumental output? Are the USSR and China systems of this nature? If low affect can be combined with high instrumental output, what special mechanisms are required? Will such systems tend to be coercive?

It is hoped that the attempt to relate small group studies of a significant leadership problem with that problem as it exists in on-going systems has suggested an important political relationship that deserves further study.

Chapter VIII

LEADERSHIP AND THE NORMS
OF THE GROUP

Norms, we have suggested, play an important part in the ability of the leader to direct his group. But group norms also limit the leader. Insofar as his control is legitimized by a set of group norms, he as well as the other group members will be expected to obey those norms. In fact, group leaders are probably under greater pressure to conform to the expectations of the group than are the other members. This pressure to conform conflicts with another aspect of the leader's role. The group leader may be called upon to play a major innovating role—especially when demands for change are placed upon the group. As the most influential member, the leader will be expected to respond to these new demands. Such response may require violation of the group norms. Thus we have another leadership conflict similar to that between the affective and instrumental aspects of leadership. And like the leadership conflict discussed in the previous two chapters, this conflict affects political leaders as well as leaders in small groups. Political leaders are expected to conform to group norms and yet to respond to demands for innovation. This leads to special tensions when attempts are made to change group attitudes or behavior in some significant way. Can the leader be at the same time a group leader and a follower of group norms? Can he be at once innovator and conformist? This chapter will discuss this conflict, pointing first to some of the conflicting pressures for conformity and innovation, and then turning to a discussion of the resolution of these pressures. Again the leader-follower relationship in small groups will be used as a model for the analysis of the analogous relationship in on-going social systems.[1]

[1] The approach in this chapter will be similar to that in the previous. Findings in small group literature will be compared with findings about analogous processes in other social situations. However, since there are fewer laboratory experiments on group norms that are relevant for our

The Leader as Conformist

The leader may be the most influential group member; he is also the most influenced. Homans has formulated one of the basic hypotheses of small group research: ". . . the higher the rank of a person within a group, the more nearly his activities conform to the norms of the group."[2] The relationship between rank and conformity is mutual—the higher one's rank, the closer one conforms to the norms; the closer one conforms to the group norms, the higher one's rank. The group's demand for conformity to its norms and the special need of the leader for acceptance by the group combine to place stronger demands for conformity upon the leader than upon any other group member. The leader of a group, Homans concludes, ". . . is not the most but the least free person within it."[3]

Numerous studies of face-to-face group situations support the hypothesis. Newcomb in his study of Bennington College found that campus leaders and highly selected girls tended to be the most liberal girls in a community that valued liberalism highly. Roethlisberger and Dickson, as well as Homans, found that those workers who were highly chosen on a sociometric test had output records that were neither high nor low, but that ranked near the mean of the group. Studies of children's play groups have indicated that group leaders will be more intelligent than other group members, ". . . but not too much more intelligent." And the authors of the Elmira voting study found that the leaders of face-to-face opinion groups supported the opinion of their group more strongly than did the other members. They tended ". . . to be like everyone else, only more so. . . ."[4]

Conformity of the leader to the standards of the group is

---

present discussion, more emphasis will be placed upon field experiments and non-experimental small group research.

[2] Homans, *Human Group*, p. 141.   [3] *Ibid.*, p. 149.

[4] Theodore M. Newcomb, "Some Patterned Consequences of Membership in a College Community," in Newcomb and Hartley, eds., *Readings in Social Psychology* (New York: Henry Holt, 1947), pp. 345-58; Roethlisberger and Dickson, *Management and the Workers*, pp. 409-548; George Homans, "The Cash Posters," *Am. Soc. Rev.*, *19* (1954), pp. 724-32; P. Pigors, *Leadership or Domination*, p. 12; and Berelson, *et al.*, *Voting*, p. 113.

characteristic of many political situations—especially of those in which the leader is to some extent dependent upon the voluntary acceptance of his directives by his followers. Many electoral systems have institutionalized a process whereby candidates are selected who reflect the characteristics of the voters—who match the dominant religious breakdowns of a community or conform to the policy expectations of a wide range of voters. In non-democratic political systems as well, leaders will conform to group norms, especially when their leadership depends upon acceptance by their followers. It has thus been suggested that great mass leaders embody the expectations of their followers. The charismatic leader whose "gift of grace" sets him apart from ordinary men and endows him with powers approaching the supernatural may reflect the strivings and desires of those he leads. Paul Halmos, in an interesting study of abnormality and leadership, follows up Weber's suggestion that charisma derives from the internal suffering of the leader by suggesting that ". . . the charismatic leader is no other than the one whose private misery is the ideal type of the misery prevalent in his culture."[5] Fromm's analysis of the reasons for Hitler's success supports this view. "I have tried to show in Hitler's writings the two trends that we have already described as fundamental for the authoritarian character: the craving for power over men and the longing for submission to an overwhelmingly strong outside power. Hitler's ideas are more or less identical with the ideology of the Nazi Party. . . . This ideology results from his personality which, with its inferiority feeling, hatred against life, asceticism, and envy of those who enjoy life, is the soil of sadomasochist strivings; it was addressed to people who, *on account of their similar character structure*, felt attracted and excited by these teachings and became ardent followers of the man who expressed what they felt."[6]

[5] Paul Halmos, *Towards a Measure of Man: The Frontiers of Normal Adjustment* (London: Routledge and Kegan Paul, 1957), p. 134. See also Max Weber, *From Max Weber: Essays in Sociology*, translated and edited by H. H. Gerth and C. Wright Mills (New York: Oxford University Press, 1946), pp. 245-64.

[6] Fromm, *Escape from Freedom*, p. 236; italics mine.

187

CONFORMITY AS A KEY TO INFLUENCE: The willingness of the followers to accept the directives of the leader depends in part, as Pigors suggests, upon their perception of the leader as being similar enough to them to share a common goal.[7] That conformity to the group norms is a key to influence within the group is supported by an experimental study by Merei. Children who had been judged to demonstrate leadership in play-groups were removed from these groups. While the previous leaders were absent, the group was induced to develop new play norms. When the previous leaders were returned, it was found that they had to adapt to the new group norms if they were once again to exercise leadership over the group—this despite the fact that they had previously been judged to have been the most influential group members. "The leader is stronger than any group member. (He gives orders—they obey.) He is weaker than *group traditions*, and is forced to accept them. He is stronger than the individual member, weaker than the 'plus' which a group is over and above the sum of the individuals in it. He is stronger than the members, weaker than the formation."[8]

WHY MUST THE LEADER CONFORM? Some of the reasons why the leader must conform were discussed in Chapter II when we dealt with the pressures upon group members to conform to the group norms. The leader as a group member is subject to the same internal and external pressures that ensure the conformity of the ordinary member. Violation of group norms brings sanctions from the other members—negative reactions ranging from mild disapproval to expulsion from the group. And these negative reactions would naturally lower the influence of the leader in the group.

The leader is also subject to pressures to conform not felt by the ordinary group member. These pressures derive from the special position of the leader in the internal structure of the group, as well as from his position vis-à-vis the group's external environment. As has been suggested within the internal structure of the group, the leader derives a large part

[7] Pigors, *op.cit.*, pp. 14-15.   [8] Merei, *Hum. Rel.*, 2 (1949), p. 28.

of his influence from his position at the center of communications. A central position in a communication net improves the chances that an individual will assume a leadership role.[9] Similarly, Homans makes the point that the leader receives and sends more communications than any other group member.[10] But just as the communication position of the leader gives him control over the group, so does this position increase the control of the group over the leader. It is easier for the leader to express his opinion to other group members, but it is also easier for the members to express their views to the leader. Shaw corroborates this point in an experiment using communication nets similar to those of Bavelas. He finds that the individual in the center of a communication network is more active in trying to influence the opinions of those on the periphery than is any individual periphery member, but that he is also more open to influence from the other members than is any single periphery member.[11]

Special pressures for conformity to the norms of the group are also placed upon the leader by his position in relation to the external environment of the group. One of the most important of leadership functions is the representative function. In numerous contacts with the external environment, the leader will represent the group—not himself or any sub-group. In his role as group representative before non-members of the group, he will be expected to some extent to symbolize the values and standards of the group.[12]

The Leader as Deviant

One horn of the leadership dilemma discussed in this chapter is the pressure upon the leader to conform to the norms of the group. The other horn is the pressure placed upon the leader to differentiate himself from his group, to violate its norms in some way. Leaders are by definition different in some respects from the other members of the group. They

9 See Chapter V.
10 Homans, *Human Group*, pp. 148-49.
11 M. E. Shaw, *et al.*, "Decision Processes in Communications Nets," *J. Abnorm. Soc. Psych.*, 54 (1957), pp. 323-30.
12 Cf. Sutton, unpublished S.S.R.C. paper (1955), pp. 12-16.

exert higher amounts of interpersonal influence and perform special functions. This special position often leads to attitudes and standards different from the rest of the group. Furthermore, external demands for change place special pressures on the group leader. If the demands upon the group are such as to require some change in the norms of the group—some new behavior or orientation to some new task—the leader by token of his position in relation to the external environment and his influence within the group will be under pressure to direct the group toward that change. His special situation places him under cross-pressures. To direct the group toward some new solution of a task facing it, the leader must risk rejection by the group and loss of his leadership position. Yet if he does not direct the group toward the changes demanded by the group's environment, he will not be an effective leader. We have seen how this dilemma was faced by leaders of traditional groups in an environment that was rapidly modernizing. Conformity to the demands of the external environment meant violation of the norms of the group; conformity to the standards of the group meant ignoring certain demands for adjustment to the external situation.

This conflict is especially acute when a new leader has been appointed to a group by external authority with orders to direct some change in the group. If he does not observe the norms of the group he risks rejection. If he accepts the norms of the group completely he will not carry out the task he was given. In either case, the planned change will not be accomplished. Fainsod points out an interesting example of this process in Russia during the 1930's when party zealots were sent into rural villages with orders to introduce numerous drastic changes, including collectivization. Few, it would seem, avoided the poles of rejection or seduction. "In some cases they were drawn into the family circle of village power; in others the whole village was mobilized to discredit them."[13]

The leadership dilemma is heightened in two ways by the position of the leader in relation to the external environment of the group: as group representative he is under special pres-

[13] Merle Fainsod, *Smolensk Under Soviet Rule*, p. 149.

sures to symbolize the group norms to the outside world, while as communicator with the external system he will have to transmit demands for change from the external system to the group. The leader's relations with the external system can heighten the dilemma in a third way. The contact that the leader has with the norms of the external environment, coupled with his need for some acceptance by that environment if he is to be an effective group leader, may place upon him pressures to conform to norms of the external system that are in conflict with those of the group he leads. This is especially likely when the group is "underprivileged"—when, in some way, the norms of the external environment are more highly valued than those of the group. In cases of this nature, the leader may be expected to adopt some of the norms of the external environment and to isolate himself from the group he leads. Lewin suggests that this is a major problem among minority group leaders. Their acceptance in the external environment depends upon achievements highly valued in that environment—high economic or professional status, for instance. This, coupled with their greater contacts with the external environment, cuts them off from their followers and makes them less effective leaders.[14] Michels discusses a similar tendency of the Socialist party to "deproletarianize some of the most capable and best informed of its members" by promoting them to positions of leadership where they mingle with and learn the values of the bourgeoisie. "The leaders of the American proletariat," he cites as an example, "have merely followed the lead of the capitalism by which the life of their country is dominated. The consequence is that their party life has also become essentially plutocratic. When they have secured an improved rate of wages and similar advantages, the officials of the trade unions, wearing evening dress, meet the employers at sumptuous banquets."[15] Of course, their group effectiveness is lowered.

[14] Lewin, "The Problem of Minority Leadership," in *Resolving Social Conflicts*.
[15] Michels, *Political Parties*, pp. 279 and 311.

The Content of Conformity

THE SEVERAL MEANINGS OF "GROUP NORMS": How can this dilemma be resolved? How can leaders be both innovators and conformists? And, above all, how can change be brought about in groups if the change must be directed by a group leader who is most highly committed to the traditional way of life of the group and who risks rejection if he attempts to initiate change? To answer these questions, we must look more closely at the concept of group norms and at what is meant by conformity to them. Several different concepts of group norms may be found in the literature. The most usual definition in sociological literature has two aspects: norms are expected behaviors that *ought* to be carried out, and their violation is followed by some negative reaction within the group. Thus, in Homans' definition: "A norm . . . is an idea in the minds of the members of a group, an idea that can be put in the form of a statement specifying what the members or other men should do, ought to do, are expected to do, under given circumstances." Furthermore, he makes the point that statements of expected behavior are considered norms only if behavior that violates them is followed by punishment.[16] The last qualification is significant for developing valid measures of the existence of norms. The expectations of the group members cannot always be measured directly—e.g., if they are asked to describe what behaviors a group member *ought* to manifest, they may give lip service to a standard to which conformity is not actually expected. The existence of some form of group punishment for deviance is a useful clue to the existence of actual norms.

One of the difficulties in relating this definition of norms to small group studies is that most small group studies do not deal with norms as expectations. We have discussed in the previous chapter the fact that a group role—i.e., a set of norms

---

[16] Homans, *op.cit.*, p. 123. Similarly, Bates and Cloyd define norms as ". . . evaluations of anticipated behavior consciously shared by the group members." Alan P. Bates and Jerry S. Cloyd, "Toward the Development of Operations for Defining Group Norms and Member Roles," *Sociometry, 19* (1956), pp. 26-39.

associated with a particular status in the group—is defined in small group studies not as a set of expectations but as an orderly pattern of behaviors. Similarly, small group studies that deal with pressures to conform within groups deal with conformity not to group expectations but to certain average characteristics of the group—average group performance, average qualities of group members, or average opinion of group members. Thus, the studies of the pressure of group opinion upon the opinion of the members deal with the average opinion of the group members, not with member expectations of conformity to these opinions.

A field study by James March, designed to test the Homans hypothesis that group leaders conform to the norms of the group more than other members, illustrates some of the difficulties in defining norms as population averages rather than as expectations.[17] March studied the League of Women Voters in Connecticut. The norms of the group were assumed to be those characteristics that differentiated the League members from other Connecticut women. Four such characteristics were selected. In comparison with other Connecticut women, the League members were found to have had a higher education, to be married to men of higher income, to be less likely to be Republicans, and to be more independent of the political views of their husbands. The hypothesis was that the active group members would differ from the rest of the group members in the same direction as the group members differed from the overall population.

The results give only partial support to the hypothesis. The active members of the organization were found to be significantly different in the predicted direction from the other members in two characteristics—degree of Republicanism and independence from husband's political views. But there was no significant difference between the group leaders and members in income or education. It is, in any case, difficult to tell the extent to which these four characteristics selected by March represented expectations of the group members. That the

[17] James March, "Group Norms and the Active Minority," *Am. Soc. Rev.*, 19 (1954), pp. 733-41.

average member was wealthier than the average non-member does not necessarily imply that the members expected fellow members to be wealthier than non-members. It is possible, on the other hand, that the results do support the Homans hypothesis. His hypothesis holds for the two measures of political attitude—degree of Republicanism and degree of independence from husband's political views—but not for the income and education measures. The first two measures, one would guess, are relevant to the aims of the organization—non-partisan political activity by women—while the latter two are not necessarily relevant. It is possible that organization members would expect fellow members to have these political attitudes. But in the absence of either direct measures of expectations or evidence of sanctions for violation of an assumed expectation, we cannot be sure that what are measured here are group norms in the sense used by Homans.

The study of the degree of leader conformity to the group norms, when those norms are defined as population averages, illustrates another problem of the analysis of conformity to norms. If we know the average wealth or the average opinion or some other average characteristic of a group, what shall we consider a position of high conformity to that norm? Does high conformity imply being as much like the average group member as possible—i.e., having an opinion or income near to the mean opinion or income of the group? Or does conformity imply being different from the group members in the direction which differentiates the group from the rest of the population—i.e., being the wealthiest in a wealthier than average group? Each of these alternatives has a certain face validity, but without more direct evidence of expectations it is impossible to say which alternative represents conformity to the expectations of the members—behavior that approaches the mean of the group, or behavior that represents the "ideal" of the group.

MULTIPLE NORMATIVE EXPECTATIONS: This illustration of two possible forms that conformity to group norms can take suggests one of the complexities of the problem of conformity—a complexity which, we shall see, helps to explain the way in which the conflict between leader conformity and leader innovation is resolved. When we speak of conformity of the leader to the norms of the group (in terms of expectations of the members), we may be speaking of characteristics that are similar to those of the other group members, or we may be speaking of characteristics that differentiate the leader from the other group members. In the industrial group situations cited above, the group leader produced at a rate of output close to the mean group output. In the street gang called the Nortons, on the other hand, Doc, the leader, was expected to achieve the best score in bowling in this group that valued bowling highly.[18] Conformity in this latter case represented behavior that differentiated the leader from the other group members.

Political leaders may be subjected to demands for either type of conformity. In some cases leaders may be expected to have had the same experiences as the other group members. Thus, in a survey in post-war Austria, respondents were asked ". . . their feelings about according position leadership to Schuschnigg and others who had been exiles during the war. A considerable number of the respondents were opposed to their returning to positions of leadership in Austria for one of two reasons: either they felt that these individuals by virtue of their exile had not suffered the same deprivations that those who stayed behind had, and therefore had no right to be leaders again. Or they said that these individuals had been away, and did not have the benefit of the experience of the war period and therefore would not understand the problems involved."[19] Leaders, on the other hand, may often be expected to have engaged in activities that differentiate them from the other members of the group. These activities will, however, usually be highly valued in the group. Thus, in societies that highly value prowess in hunting, leaders may be selected from among those who are the best, not the average, hunters;

[18] See the description in Homans, *op.cit.*, pp. 179-80.
[19] From a survey conducted by Herbert Hyman, quoted in Hartley and Hartley, *Fundamentals of Social Psychology*, p. 618.

or in societies that highly value wealth, leaders may tend to be chosen from among the wealthy.[20] The family origin of political leaders may either be expected to conform to the family origin of the average supporter—thus making the leader similar to the other group members—or be expected to conform to certain values of the society that differentiate the leader from the other members. In some cases, leaders may be expected to have ethnic backgrounds similar to those of their followers,[21] while in other cases they may be selected because of noble or high-status birth.

The relationship of the leader to the normative expectations of the group members is thus complex. He may be expected to exhibit qualities or behaviors similar to those of the average member of the group, or he may be expected to exhibit qualities or behaviors different from those of the other members of the group. More likely, leaders will be subject to both types of expectation. Similarities may be expected in some respects; divergencies expected (or at least tolerated) in others. In the United States, political candidates from wealthy and high-status families may not be rejected for their high-status birth; they may even receive additional support because of this characteristic that differentiates them from the average man. But they will be expected to conform in dress, behavior, and manner to the ways of the man in the street. The 1958 gubernatorial race in New York State between Nelson Rockefeller and Averell Harriman is a clear example. Their family origins differentiated them greatly from the ordinary man, but "the minute rituals of democracy" had to be performed by both candidates. "Mr. Rockefeller, for example, shows himself in blue jeans, suited to a plain man of the people. Mr. Harriman and his missus drop in, country-style, for a backyard patio lunch in the Levittown home of William Reilly and

[20] See Lasswell and Kaplan, *Power and Society*, pp. 207-14.
[21] See, for instance, Warren Moscow, *Politics in the Empire State* (New York: Alfred A. Knopf, 1948), chap. 3; and Whyte, *Street Corner Society*, part IV. In a study of city bosses, Zink found that three-quarters were either foreign-born or the children of foreign-born. They came from ethnic groups that predominated in their cities. H. Zink, *City Bosses in the United States* (Durham, N.C.: Duke University Press, 1930), p. 7.

his missus; and, on the way out, the first missus asks the second missus whether she can have the recipe for the simply delicious chicken salad."[22] A survey conducted for the Massachusetts Republican Committee of the voters' image of Senator Saltonstall (another political leader whose background could hardly be called that of the average man) reports similar results. Respondents perceived him as "a 'distinguished, fine' man from an 'old New England family,' and a 'man of means.' . . ." But the Senator's difference in origin was balanced by his similarity in appearance. "The Senator's 'South Boston face' and the way he dresses help make him look like the everyday man."[23]

The dual image of the leader as both man of the people and unique individual is well exemplified among great mass leaders. The habit of common dress was noted above as a means by which upper-class political aspirants can maintain a symbolic identification with the people. Leaders of mass movements have also identified with their followers in their "principled shabbiness. . . . Hitler carefully maintained his public image as a mass militant, ornamented only by the Iron Cross, second class, which had become the plainest and most widely held distinction of the German common soldier. Before the war situation, he continued to represent himself, even as the head of the state, as a hatless, demobilized soldier in a trench coat. . . . Stalin, particularly at the annual Red Square ceremonials, usually remained simply the party secretary, clothed in the unrelieved drabness of his high-buttoned tunic. And at Stalin's funeral, Malenkov legitimated his succession to the mass party leadership with visual immediacy by assuming precisely the same dress image. Mao still wears, as his public mask, the shabby uniform of the Long March, and this is the general dress habit of the Chinese leadership."[24] And the

[22] Sidney Hyman, "The Log-Cabin Myth Comes to an End," *New York Times Magazine*, September 21, 1958, p. 26.

[23] From an unpublished report to the Republican State Committee of Massachusetts. I am indebted to Prof. Stanley Kelley for allowing me to see this material. De Tocqueville was, of course, one of the first to comment on the "democratic manners" of American leaders.

[24] Philip Rieff, "Aesthetic Functions in Modern Politics," *World Politics*, 5 (1953), p. 485.

description by Lowenthal and Guterman of the native fascist leader also describes a leader as at once common-man and un-common-man. The fascist agitator is ". . . one of the plain folk and the sanctified leader; the head of a bedraggled family and a man above all material considerations; a helpless victim of persecution and a dreaded avenger with fists of iron. . . .[He is the] great little man acting as leader."[25]

Thus the variety of expectations that followers may simul-taneously hold of the behavior of leaders helps to explain the dual position of the leader—as both group member like every-one else and unique individual in some ways cut off from the group. Furthermore, the high level of identification with group members that the leader can attain by being perceived as similar in some ways to the group members may allow him greater flexibility in other respects. This, as we shall see, is one way of resolving the conflict between conformity to the group norms and instrumental leadership. It is to the means of resolving this conflict that we now turn.

Group Change and the Conformist-Innovator Dilemma

The leader of a group, it has been pointed out, is under strong pressure to conform to the group norms; he is also under pressure to violate these norms. The latter pressures arise when there is some demand for change placed upon the group, when group traditions must be changed to meet a new external demand. In such change situations, the group is in what Lewin would call "quasi-stationary equilibrium."[26] The leader's introduction of new forces into the group in response to a new situation will be met by other forces that tend to return the group to its original activity level. The leader who introduces changes in the traditional patterning of group be-havior risks negative reactions for violating the group norms, negative reactions that serve to counteract the changes in the group tradition which he attempts to initiate. We shall try to suggest several ways in which the group can be moved to

[25] Leo Lowenthal and Norbert Guterman, "The Self-Portrait of the Fascist Agitator," in Gouldner, ed., *Studies in Leadership*, p. 99.
[26] See Chapter X.

a new equilibrium level and permanent change be introduced into the group.

NON-CONSENSUAL CHANGE: Not all group change need be on a consensual basis. It is possible that under certain circumstances a leadership structure may be replaced by what Gibb calls a "headship" structure, in which the acceptance of instrumental directives by followers plays little or no part. Leadership of this form is more likely to arise at times of great stress or emergency.[27] Furthermore, since group members will reject leaders who are perceived as distant from followers and who represent norms not shared by the followers, these leaders will be forced to depend more upon non-consensual techniques of direction. Such a leadership structure can induce change in a political system, but that change will require coercion. The relationship between deviation from the group norms and non-consensual leadership is suggested by Michels, who claims that democratic consensual leadership can be maintained only if the group leaders do not develop a separate and distinct style of life from that of the rank and file members: ". . . the most ominously dictatorial tendencies of the leaders can be weakened, if not altogether suppressed, by one prophylactic means alone, namely by the artificial creation of a social homogeneity among the various strata and fragments of which the revolutionary socialist party is composed. It thus becomes a moral postulate that all members of the party should live more or less in the same manner. The homogeneity of life is regarded as a safety-valve against the development of oligarchical forms within the working class parties."[28]

The effectiveness of this prophylactic is suggested by the study of democracy in the International Typographical Union conducted by Lipset, Trow, and Coleman. They stress the relatively high wages and status of the printing trade as one of the reasons why democracy in the union has been successful. This leads to a relatively small differential between the way

---

[27] Cf. Pigors, *Leadership or Domination*, pp. 125-27.
[28] Michels, *Political Parties*, p. 343. Michels feels, however, that the attempt to level the style of life of the party leaders will not be successful.

of life and income of the rank and file and that of the union leaders. Furthermore, the ability of the union leader to return to a rank-and-file position with little loss of status or income fosters the circulation of leadership.[29] Thus, it is suggested that group change will have to rely on non-consensual means if normative expectations are not considered. But changing the group through non-consensual means is not of major interest to us here. We are interested in explaining how leaders who depend upon the acceptance of the followers are able to induce change without losing the acceptance of the group.[30] A review of the relationship of the group leader to the norms of the group suggests that there are several situations in which change can be induced by a group leader without the use of coercive means: (1) if there is a group norm requiring the leader to deviate from the group in some respects; (2) if the leader risks his position by using up some of his "acceptance capital"; (3) if the leader uses up all his "acceptance capital" and yields the leadership position; (4) if the leader uses his ability to define the norms of the group; or (5) if the leader can succeed in projecting the burden of his norm-violating directives onto someone else. We will now look briefly at each of these techniques of resolving the conflict between innovation and conformity.

GROUP NORMS REQUIRING DEVIATION: Leaders, one may argue, are often expected to do what is not immediately acceptable to their followers. One norm that may be associated with the leadership role is that he violate other group norms in order to accomplish some task. Political leaders are sometimes expected to do unpopular things when the situation demands

[29] Lipset, Trow, and Coleman, *Union Democracy*, chaps. 10 and 11.
[30] It should be stressed that the problem of consent is significant not only in situations in which leaders are elected by formal democratic means—i.e., those in which a deviant leader risks rejection at the polls. Lack of consent by followers can seriously limit the effectiveness of leadership directives even in those situations that are formally non-consensual. Thus, though the hierarchy of an industrial organization is not formally required to obtain the consent of the workers on many decisions affecting the work task, numerous studies have pointed out the ways in which subordinates who do not accept directives from an organizational hierarchy can lower the effectiveness of that directive by informal resistance.

it—e.g., when there is a great challenge to the system. Insofar as the norm requiring deviation from other norms has a higher place in the group hierarchy of norms (i.e., conformity to the "deviation" norm is more highly rewarded and nonconformity more severely punished than is the case with other norms), the leader will be able to introduce change without risking his position. He may in fact risk his position by *not* introducing new behaviors and norms into the group. Such group norms institutionalizing change enable systems to be moved to new levels of activity.

RISKING THE LEADER'S "ACCEPTANCE CAPITAL": We have suggested above that there is a wide variety of ways in which leaders conform to the expectations of the group members. Through this conformity leaders build up a fund of acceptance by the group which allows them some leeway for deviation. Thus the degree to which the charismatic leader identifies himself with the masses gives him leeway to act in ways quite different from the average group member. If the leader can develop sufficient high, generalized status by conforming to the expectations of his followers, he will be able to deviate in some respects from the group without facing rejection. Merei's study of the strength of the group norms supports this proposition. Some returning group leaders were able to change the norms of the groups they had once led—but only after they had reassumed their leadership position by conforming to the new norms that had developed in the group during their absence.[31]

High, generalized status also affects leader motivation. The more secure a leader is in his acceptance by the group, the more willing he will be to deviate from a group norm when he feels that deviation is necessary for the good of the group. This is demonstrated in an experimental study by Kelley and Shapiro. High-status group members who were secure in their group relations deviated more from group

[31] Merei, *Hum. Rel.*, 2 (1949).

norms when those norms were detrimental to the group than did group members who were less accepted.[32]

CHANGING LEADERS: One mechanism for inducing change in groups is a shift of leadership from one individual to another. There are two reasons for the usefulness of this mechanism—one lying in the internalized attachment of the leader to the group norms, the other in the external pressures from the group for him to conform. Insofar as the leader has internalized the group norms more strongly than have the other group members, his commitment to these norms may prevent him from dealing with demands for change in the group. In cases of this sort, the external demands upon the group will lead to the development of a new leadership structure better able to handle the instrumental group tasks. We have cited the works of Eisenstadt and Lerner indicating that traditional groups in modernizing societies will develop new leaders better able to meet the needs of these groups in relation to their external environment. Similarly, Selznick describes the process of change in unions from militant organizations to accepted institutions in the industrial scene. One concomitant of this change is the development of a new leadership structure better able to deal with the new tasks. "After the union achieved its initial aims, the older methods of direct strike action, associated with a class struggle outlook, became inappropriate and sometimes even harmful. Work stoppages were costly for both labor and management. While they might be thought indispensable as demonstrations of power by a group struggling for recognition, they could not be satisfactory as a permanent way of dealing with management. As this became clear, new leadership—locally and nationally—was indicated. . . . There began a movement away from militance, toward more astute negotiating techniques. To implement this change, a widespread turnover of personnel was required."[33]

[32] H. H. Kelley and M. M. Shapiro, "An Experiment in Conformity to Group Norms Where Conformity Is Detrimental to Group Achievement," *Am. Soc. Rev., 19* (1954), pp. 667-77.
[33] Philip Selznick, *Leadership in Administration* (Evanston, Ill.: Row, Peterson, 1957), pp. 108-9.

Leadership change is thus a useful mechanism for changing group norms when the older leadership is so committed to previous group norms as to be unwilling or unable to meet the new situation. Similarly, leadership shifts are useful because of the external pressures upon the leader to conform. Leaders, faced with a problem that must be solved, may be forced from their position because of the unwillingness of followers to allow them to institute change. But this rejection of one leader may aid the processes of change because of the tendency of followers to "suspend the rules" for newly selected leaders and to allow them, at least temporarily, a wider range of discretion. This, it has been suggested, was a major means of achieving change within the French Fourth Republic. A cabinet crisis and the selection of a new premier often preceded a major policy change—restrictions placed upon the older leader being lifted during the short "honeymoon" period with the new leader.

> . . . on the evidence of three crises more and more observers have come to the conclusion that in the current state of French institutions and political divisions the crisis system appears to be the only means of bringing about a policy shift.
>
> Thus what parliament refused to Premier Guy Mollet—new taxes—it gave, after a prolonged crisis, to Maurice Bourges-Maunory, his successor. What the Deputies denied to M. Bourges-Maunory—an Algerian reform law—they voted to Felix Gaillard, who is next in line.
>
> Finally the policy that caused the fall of M. Gaillard twenty-four days ago—essentially a policy of conciliation with North Africa nationalism—will almost certainly be carried out by his successor, when one is found.[34]

[34] Robert Doty, "The French Crisis System," *New York Times*, May 10, 1958, p. 3. Certainly the rules in 1958 were suspended for M. de Gaulle—in this case, formally suspended. But he represents such a special case that it might be well not to consider him within the same framework as the other Premiers. De Gaulle probably falls under our first category of change—a leader who is expected to introduce new normative patterns into the group. Though these innovations may violate certain expectations of the population (and especially of certain groups), they will be greeted with less dissatisfaction than if he had refused to introduce any change. See also Philip Williams, *Politics in Postwar France* (New York: Longman's, Green, 1954), p. 399; and Maurice Duverger, *The French Political System* (Chicago: University of Chicago Press, 1958), p. 138.

THE LEADER'S ABILITY TO SET THE GROUP NORMS: The discussion of the latitude allowed the high-status group leader and the new leader during the "honeymoon" period suggests a fourth way in which leaders can challenge the established norms of the group without negative reactions. This fourth mechanism is the ability of the group leader to define the norms of the group. The leader is expected to conform to those norms, but he still has the greatest voice (greater than that of any group member, although not greater, as Merei points out, than that of the group itself) in setting the group norms. Talland suggests that one reason group leaders have been found to be better able to estimate the norms of the group is that they participate in the formation of these norms. "Leaders may best know the opinions of their groups because they, more than any other member, were influential in formulating these opinions."[35] The development of new group norms is, according to Chester Barnard, the "highest exemplification of responsibility" by the executive. He stresses, as we have stressed here, that the executive will be expected to adhere to a large number of organization norms (he calls them "morals" or "codes of conduct"). But creative change in the organization comes about through the ability of the executive to redefine the norms of the organization so that new activities, carried on to meet new problems, will be felt to be in accord with the norms of the organization.[36]

PROJECTION OF RESPONSIBILITY: Lastly, the conflict between innovation and conformity may be solved by projecting the responsibility for violation of the group norms. If some object other than the group leader is perceived to be responsible for the change in the group, change can be introduced without risking rejection of the leader. In the previous chapter we have discussed at length some examples of this projection of responsibility onto a scapegoat leader or onto the "demands of the situation." In these cases, negative reactions

---

[35] G. A. Talland, "The Assessment of Group Opinion by Teachers and Their Influence on Its Formation," *J. Abnorm. Soc. Psych.*, 49 (1954), pp. 431-34.
[36] Barnard, *Functions* . . . , pp. 279-81.

were channeled into harmless directions—that is, in directions where they would not negate the effects of the introduced change. Another form of projection consists of bringing the group members into the decision that initiates change and having them share the responsibility for innovation. This method of inducing change in groups through the participation of the group members has received much study in the field of small group analysis. The problem of participation in decision-making is also of high relevance in political behavior. For these reasons, the question of group change through group participation deserves full consideration in this study. Chapters IX and X will consider it.

Chapter IX

THE PARTICIPATION HYPOTHESIS
1: THE APPLICATION
OF A SMALL GROUP FINDING

FEW HYPOTHESES derived from the study of small groups have received as much attention and general acceptance as the "participation hypothesis." This hypothesis states that ". . . significant changes in human behavior can be brought about rapidly only if the persons who are expected to change participate in deciding what the change shall be and how it shall be made."[1] The participation hypothesis was the subject of one of the best-known sets of group experiments—that conducted by Lewin, Lippitt, and White at the State University of Iowa in the late 1930's. These experiments on three leadership styles—democratic, authoritarian, and laissez-faire —had an impact not only on the field of small group experimentation (on which they had substantial influence), but on numerous related fields as well. The techniques and findings of these experiments had an effect on educational and industrial psychology; on leadership training programs in business, government, and the military; on work in the art and science of persuasion; and on community planning. In all these fields there have been follow-up experimental and semi-experimental studies, as well as attempts to apply the findings of the experiments. Furthermore, these studies have been cited as "scientific" demonstrations of the superiority of democratic methods over autocratic ones. Thus Wolpert comments that these studies represent ". . . the empirical demonstration of the functional superiority of a democratic form of organization. . . . Even to a limited extent, it can be seen that science can bolster the claims of a democratic form of authority, and it

---

[1] Herbert Simon, "Recent Advances in Organization Theory," *Research Frontiers in Politics and Government* (Washington: Brookings Institution, 1955), pp. 28-29.

would therefore seem that on scientific grounds, it is the duty of the scientist to take the side of fostering democracy. . . ."[2]

The body of material on democratic and autocratic leadership commends itself to this study. It represents the most ambitious attempt to connect significant laboratory findings with leadership phenomena as they exist in on-going social systems. As such it is a useful case study of the applicability of small group research to political behavior. Furthermore, the particular leader-follower relationship to be discussed is of obvious political significance. The problem that the small group studies of the participation hypothesis deal with is essentially: How does participation in the making of a decision affect the nature of that decision and its acceptability? At a time when politics throughout the world is characterized by the entrance of many new groups into political participation and by conflicts between participatory and non-participatory political systems, this problem is of great moment. Can the study of this problem in the micro-situation of the small group increase our understanding of on-going political processes? One will not be able to transfer directly from the small group level to that of the political system—in fact, one of the burdens of this chapter and the next will be to point out the weaknesses in attempts to make too easy a transfer between the two levels.

[2] Wolpert, "Toward a Sociology of Authority," in Alvin W. Gouldner, ed., *Studies in Leadership* (New York: Harper, 1950), p. 699. In a chapter on experimental studies of democracy and their relation to democracy in political systems, some attempt must be made at the beginning to define democracy. Democracy is here defined as a method of decision-making in which the maximum participation of the members of the unit is institutionalized. Insofar as authoritative decisions are made that affect the unit, those making the decisions are responsible to the members of the unit (or at least to a majority of them). Furthermore, some means by which the members of the unit can challenge the decision both before and after it is made is also institutionalized. This definition does not attempt to deal with the complexities of this subject but it is useful for our purposes. As will be noted later, this definition is compatible with the emphasis on participation as the main characteristic of democratic small groups. Certain significant features of the small group definition of democracy and participation will be dealt with later. For a lucid analysis, see Robert A. Dahl, *A Preface to Democratic Theory* (Chicago: University of Chicago Press, 1955).

The terms democratic and autocratic, participatory and non-participatory, group-centered and leader-centered, are all used in the literature to refer to the processes of decision-making we are considering here.

But, nevertheless, the small group literature on participation should be suggestive for the study of politics.

The Iowa Experiments

THE THREE LEADERSHIP CLIMATES: The experiments in leadership climate carried on by Lippitt and White under the direction of Kurt Lewin represent the first attempt to deal systematically with a wide range of relatively free behavior in an experimental situation.[3] Using groups of ten-year-old boys, the authors attempted to measure the effects of three experimentally created leadership climates. Each group was exposed to all three leadership styles. The adults who acted as leaders alternated in the three roles so as to eliminate as much as possible the personal factor in their leadership behavior. The three leadership climates are described as follows:

AUTHORITARIAN	DEMOCRATIC	LAISSEZ-FAIRE
1. All determination of policy by the leader.	1. All policies a matter of group discussion and decision, encouraged and assisted by the leader.	1. Complete freedom of individual or group decision, with a minimum of leader participation.
2. Techniques and activity steps dictated by the authority, one at a time, so that future steps were always uncertain to a large degree.	2. Activity perspective gained during discussion period. General steps to group goal sketched, and when technical advice was needed, the leader suggested two or more alternative procedures from which choice could be made.	2. Various materials supplied by the leader, who made it clear that he would supply information when asked. He took no other part in work discussion.
3. The leader usually dictated the particular work task and work companion of each member.	3. The members were free to work with whomever they chose, and the division of tasks was left up to the group.	3. Complete non-participation of the leader.

[3] These experiments have been reported in numerous places. See White and Lippitt, in Cartwright and Zander, eds., *Group Dynamics*; Lewin and Lippitt, in Hare, Borgatta, and Bales, eds., *Small Groups*; and Lewin, Lippitt, and White, "Patterns of Aggressive Behavior in Experimentally Created Social Climates," *J. Soc. Psych.*, *10* (1939), pp. 271-99. The description of the experiments in the text is taken from these various sources. For a discussion of the measurement techniques used and the innovations in observational techniques introduced by these experiments, see above, Chapter III.

4. The dominator tended to be "personal" in his praise and criticism of the work of each member; remained aloof from active group participation except when demonstrating.

4. The leader was "objective" or "fact-minded" in his praise and criticism, and tried to be a regular group member in spirit without doing too much of the work.

4. Infrequent spontaneous comment on member activities unless questioned, and no attempt to appraise or regulate the course of events.

The significant differences between the authoritarian and the democratic systems (the two systems of major interest to us) are to be found: (1) in the decision method (decisions by the leader vs. decisions by the group); (2) in the time perspective (step-by-step direction vs. broad time perspective); (3) in the degree of freedom of movement of the group members (highly structured behavior controlled by the leader vs. freedom of movement within the activity pattern); (4) in the group atmosphere (impersonal and cold vs. friendly and warm); and (5) in the leader's criteria for criticism of the group members (personal and arbitrary vs. objective and fair). Both the democratic and the authoritarian leaders, however, were active participants in the group process, in contrast to the passivity and lack of activity of the laissez-faire leader. The precise recording of the frequency of various types of behaviors indicated that, in fact, the leaders were playing the roles assigned to them.

EFFECTS ON THE GROUP: The reactions of the groups to the various forms of leadership were strikingly different. Member satisfaction was higher in the democratic group than in the autocratic—nineteen out of twenty boys preferred the former to the latter when asked to rate them on a post-test. Autocratic groups also tended to be more aggressive. Some autocratic groups manifested high rates of overt aggression, usually directed at a scapegoat, the group leader, or some other group. Other autocratic groups were overtly apathetic rather than aggressive, but there is evidence that these had a high level of suppressed aggression. When the leader left the room (one of the planned standard events in all groups) or the group was switched to another form of leadership, aggression increased tenfold.

Productivity was also affected. The actual output was about the same for both groups. But though the autocratic groups spent a larger proportion of the time working on the masks— the groups were children's clubs brought together to make masks—the quality of the work in the democratic groups was higher. The democratic groups also showed greater interest in the work. This is illustrated by what happened when the leader was called out of the room. In the autocratically run groups, the amount of time spent on work fell from 52 to 16 per cent for the aggressive groups and from 74 to 29 per cent for the apathetic groups. In the democratic groups, on the other hand, the amount of time spent on work fell insignificantly, from 50 to 46 per cent. The experimental results clearly indicate that for groups of this nature, democratic leadership will produce more member satisfaction, more enthusiasm for the work at hand, and at least as much actual production.[4]

FOLLOW-UP STUDIES: The effectiveness of the democratic form of leadership in satisfying the group members and in increasing the motivation of the members has led to further studies of these processes and to attempts to put them to work in directing social change. Numerous studies in industrial situations have confirmed the participation hypothesis. The typical study is one in which matched work units receive either participatory or non-participatory leadership in instituting some change. Results indicate that satisfaction and productivity are greater when participatory leadership is used. Coch and French, for instance, report that the rate of recovery of job efficiency after the change ". . . is directly proportional to the amount of participation," and that ". . . rates of turnover and aggression are inversely proportional to the amount

[4] We have contrasted the effects on the members of the different leadership styles of the democratic and autocratic groups. It is interesting to note the great difference between these groups and the laissez-faire groups. The latter manifested the lowest levels of satisfaction and of output. These groups spent less time on the task, fell apart into conflicting sub-groups more easily, and produced much less. Furthermore, the lack of leadership behavior on the part of the laissez-faire leader caused him to be the least liked of all the leaders.

of participation."[5] Similar results are reported from a large-scale questionnaire study of naval personnel conducted by the Ohio State Studies in Leadership. The most effective leader, it was found was one who delegated authority to subordinates, allowed subordinates to participate in decisions, and generally allowed them greater freedom of movement.[6]

A series of experiments on the relative effectiveness of a lecture and group discussion in changing group habits also supports the participation hypothesis. Lewin found that women were more likely to change their eating habits (eat more organ meats) and their baby-feeding habits (feed more orange juice and cod liver oil) if the advantages of these new habits were communicated to them in a group discussion rather than in a lecture. Lewin ascribes the greater effectiveness of the group discussion to three factors: (1) involvement is greater in group discussion than in the passive lecture situation; (2) in the group situation, the women are able to observe the formation of a new group norm to replace the old one that was inhibiting change; and (3) in the group situation, the women make a positive decision at the end of the meeting.[7]

[5] Coch and French, in Cartwright and Zander, eds., *Group Dynamics*, p. 270. See also the work of Alex Bavelas, reported in J. R. P. French, "Field Experiments," in James G. Miller, ed., *Experiments in Social Process* (New York: McGraw-Hill, 1950); L. C. Lawrence and P. C. Smith, "Group Decision and Employee Participation," *J. Applied Psych.*, 39 (1955), pp. 334-37; and H. Baumgartel, "Leadership Style as a Variable in Research Administration," *Administrative Science Quarterly*, 2 (1957), pp. 344-60.

[6] Ralph M. Stagner, in Hulett and Stagner, eds., *Problems in Social Psychology*, p. 150.

[7] Lewin, "Group Decision and Social Change," in Newcomb and Hartley, eds., *Readings in Social Psychology*, pp. 330-44. In a number of follow-up studies on the relative effectiveness of lecture and group discussion, several biases in the Lewin design have been removed. In the Lewinian experiments, those participating in the discussion group were told that there would be a check at a later date to see if they accepted the suggestions in the discussion. Those receiving the lecture treatment were not told this. Levine and Butler eliminated this possible bias and report results that confirm the Lewinian finding as to the effectiveness of the discussion method. (Jacob Levine and John Butler, "Lecture v. Group Discussion in Changing Behavior," *J. Applied Psych.*, 36 [1952], pp. 29-33.) A study by Bennett, however, casts some doubt upon the participation hypothesis. Bennett attempted to isolate the effect of the group discussion from that of the decision taken at the end of the meeting. She exposed groups drawn from a psychology course to three forms of influence in favor of volunteering for a psychological experiment—a lecture, a discussion, and a control group receiving no influence. Three different decision situations at the end of the meeting

Similar effects have been found in training programs for playground supervisors, in studies of community change, and in studies of classroom situations. Bavelas found that those playgroups that were led by supervisors trained in the participatory technique enjoyed the play more, were more energetic, and formed sub-groups more freely. Community planners have found that a high degree of participatory decision-making is an effective means of introducing change. And studies in classroom situations have found that participatory classrooms (employing what is sometimes called permissive teaching or student-centered teaching) have less hostility toward the teacher, less tension among the students, greater satisfaction with the learning process and, in some cases, greater actual learning.[8]

Democracy in Small Groups

The results cited above from many different fields lend strong support to the participation hypothesis. Can these

---

were used—a public decision, a private decision, and no decision. (There were thus nine possible types of groups.) There were two post-session tests of the amount of influence exerted by the various techniques: (1) did the individual in fact volunteer for a psychological experiment when later solicited, and (2) did he favor volunteering in a post-session opinion test? She found that the discussion situation, when isolated from the decision at the end of the meeting, had no effect upon the amount of influence exerted as measured by later behavior and attitude tests. On the other hand, there was a tendency for those who had been in the groups in which a decision was made at the end of the session (either private or public) to accept the value of volunteering for these experiments more frequently than did those in no-decision groups. Edith Bennett, "Discussion, Decision, Commitment, and Consensus in 'Group Decision,'" *Hum. Rel.*, 8 (1955), pp. 251-73.

8 Alex Bavelas, "Morale and the Training of Leaders," in G. Watson, ed., *Civilian Morale* (Boston: Houghton-Mifflin, 1942). The community studies include Richard W. Poston, *Democracy Is You* (New York: Harper, 1953); Ronald Lippitt, *Training in Community Relations* (New York: Harper, 1949); and Lippitt, Watson, and Westley, *The Dynamics of Planned Change*. On the classroom situation, see Everett W. Bovard, "Group Structure and Perception," *J. Abnorm. Soc. Psych.*, 46 (1951), pp. 398-405, reprinted in Cartwright and Zander, eds., *Group Dynamics*, chap. 14, pp. 78-79; and M. Asch, "Non-directive Teaching in Psychology: An Experimental Study," *Psych. Monographs*, 65 (1951), No. 4, entire number, particularly pp. 1-2. The finding that there is less tension and more satisfaction in the participatory situation is reported by Bovard, *op.cit.*; V. Faw, "A Psychotherapeutic Method of Teaching Psychology," *American Psychologist*, 4 (1949), pp. 104-9; and Ned A. Flanders, "Personal-Social Anxiety as a Factor in Experimental Learning Situations," *J. Educ. Res.*, 45 (1951), pp. 100-10.

results be related to studies of political democracy? Do they, for instance, tell us something about the relative effectiveness of democratic and authoritarian political systems? In order to deal with the possible application of these results to studies of political democracy, we must look a bit more closely at what is meant by democracy or participation in the decision-making groups cited above.

THE "TONE" OF THE GROUP: One of the main components of the democratic leadership technique is the "tone" of the group. Leaders attempt to be friendly, to minimize their hierarchical position (teachers, for instance, sit with the students in a circle, rather than in front of the group), and to develop a relaxed, tension-free atmosphere. The importance for a democratic system of a friendly, warm attitude on the part of leaders is difficult to assess. Certainly, it is not necessary in a formal sense. On the other hand, at least in our country, it is expected from political leaders. In any case, the degree of friendliness of the group leader and the atmosphere of the group do not go to the heart of the democratic system as it is known in political science.

SELECTING THE LEADER: Of greater importance in relating the concept of democracy in these groups to the political concept of democracy are two aspects of leadership structure—the manner in which leaders are selected and the method of decision-making in the group. Alex Bavelas differentiates between the method of selection of leaders in democratic and authoritarian systems. "In the authoritarian setting, the leader of a group is not usually a member of the group itself, but is often a member of a 'higher' class. He is set over the group without consultation of the group's wishes. . . . His stay in office does not basically depend upon the support of the group." On the other hand, the "typical democratic leader is a member of the group he leads and has been 'elected' by that group. . . . His term of office is usually predetermined, and only by the group's support can he remain in the position of leadership."[9] Though this description of democratic and authoritarian lead-

---

[9] Bavelas, in Watson, ed., *Civilian Morale*, p. 144.

ership is by one of the leading exponents of the Lewinian participation hypothesis, it is not that of the democratic leader in the Lewinian "group dynamics" tradition. In none of the studies of democratic and authoritarian leadership cited above —the original Iowa studies, the industrial studies, the educational studies—was the democratic leader a group member, selected by the group, and responsible to the group for his term in office. Rather, like the authoritarian leaders described by Bavelas, the leaders of these groups were all appointed by some outside authority: in the Iowa experiments, the leaders were appointed by the experimenters; in the industrial studies, the leaders were supervisors who owed their position to the organizational hierarchy; and in the educational studies, the leaders were the classroom teachers. Furthermore, these leaders were all of higher status than the followers on the basis of criteria external to the group they led—they were adults dealing with children, teachers dealing with pupils. Whatever is meant by democratic leadership in these studies, it does not refer to selection by the group.

THE DECISION-MAKING PROCESS: If the democratic leader is not selected by the group, the characteristics that differentiate him from the autocratic leader must lie in decision-making processes under the two leadership types. Of particular importance in analyzing the difference between the two forms of decision-making is the way in which the decision process is divided up between the leader and his followers. A decision is a choice of one of several alternative projects in anticipation of the achievement of certain expected consequences.[10] Decision-making involves: (1) learning of the possible alternative actions (or of some of the alternatives); (2) defining the probable consequences of these alternatives; and (3) selecting from the alternatives both a desired consequence (end) and a desired technique for achieving that consequence (means). In the authoritarian leadership groups, as exemplified by the description of the authoritarian leader in the Iowa experiments, all aspects of this process were in the hands of the leader. In

[10] Cf. Snyder, Bruck, and Sapin, *Decision-Making . . .* , pp. 57-58.

fact, by maintaining a limited time perspective, the leader kept the group relatively in the dark as to its ultimate goal. In contrast, the democratic leader did not monopolize the decision-making process. Though the overall goal of these groups (making masks) was, in a sense, presented to the group by the experimenter, the techniques used in reaching the goal— the methods of making the masks, who worked with whom, how much time was spent on work and how much on play, etc.—were left to the group to decide. When there were several alternatives open to the group, the leader attempted to encourage a group choice among these alternatives. Though the leader did often perform the first part of the decision-making process discussed above (discovering alternatives), and at times the second (evaluating the probable consequences of the alternatives), the group members were free to choose among them. And in wide areas they were free to develop specific work techniques on their own.

POSITIVE FUNCTIONS OF THE DEMOCRATIC LEADER: In the Iowa experiments, then, the democratic leader differed from the autocratic leader in terms of the amount of decision-making left to the group members. But it is important to note that the democratic leader was not a passive leader. The contrast between the democratic and the laissez-faire leader was perhaps as strong as that between the democratic and the autocratic leader. The laissez-faire leader was instructed to take as little part as possible in group activities, while the democratic leader was active in presenting alternatives to the group, in suggesting that group decisions be made, and in encouraging members to participate in these decisions. The democratic leader thus performed significant positive functions in maintaining a participatory decision-making process in the group.

Several studies have illustrated the importance of this positive democratic leadership as compared with passive laissez-faire leadership. In the Lewin, Lippitt, and White work itself, it was noted that the laissez-faire leader was least liked and that the quantity and quality of performance in these groups were lower than under either democratic or autocratic leadership. Members were discouraged and disorganized, and at least some of the aggression in the group can be directly traced to the lack of leadership.[11] Maier and Solem present evidence that active democratic leadership results in greater group productivity than does laissez-faire leadership. Group members were asked individually to write their solutions to a mathematical puzzle before the group session. They then took part in group discussions of the problem—some in groups led by leaders instructed only to observe but not to participate in the discussion, and others in groups in which the leaders were instructed to encourage member participation but to make no substantive suggestions themselves as to the correct solution. After the group session, the members were again asked to write down their solution to the puzzle. The test of the effectiveness of the two types of leadership was the extent to which the percentage of group members having the correct answer rose between the pre- and the post-tests for the two leadership styles. In the groups with the inactive, laissez-faire type leader, the percentage of individuals having the right answer rose from 44.3 per cent on the pre-test to 71.6 per cent on the post-test; an improvement of 61.6 per cent. In the groups with the more active leader, the percentage of correct answers rose from 45.6 to 83.6 per cent; a gain of 82.5 per cent. The better performance of the groups with the more active leader was significant at the .01 level of confidence.

In understanding why the groups with the active leader were more effective, it is important to note that the difference in the results of the two leadership styles was greatest in those cases where a minority of the group had the correct answer on the pre-test, while the group majority had the wrong answer. The difference in the percentage improvement between the groups with active and inactive leaders was 26.8 per cent for those cases in which there was such a minority with the correct answer, and only 8.2 per cent in those cases where such a minority was not present. The results suggest that the main contribution of the active leader to group task accomplish-

[11] White and Lippitt, in Cartwright and Zander, eds., *Group Dynamics*, pp. 597-98.

216

ment was that he allowed minority opinions to be heard and prevented majority opinion from dominating the group discussion. In those cases where the minority happened to have the correct solution, this interchange upgraded the group's performance. In a sense, the active participatory group leader legitimized the expression of minority opinion and allowed it to make its full contribution to the group task. As Maier and Solem conclude: "To the extent that minority opinions are superior to those of a majority, they should be allowed to exercise an influence. If a minority's opinion has reality on its side, it should be capable of influencing the quality of a group's thinking. However, if a minority opinion cannot be adequately expressed, this opportunity to upgrade a group's thinking will be lost. The function of a discussion leader is to permit the expression of various viewpoints."[12] The democratic, participatory leader, therefore, performed the important function of maintaining an "open" decision-making process—one in which the expression of minority opinion in decision-making by the group is institutionalized.

Strains on Democratic Leadership

The democratic leader stands between the autocratic and the laissez-faire leader. He does not monopolize control of the group, nor does he relinquish it completely to the group. But this middle position is difficult to maintain. Two strains that are placed upon such leadership and that may cause it to change toward a more autocratic type may be illustrated from the studies cited above.

ENFORCED DEMOCRACY: A central problem in democratic theory is suggested by Rousseau's question: Can people be forced to be free? Can a system of participation in decisions be introduced or maintained if the members of the system are

---

[12] Maier and Solem, in *ibid.*, chap. 38. See also N. F. Maier, "The Quality of Group Discussion as Influenced by the Leader," *Hum. Rel., 3* (1950), pp. 155-74; Hare, in Hare, Borgatta, and Bales, eds., *Small Groups*; and M. G. Preston and R. K. Heintz, "Effects of Participatory and Supervisory Leadership on Group Judgment," *J. Abnorm. Soc. Psych., 44* (1949), pp. 345-55, reprinted in Cartwright and Zander, eds., *Group Dynamics*, chap. 39.

not in favor of it? The experience of the Iowa researchers in trying to shift groups from laissez-faire or autocratic leadership to the democratic leadership style illustrates this problem. In attempting to introduce a more democratic decision-making system, the leader was forced to engage in activities incompatible with the system he was trying to initiate.

> In regard to change toward democracy, this paradox of democratic leadership is still more pointed. In an experimental change, for instance, from individualistic freedom (laissez-faire) to democracy, the incoming democratic leader could not tell the group members exactly what they should do because that would lead to autocracy. Still some manipulation of the situation had to be made to lead the group into the direction of democracy. A similar difficult problem arose when the autocratic group was to be transformed into a democratic one. Relaxing the rules frequently led first to a period of aggressive anarchy.
>
> To instigate changes toward democracy a situation has to be created for a certain period where the leader is sufficiently in control to rule out influences he does not want and to manipulate the situations to a sufficient degree. The goal of the democratic leader during this transition period will have to be the same as that of any good teacher, namely, to make himself superfluous, to be replaced by indigenous leaders from the group.[13]

In the highly structured situation of the Iowa experiments, the change to a democratic form of leadership from a non-democratic form was accomplished with relatively little strain. But the situation is more complex within political systems. Leaders who have assumed directive roles in order to induce change toward citizen participation may be unable or unwilling to relinquish that role. They may not desire to become superfluous. Furthermore, if the directive leadership structure does wither away, it may leave behind followers ill-prepared for the political role they must assume because their experience under the directive leader provided no training.[14]

[13] Lewin, *Resolving Social Conflicts*, p. 39.
[14] John D. Montgomery, *Forced to Be Free* (Chicago: University of Chicago Press, 1957), chap 5, suggests some of the difficulties encountered by an external authority attempting to introduce democratic systems through

The positive role that the leader must take during transitional periods in groups not "prepared" for democracy represents, as the Lewinian experiments demonstrate, a strain upon the maintenance of a democratic form of leadership. But this in itself is not incompatible with a definition of democratic leadership that involves the maximization of group participation in decisions. There is, however, another strain placed upon the democratic leader by his active role in the group—a strain that, as illustrated in the small group work, represents a greater challenge to the maintenance of a democratic decision-making process.

PSEUDO-DEMOCRACY: It was suggested above that it is not inconsistent with democratic leadership for the leader to perform the first two steps of the decision-making process: the specification of alternative actions and the analysis of their consequences. Effective member participation is still possible through choice among the alternatives presented by the leadership structure. This is essentially the justification given by those political scientists who favor a responsible party system made up of political parties with strong internal discipline. The voter has little voice in the parties' selection of alternatives to offer the electorate, but can choose from among these alternatives. There is, however, a significant difference between this situation and the scope of decision-making left to the group members in the small group situation. Under the political party situation, there are at least two parties presenting alternatives. This institutionalizes a process whereby "attractive" alternatives will be presented to the voter. Each party must attempt to select those alternatives that the voter would want for fear that he will otherwise support the opposition. As Schattschneider puts it, the selection of choices by a hierarchy over which the voter has no control does not limit the voter's rights, because he still has the "privilege of being courted by *both* parties."[15]

---

planned peaceful revolutions in Germany and Japan—two nations with little experience with the forms which were being introduced.

15 E. E. Schattschneider, *Party Government* (New York: Rinehart, 1942), p. 61.

But in most of the work on democratic groups discussed above no alternative policies are offered. Participation is in most cases limited to member endorsement of decisions made by the leader who, as was mentioned earlier, is neither selected by the group nor responsible to the group for his actions. In group discussions the leader does not present alternatives to the group from which the members choose. Rather, the group leader has a particular goal in mind and uses the group discussion as a means of inducing acceptance of the goal— whether this be changing diet habits, increasing production, or participating in play groups in the desired manner. As used in much of the small group literature, participatory democratic leadership refers not to a technique of decision but to a technique of persuasion.

The experiment by Bennett on participatory and directive leadership is a good example of this persuasive technique. The directive leader presented the case for volunteering for a psychological experiment in a lecture. The non-directive leader proceeded in the following manner: "The leader introduced the topic of the necessity of volunteer subjects in social science research. A few words were said about the value of research as against folk-lore or arm-chair theorizing. He opened discussion by asking students how they felt about being subjects, and tried to elicit participation from all or most group members. He tried to get at least some members to offer all the relevant objections. . . . He accepted all objections without implied disapproval, supporting the members' right to and reason for objections. When, however, no member seemed inclined to meet an objection with a positive argument, the leader opened new lines of discussion that could be expected to arouse such positive feelings. . . . *His objective was persuasion of as many members of the group as possible that being a subject would be a worthwhile, interesting, and valuable experience.*"[16]

In the field of industrial psychology, participatory leader-

16 Bennett, *Hum. Rel.*, 8 (1955), pp. 255-56; italics mine.

ship has become somewhat of a cult.[17] And it is in this field more than any other that participatory leadership has become a technique of persuasion rather than of decision. In the work of Coch and French, for instance, the group given the autocratic treatment was merely told what the new work arrangements would be. In the participatory groups the new work arrangements were "dramatically" presented and discussed. The group then "approved the plans."[18] In both the participatory and the non-participatory techniques the workers were informed of a decision made by management, though the mode of communication differed. A similar but more subtle technique was employed in a field experiment described by Levine and Butler. In this case the hierarchical goal was not communicated directly by the group leader. Rather the group leader by asking the right questions and presenting the problem in a particular way induced the group members to suggest the policy he wanted enacted.[19] As Stanley Seashore has put it: "It is not inconsistent with participatory leadership that objectives and limiting conditions should be set by higher authorities."[20] The goal of this approach to democratic leadership seems to be to inculcate in followers the belief that they are participating—whether or not there is actual participation. A leading handbook on practical human relations techniques describes "democratic leadership" as ". . . *leading in ways that give the followers a feeling of taking part in setting the goals and methods of their groups.*"[21] The essential aspect of the definition is the "feeling" of participation. As the same book indicates, basic decisions as to goals and methods are still to be made by the organization.[22]

---

[17] See the excellent discussion of the fad of "pseudo-participation" in Argyris, *Personality and Organization*, pp. 132-69.

[18] Coch and French, *op.cit.*, pp. 266-67.

[19] Levine and Butler, in Cartwright and Zander, eds., *Group Dynamics*, p. 282.

[20] Seashore, in Likert and Hayes, eds., *Some Applications of Behavioral Research*, p. 48.

[21] Donald A. Laird and Eleanor C. Laird, *The New Psychology of Leadership: Based on Researches in Group Dynamics and Human Relations* (New York: McGraw-Hill, 1956), p. 52.

[22] *Ibid.*, pp. 9-11. See also François Bourricaud, "La 'Démocratie' dans

THE "NO-CONFLICT" ASSUMPTION: The particular form that participatory decision-making has taken among those who have tried to apply some of the findings of the original Iowa studies illustrates one of the difficulties of moving from the level of the small experimental group to that of the on-going social system. In applying the techniques learned in small experimental groups, the members of the "group dynamics" school have carried over an assumption that may be valid in the small group experimental situation but that is not valid in an organizational context. This may be called the "no-conflict" assumption: that there is a single group goal or a single method of attaining a group goal that is in the best interests of all concerned—both leaders and followers. If this single goal or means of attaining a goal is suggested by the group's expert leadership—using the proper technique of presentation—it will lead to a recognition by the followers that it is in their best interests. The assumption is valid for a large number of small experimental groups artificially insulated from external pressures. Decisions in small face-to-face groups, we have suggested, are often made on the basis of consensus rather than on the basis of formal vote and majority rule. In a small face-to-face group made up of peers and relatively isolated from external pressures, there may well be a single group goal or a single means to that goal that is in the best interests of all members.

---

les Petits Groupes," *Cahiers Internationaux de Sociologie, 19* (1955), pp. 109-10.

Tannenbaum and Massarik argue that choice among alternatives by the organizational hierarchy is not incompatible with democratic leadership. In what is essentially an inversion of the argument we used earlier, they maintain that subordinates can participate in suggesting alternatives and the possible consequences of these alternatives. However, "The actual choice between relevant alternatives must be made or accepted by the manager." R. Tannenbaum and F. Massarik, "Participation by Subordinates in the Managerial Decision-Making Process," in Dubin, ed., *Human Relations in Administration* (New York: Prentice-Hall, 1951), p. 224.

But such a democratic system, in which participation exists in the pre-decision stage but not on the decision itself—the sort of democratic central-ism which friendly critics of the USSR, as Dahl points out, used to attrib-ute to Soviet "democracy"—cannot lead to effective participation. In the pre-decision stage, the inequalities of access to means of influence will greatly enhance the power of the few over the many. See Dahl, *Preface to Democratic Theory*, pp. 64-67.

The work of Mary Parker Follett—one of the first to stress the significance of primary groups and participation in organizations—illustrates the attempt to apply the no-conflict assumption to on-going systems. Decisions in organizations can, according to her, be made on the basis of domination, compromise, or integration. Neither domination ("a victory of one side over the other") nor compromise ("each side gives up a little in order to have peace") is a satisfactory means of decision-making. Under domination one side is unsatisfied; under compromise neither side gets what it wants. Integration, on the other hand, "means finding a third way which will include both what A wishes and what B wishes, a way in which neither side has had to sacrifice anything." Miss Follett gives an example of integration: "In a University library one day, in one of the smaller rooms, someone wanted the window open, I wanted it shut. We opened the window in the next room where no one was sitting. There was no compromise because we both got all we really wanted. For I did not want a closed room, I simply did not want the north wind to blow directly on me; and he, the man in the room with me, did not want that particular window open, he merely wanted more air in the room."[23] While it is true that such "best-for-all-concerned" solutions exist in some situations, politics would hardly be as complex and frustrating as it is—both for the scholar and the practical politician—if all conflicts could be so easily resolved. This approach to decision-making ignores the myriad complex social situations in which the goal of some members of the system may not be the same as that of the others, and the best solution for some participants will not be the best for others. There are numerous cases where the goal of an organization is congruent with the goal of the small groups and individuals of which it is composed. But there are also significant situations in which these goals are in conflict. In complex social situations—especially those studied by the political scientist—there is often no window in the next room that can be opened.

[23] Follett, *Freedom and Coordination*, pp. 65-66.

Under the "no-conflict" assumption, leaders aim at unanimous, not majority, decisions. Formal votes are avoided since they tend to highlight intra-group conflicts and leave a dissatisfied minority after the decision—a factor that might lead to resistance. According to Maier, pure democracy exists only when authority lies in the group as a whole. A majority-rule system is a "mixed-type" democracy because of the imposition of control by the majority over the minority. "The objective of discussions under democratic leadership is to obtain *unanimous* agreement, and the skilled leader can obtain this degree of agreement in a high percentage of cases."[24] The contrast between this notion of democracy and that of political democracy is striking. While it is true that democratic thinkers have not associated democracy with majority rule, pure and untrammeled,[25] the notion of a "pure" democracy in which all participants can agree that a particular policy is in the best interest of all concerned is surely Utopian. Within larger social systems, consensus decisions become decisions that are in the interest of the organizational hierarchy and to which group members are induced to agree through the use of some techniques of pseudo-participation.

That participatory decision-making when applied in ongoing social systems has often been in actuality subject to indirect directive leadership is probably a reflection of the fact that it has been put into effect in organizational situations where decision-making on a broad participatory level is incompatible with organizational efficiency and where some central direction is necessary. The impetus for the introduction of this pseudo-participation may come from two sources. In the first place the participatory technique is an effective way of communicating the organization goal to the members of the organization. As Marquis, Guetzkow, and Heyns found in a study of numerous decision-making groups, satisfaction with a group decision is related to the degree to which the group member *perceives* himself as having been able to participate in a group discussion (as measured on a post-test) rather than

[24] Maier, *Principles of Human Relations*, pp. 21-22.
[25] See Dahl, *Preface* . . . , p. 36.

to the degree to which the member actually did participate in the discussion (as measured by an interaction count).[26] Thus, even if there is no actual participation in an organization decision, this technique may be useful in increasing the acceptance of that decision. And secondly, participatory leadership probably has a certain attraction in our culture where, as was suggested earlier, the exercise of interpersonal influence is in conflict with certain social norms. Participatory leadership reduces the visibility of control. It is a way to exercise such control—control that is needed in an industrial society—and at the same time to deny that such control exists. The attempt to apply the findings of the Lewinian experiments to on-going groups and organizations has been dominated by practical desires that have led to a distortion of the meaning of participatory leadership in the process of transference from the experimental to the non-experimental level.

[26] D. G. Marquis, H. Guetzkow, and R. W. Heyns, "A Social-Psychological Study of the Decision-Making Conference," in Guetzkow, ed., *Groups, Leadership and Men*, pp. 55-67.

Chapter X

THE PARTICIPATION HYPOTHESIS
2: THE GENERALITY
OF A SMALL GROUP FINDING

Why Participation Works

THOUGH the meaning of democratic leadership may have been changed in the application of the findings of the Iowa studies, this does not *per se* destroy the validity of the finding that participation in a decision (or the perception of having participated) increases the degree to which followers support the decision; nor does it destroy the importance of this finding for political science. To analyze more fully the validity of this hypothesis and to evaluate its usefulness for political studies we must explore two questions: the reasons why participation increases group effectiveness, and the degree of generality we can ascribe to the participation hypothesis. We shall deal with the former question first, as it offers some clues to the extent of the generality of the hypothesis.

FIELD THEORETICAL EXPLANATION: The effectiveness of participatory decision-making is explained by Kurt Lewin in terms of the field of forces (pressures) acting upon group members.[1] A group norm, whether it be an attitude toward serving certain foods, a production level, or a prejudice against an out-group, will be associated with a certain field of forces that maintains adherence to that norm. The group is conceived of as being in a condition of "quasi-stationary equilibrium." This has the following characteristics: (a) the level of forces tending to move the group in one direction is equal to the level tending to move it in the other (e.g., the pressure to increase output due to a raised piece-rate is balanced by the

---

[1] For a discussion of Lewinian field theory, see Kurt Lewin, *The Conceptual Representation and Measurement of Psychological Forces* (Durham, N.C.: Duke University Press, 1938); and *Field Theory. . . .* See also Morton Deutsch, "Field Theory in Social Psychology," in Lindzey, ed., *Handbook . . .* , Vol. I, chap. 5.

group norm holding production down); and (b) a movement of the level of group activity will lead to countervailing forces that tend to return the group to its original level of activity (e.g., an increase in production by a single member will lead to sanctions against him and a return to the original level). The strength of the opposing forces (say, that raising production and that holding production down) determines the tension level of the group. It is possible to increase the forces in each direction without changing the group norm. In this case, the group will continue to behave as before, but at a higher level of tension.

Change in group behavior can be brought about either by increasing the forces in one direction (increasing the piece-work rates) or by lowering the forces opposing movement in that direction (changing the group norms against higher production). The value of the second method is that change is accomplished without raising the level of tension in the group. This value accrues to the democratic participatory decision-making process. Directives from an external authority, on the other hand, operate by increasing forces; and thus create conflicting pressures on the group members. The external pressures push them in the direction of a new activity; the internal norms oppose it. Under such a situation, tension will increase and may be released in the form of aggression. Furthermore, the increased tension within the group will lead to a demand for more directive control, if the group task is to be accomplished. In this way a "spiral" of control is set in motion—repressive measures engender a need for further repressive measures.

Participation by group members in the decision-making process avoids this spiral of tensions and controls. In the group decision situation, a group norm can be changed without any accompanying increase in internal tensions. In the discussion process, the individual makes a personal, internalized commitment to the new norm. Furthermore, the new norm is sanctioned in his eyes by the fact that he can observe the others in the group adopting it. In this way, new norms are created and group performance can be "frozen" at a new level of activity. The important characteristics of group participation are: (1) the members make a positive commitment by actively discussing the subject; (2) the force for the decision seems to come from the group; and (3) the members perceive other members as changing.[2]

To revert to language other than that of field theory, the participation of the group members legitimizes the decision and makes it proper that the members follow it. The participation of the individual member prevents his opposition: ". . . a person ceases to be reactive and contrary in respect to a desirable course of conduct only if he himself has had a hand in declaring that course of conduct desirable."[3] As Lipset, Trow, and Coleman suggest in a study of organizational change in a trade union: "The greater the changes in the structure of society a governing group is attempting to introduce, or the greater the changes in the traditional functions of unions that a union leadership is attempting to effect, the more likely the leadership is to desire or even to require a high degree of participation in various groups by citizens or members. The radical changes that accompany social revolution, or on a smaller scale the transformation of a trade union into a political weapon, put severe strains on group loyalties and create a potential for strong membership hostility toward the leadership. A high level of controlled and manipulated rank-and-file participation is perhaps the only way, given the leadership's purpose, of draining off or redirecting the discontent created by violent changes in traditional patterns and attitudes."[4]

UNITING GROUP AND INDIVIDUAL GOALS: The language of

---

[2] This technique of changing the group norms is the one mentioned at the end of Chapter VIII. By bringing the group into the decision, the leader averts the negative reaction that might otherwise accompany his attempts to change group norms.

It is important to note that Lewin does not maintain that this is the only technique to avoid such strains. Autocratic control can operate without starting a spiral of tensions and controls if (1) the individual accepts "blind obedience to the leader," or (2) if the tensions engendered by the autocratic direction can be directed toward some external outlet—scapegoats, other groups—and away from the group leader.

[3] Gordon W. Allport, "The Psychology of Participation," *Psych. Rev.*, 53 (1945), p. 123.

[4] Lipset, *et al.*, *Union Democracy*, p. 79.

field theory is a bit awkward, but it is useful in highlighting some of the relationships that explain the greater effectiveness of the participatory method. Of particular significance is the conceptualization of the force engendered in group decisions as an "own-force" coming from the group and/or the individual members, rather than from some external source. The effect of participatory decision-making can be made clearer if we look again at the general tasks of groups and organizations. It was suggested above that groups and organizations must satisfy the individual demands of the participants at a high enough level so that they will contribute their time and re-sources to the group. At the same time, the group or organiza-tion must deal rationally with the external instrumental task for which it came together. Relationships within the group must be so ordered that the group can deal with both its instru-mental task and the satisfactions of the members at the same time. The autocratic leadership system deals with the instru-mental task and the satisfactions of the members separately. Under this system, the instrumental task activities are directed by the group leadership structure, while individual satisfac-tions are derived from group outputs not directly connected with the instrumental task—the payment of wages, avoidance of sanctions, etc. Under participatory decision-making, the sat-isfactions of the individual members are more closely con-nected with the instrumental task. Members decide what the task shall be or, at least, how one goes about achieving it. In this way members identify with the external task and derive satisfactions directly from the accomplishment of that task. Greater productivity or greater rationality in approaching the task becomes *per se* rewarding for the group members.[5]

The development of this fusion of individual and group goals through participation is documented in the literature on laboratory and field experiments using this technique. Coch and French describe the reactions to directive and participatory

[5] The process of linking individual and group goals has been called the "fusion process" by E. W. Bakke, in *The Fusion Process* (New Haven: Yale University, Labor and Management Center, 1955). According to Argyris, the creation of such a fusion is the most important task of organizational leadership. *Personality and Organization*, pp. 211ff.

leadership: "The grievances, aggression and tension in the non-participation group . . . indicated that they rejected the force toward higher production induced by the management. . . . The non-participation procedure did not convince them that the change was necessary, and they viewed the new job and the new piece rates set by management as arbitrary and unreasonable. The other experimental groups, on the contrary participated in designing the changes and setting the piece rates so that they spoke of the new job as 'our job' and the new piece rates as 'our rates.' Thus they accepted the new force toward a higher production."[6]

The difference in the effects of the two forms of leadership may not always be immediately apparent. Both types may lead to public conformity. The argument above suggests, however, that participatory decision-making will lead to private conformity as well. In the absence of such private acceptance under authoritarian leadership, the removal of the external pressures will result in a reversion to the original level of group activity. This is illustrated in the Iowa experiments. When the democratic leader left the room, task activity remained at essentially the same level. When the autocratic leader left the room, the level of activity fell considerably.[7] Raven and French report similar results. They compared groups whose leaders had been selected by the group with groups whose leaders had assumed that role without support from the group. Both groups conformed overtly to the directives of the leader, but those who had selected the leader were more likely to accept privately his evaluation of their rates of output.[8]

[6] Coch and French, in Cartwright and Zander, eds., *Group Dynamics*, p. 276. Participation was in this case what we have called pseudo-participation. But, as was pointed out earlier, this can have the same effect as genuine participation.

[7] Similarly, Coch and French report the activities of one worker whose production was kept down by the pressures of the other workers. But when he was left to work alone, his production rate returned to the level at which it had been before the external group pressures were applied. *Op.cit.*, p. 276.

[8] Raven and French, *Sociometry*, 21 (1958). This is one of the few studies in which the effects of leaders chosen by the group and those not so chosen were compared. The two leaders in this study differed not in their style of leadership, but in their origin. Half of the leaders had been selected by the group before the experimental session, while the others took over the leadership role without group sanction.

FACE-TO-FACE DECISIONS: A significant factor in the individual's acceptance of the group goal as his own is that, in the above examples, this acceptance takes place in a face-to-face group. We have stressed up to now the participatory or non-participatory quality of the group situation. But of equal significance in the studies discussed in this chapter is the group context of the decision. It is the perception of other group members taking a similar position that leads to the acceptance of a new norm by the individual members. Radke and Klisurich found that a group decision was not only more effective than a lecture; it was more effective than individual instruction. New mothers were exposed to communications in favor of feeding children orange juice and cod-liver oil, some in six-member discussion groups and others in individual sessions with a nutritionist. The same amount of time was spent in the group discussion as in the individual communication. Yet the group session proved more effective. After four weeks, 90 per cent of the mothers who had participated in the group discussion were feeding their children cod-liver oil and 100 per cent were feeding them orange juice. Among those mothers who had taken part in the individual instruction, the figure was 55 per cent for both foods.[9] The findings suggest that a major factor in influencing change in participatory groups is the power of the group itself over its members. The opinions of one's fellow members become apparent in the discussion situation and invoke the powerful authority of the peer group. This illustrates again that the democratic groups as they are found in these studies are groups in which highly authoritative decisions are made—i.e., decisions to which compliance is expected and from which deviance will be met by sanctions. The source of authority may be different from that in the autocratic situation, but the pressure to conform to decisions will certainly be as great and probably greater.[10]

[9] Reported in Lewin, in Cartwright and Zander, eds., *Group Dynamics*, pp. 293-96.

[10] The pressure of the group upon the individual in the face-to-face decision situation points up a significant aspect of participation in small decision-making groups. The very factors that make participation of the individual easier in smaller units—visibility of the decisional process,

Does Participation Always Work?

What level of generality can one ascribe to the participation hypothesis? Does the evidence, for instance, provide a scientific demonstration of the greater effectiveness of democratic political systems? Scholarly caution and the advent of the Sputniks must certainly make us hesitate before answering affirmatively. In fact, on the level of political systems, such a question cannot be answered on the basis of experimental—or any other—study. Political systems have many goals that may

---

absence of formal mechanisms of decision-making, and assumed homogeneity of opinion—can lead to a degeneration of this system into one that is intolerant of the minority member. We have already noted the emphasis on consensus and unanimous opinions in the face-to-face group. Perhaps the best statement of the potentiality of group tyranny over the individual member in small political units is found in that classic plea for diversity, Madison's *Federalist* #10:

"From this view of the subject, it may be concluded that a pure democracy, by which I mean a society consisting of a small number of citizens, who assemble and administer the government in person, can admit of no cure for the mischiefs of factions. A common passion or interest will, in almost every case, be felt by a majority of the whole; a communication and concert result from the form of government itself; and there is nothing to check the inducements to sacrifice the weaker party or an obnoxious individual. . . . The smaller the society, the fewer probably will be the distinct parties and interests composing it; the fewer the distinct parties and interests, the more frequently will a majority be found of the same party; and the smaller the number of individuals composing a majority, and the smaller the compass within which they are placed, the more easily will they concert and execute their plans of oppression."—(*The Federalist*, New York: Modern Library, 1937, pp. 58-61.)

That the "group dynamics" school has been intolerant of the individual is a criticism that has often been leveled against the writings we have been discussing. See H. S. Kariel, "Democracy Unlimited: Kurt Lewin's Field Theory," *Am. J. Soc.*, 62 (1956), pp. 280-89; Adrian M. Dupuis, "Group Dynamics: Its Philosophical Presuppositions and Implications" (unpublished Ph.D. dissertation, University of Minnesota, 1955). The Lewinian school of group dynamics has certainly placed a high value on such group-oriented processes as cohesion, cooperation, and consensus; and has tended to consider deviance and conflict in groups as tendencies to be avoided. Group votes have been opposed in favor of unanimous, consensus decisions. And the expression of individual ideas or needs has been considered less valuable than the expression of group-oriented ideas and values. Thus one of the indices used in comparing authoritarian and democratic leadership situations in the Iowa studies is the frequency with which the pronouns "I" and "we" are used. The authoritarian group was found to have higher rates of "I" statements and other individualistic remarks. (White and Lippitt, in Cartwright and Zander, eds., *Group Dynamics*, pp. 604-5.) Similarly, Bavelas indicates that one of the goals of his training of group leaders is the development of the "we-feeling" in contrast to the "I-feeling." Bavelas, in Watson, ed., *Civilian Morale*, pp. 156-57.

be in conflict—more guns and more butter, progress in medical science and progress in space technology, etc.—and different systems will weigh these competing claims for human and physical resources differently. One cannot therefore, match two political systems, as one can match two experimental groups to see the effect of participation in decisions upon group effectiveness. However, the experimental literature does give us some clue to the answer to a more limited question: under what circumstances (for what type of task, for what type of group) is participatory or non-participatory leadership likely to be more effective? Though there are no hard and fast answers to this question, the experimental work is suggestive.

THE SKILLS OF THE PARTICIPANTS: An experiment by M. Asch on the relative effectiveness of student-centered and teacher-centered classroom techniques presents results that contradict the participation hypothesis. An examination of these results may indicate some of the limitations upon the generalizability of the participation hypothesis. Using two matched groups of students each of which had been exposed to one of the teaching methods, he found that those taught by the teacher-centered directive technique did significantly better on the final examination. The non-directive students felt more satisfaction in the classroom technique but this was not reflected in examination performance.[11]

The reason why the participatory hypothesis does not hold in this experiment becomes apparent if one examines certain differences in the situation of the Asch experiment and the situation in the bulk of the experimental work by Lewin and his followers. In the experiments on changing food habits by Lewin, and Radke and Klisurich; and in the industrial work of Bavelas, of Coch and French, and of Levine and Butler, participation tended to increase both satisfaction and productivity. But as was pointed out above, participation consisted less in group decision-making than in the communication to the group of a decision made elsewhere. The leadership technique had no effect upon the quality of the decision. The group

---

[11] Asch, *Psych. Monog.* (1951).

process affected only the motivation of the individual members to accept the decision, and productivity was measured in terms of the degree to which the decision was accepted. On the other hand, in the classroom situation studies by Asch, group effectiveness—measured by performance in a final examination—depended not merely upon the motivation of the group to accept the information presented in the classroom, but upon the quality of that information. And the means of leadership used, it is assumed, affected both the quality of the information and the degree to which it received acceptance.

Where the motivation of the individual group member to accept the leader's directive is the major determinant of the effectiveness of that directive, participatory leadership with its concomitant increase in motivation may well be more effective, but where the technique of decision-making affects the quality of that decision, democratic techniques may be less effective. This is especially the case when the group leader possesses some expert knowledge or special skill in coordination not possessed by the average member. Thus, in the Asch experiment where the non-directive teacher was prevented from using his technical skill to the fullest, the students learned less. It is interesting to note in this connection that the original Iowa experiments do not show the significant differences in productivity between the democratic and the autocratic groups that the later studies on food-habits and on work-norms show. The autocratic and democratic groups were about equally productive—this despite the greater satisfaction and motivation in the democratic group. The difference between these groups and the later Lewinian studies may lie in the fact that, in the former, the group decision affected the quality of the group performance, not merely the motivation behind it.[12]

12 The finding that directive leadership is more effective when the group leader possesses special knowledge that affects the quality of the group decision is not in conflict with the findings reported by Maier and Solem (in Cartwright and Zander, ed., *Group Dynamics*, chap. 38), that democratic leadership can upgrade the quality of a group's performance by assuring all group members a chance to be heard. This form of leadership was shown to be most effective in cases where a minority with the correct solution was opposed by a majority with an incorrect solution. Free communications protected the minority from being overwhelmed by the majority. In a sense, an authoritarian system performs the same function for the

Permissive leadership, therefore, if it is to be effective, must relate the level of skill of the group members to the group task. Calvin, Hoffman, and Hardin report an experiment on the relationship between membership skill and the effectiveness of various forms of leadership. Using a form of "twenty questions" as the experimental task, they set up four groups, differing in terms of the intelligence of the members and the style of leadership. Bright and dull groups were subjected to permissive and authoritarian leadership. Among bright students, permissive leadership led to greater productivity. Among dull students, authoritarian leadership led to significantly greater productivity.[13] (See Table 1.) Further-

TABLE 1

Type of group	Median number of questions needed to find answer	Percentage of problems correctly solved
Permissive bright	15.5	100
Authoritarian bright	18.5	87.5
Permissive dull	31	37.5
Authoritarian dull	24.5	75

more, they report that all groups enjoyed the experiment except those in the "permissive dull" situation; they were uneasy. The productivity of the participatory group depends therefore to some extent upon the skill of the group. If productivity is to increase through group participation in decision-making, the group must possess enough skill to produce high-quality decisions.

THE NEED FOR CENTRALIZED COMMUNICATIONS: For certain tasks, an effective communication network may foster directive leadership. Thus, studies of group problem-solving with a variety of communication networks have found that a centralized communication system in which all communica-

---

leader (a minority) when he possesses greater technical skill. It allows him to use his skill without being overwhelmed by the demands of the group majority.

[13] Allen D. Calvin, Frederic K. Hoffman, and Edgar L. Hardin, "The Effect of Intelligence and Social Atmosphere on Group Problem Solving Behavior," *J. Soc. Psych.*, *45* (1957), pp. 61-74.

tions must pass through one group member was more effective than a communication network to which all members had equal access. Bavelas and Leavitt found that for the solution of simple puzzles on which all members had to cooperate— e.g., making specific geometric shapes out of pieces of cardboard distributed among the members—a "wheel" communication net, in which one member was in the center of the network and all communications went through him, was more effective than a "circle" network, where all members had equal access to communications.[14] Similar results are reported by Shaw, who found that problem-solving with a centralized and directive leadership structure was more productive.[15] A study by Heisse and Miller that compares the effectiveness of various communication nets for different tasks sheds some light on the relative effectiveness of open and centralized networks. They found that a centralized network, where all communications had to pass through one member, was more effective on a task that required a high degree of integration and coordination of the individual contributions of the members. Where such coordination was necessary, the centralized network placed someone in the position to supply it. On the other hand, for a task in which the quality of the individual's participation was the major factor in determining group success or failure and where coordination of member contributions was less important, an open communication network to which all had equal access was more effective.[16] The participation hypothesis thus holds true for some groups, but not for all. In those groups where the level of skills of the participants is low relative to the task or in which the task requires a high degree of coordination of individual activities, a more centralized nonparticipatory system of leadership may be more effective.

SATISFACTION AND PRODUCTIVITY: The communication network experiments by Bavelas, Leavitt, and Heisse and Miller did, however, confirm part of the participation hypothesis.

---

[14] Bavelas, in Lerner and Lasswell, eds., *Policy Sciences*; and Leavitt, in Swanson, Newcomb, and Hartley, eds., *Readings in Social Psychology.*
[15] Shaw, *J. Abnorm. Soc. Psych.* (1955).
[16] Heisse and Miller, in Hare, Borgatta, and Bales, eds., *Small Groups.*

They found that in groups with an open communication network, though they were not as productive as those with centralized networks, the members reported themselves to have been more satisfied with the experimental session. This separation of productivity and member satisfaction is significant. It suggests that, under certain circumstances, a group's effectiveness on the external task may be increased without a concomitant increase in its ability to satisfy the individual needs of the members and, perhaps, with a lowering of member satisfaction.

An example of such an increase in productivity without an accompanying increase in satisfaction is presented by a field experiment by Morse and Reimer.[17] The authors studied four closely matched divisions of an insurance company. In two divisions much more worker participation was instituted. In the other two divisions, a much more hierarchical decision-making process than had previously existed was introduced. Over an extended period, measures were taken of both the productivity of the divisions and the satisfaction of the individual members. All divisions increased productivity after the change in leadership technique. But the divisions placed under hierarchical control increased their productivity more than did the divisions into which greater participation had been introduced. The difference in the way greater productivity was achieved in the two situations is relevant in terms of our earlier discussion of the fusion of individual and group goals under a system of participation as well as in terms of our present interest in the relation of productivity and satisfaction. In the directive sections of the company, the increase in productivity came in response to a decision by the supervisor to assign fewer workers to a particular job. In the participatory divisions, the increase came about through a group decision that when workers left the division, they would not be replaced, but the remaining workers would fill the jobs. Productivity increase was therefore slower in the participatory divisions. The difference in the way in which production was increased under the two types of supervision is reflected in

[17] Morse and Reimer, *J. Abnorm. Soc. Psych.* (1956).

the level of satisfaction. In the participatory divisions the members showed significantly higher satisfaction with the new technique than did the members of the divisions under the more directive system. All members of the participatory divisions felt that the new system was an improvement, that it has raised satisfactions, and they desired to see it continue. In the hierarchical divisions, the workers felt that the new system was not an improvement and that it had increased tension and friction on the job.

The evidence that productivity can be raised without a concomitant rise in satisfaction ought not to obscure the fact that productivity and satisfaction are mutually dependent. Low satisfaction may affect productivity and low productivity may affect satisfaction. Thus Morse and Reimer suggest that the low-satisfaction, high-productivity situation of the hierarchical divisions is temporary.[18] In the long-run the low level of satisfaction will feed back upon the productivity level and cause it to fall. Guba presents some evidence to support the proposition that productivity increases accompanied by decreases in satisfaction will be temporary. He found the level of satisfaction of group members to be positively related to their predisposition to "put forth extra effort in the achievement of group goals and objectives." In the long run, he suggests, work situations tend to stabilize into high-satisfaction, high-productivity groups or low-satisfaction, low-productivity groups. But, at least in the short run, productivity may increase independently of satisfaction.[19]

[18] *Ibid.*, p. 128.

[19] Egon G. Guba, "Morale and Satisfaction: A Study of Past-Future Time Perspective," *Admin. Sci. Quart.*, 3 (1958), pp. 194-209.

This is essentially the point made by Lewin, who discusses the problem of "freezing" of group decisions at a new level. If there is some negative reaction to the decision—as when the decision is non-participatory—the group activity level is likely to return to its position before the change was introduced. (See Lewin, in Newcomb and Hartley, eds., *Readings* . . . , pp. 340-44.) The relationship between satisfaction and productivity over time is still unclear. Fiedler, for instance, produces evidence contrary to that of Guba. (Fred S. Fiedler, *Leader Attitudes and Group Effectiveness* [Urbana, Ill.: University of Illinois Press, 1958], pp. 34-36.) Fiedler studied the relationship between sociometric choice of the foreman by an affective criterion and the productivity of the work group for open-hearth furnace crews—crews that had worked together for a number of years. He found

THE EXPECTATIONS OF FOLLOWERS: The degree of generality of the participation hypothesis is also limited by the expectations of the group members as to what the leadership structure *ought* to be. Two factors that affect the type of leadership structure expected and desired are the culture of the group and the personality of the group members. It has been suggested above that in situations institutionalized as hierarchical, the failure of a group leader to exercise hierarchical control will lead to member dissatisfaction.[20] This conflicts with many of the findings that participation in decisions (or the perception of having participated) increases satisfaction and productivity in situations ordinarily institutionalized as hierarchical—industrial plants, classrooms, the presentation of expert advice on diet. The reason may be that the latter findings apply only to cultures in which rigid hierarchical control is not expected. One wonders whether similar results would have been achieved in cultures where democratic forms of participation were not as highly valued. Does the participation hypothesis have cross-cultural generality? Some of the predispositions in favor of the democratic system of the authors dealt with in this chapter seem to have prevented an adequate consideration of this question. Thus Bavelas notes, in a discussion of the effects of participation on morale, that authoritarian systems have at times developed high levels of morale: "The authoritarian states, notably Germany, have themselves developed authoritarian methods for creating high morale—techniques based partly upon the 'leader' myth, both in regard to Hitler as the source of all leadership power and in regard to more general 'leader principle'; and partly upon methods which resemble, at least on the surface, democratic techniques. Within certain specific areas, a kind of

---

that, unlike the situation in shorter-lived groups, there was no relationship between preference for the leader and productivity. One explanation he suggests is that: ". . . personal relations in long-lived groups become more homogeneous over a period of time since people have an opportunity to arrive at some *modus vivendi*. A person who cannot work with another either gets himself transferred to another group or he eventually leaves the company. . . . It seems likely, therefore, that we are dealing here almost entirely with positive, or else compensated interpersonal attitudes in long-lived groups such as these." *Ibid.*, pp. 35-36.

[20] See Chapter VII.

status democracy has been developed; in the army, for instance, comradeship is now emphasized, with the more familiar *du* replacing the formal address." But rather than examining the serious challenge to the participatory hypothesis that this finding suggests, he dismisses the high morale level in such authoritarian systems as but a "temporary level" in contrast to the "real spirit" developed in democratic groups.[21]

Though one can admire such loyalty to democratic forms, it is nevertheless useful to inquire into the effects of participation in cultures other than our own. Does, for instance, a friendly permissive atmosphere always lead to greater satisfaction? Barschak, in a study of happiness and unhappiness in several cultures, found that German girls preferred rigid and authoritarian control by their parents and considered this a sign of parental affection.[22] Would individuals in other cultures respond to participatory and non-participatory decision-making in the same way that individuals in this culture do? Gardner Murphey reports on various attempts to change the attitudes of Indian college students toward the caste system. Both lectures and group discussions were used. The most effective technique was an emotional lecture. "Contrary to our original expectation and hypothesis, these young boys do not seem to be in a position to exploit fully the discussion technique in bettering their social relationships. Does it not indicate that our boys have got to be used to the democratic way of discussion and at present prefer to be told what are the right attitudes rather than to be allowed to talk them out?"[23]

[21] Bavelas, in Watson, ed., *Civilian Morale*, pp. 164-65.

[22] E. Barschak, "A Study of Happiness and Unhappiness in the Childhood and Adolescence of Girls in Different Cultures," *J. Psych.*, *32* (1951), pp. 173-215. See also the discussion in Chapter II, above, of the expectations developed in primary groups and their effect on later authority relationships.

In this connection it is interesting to note that the one child in the Lippitt and White experiments who preferred the autocratic leader over the democratic leader was, as they note, the son of an army officer. (Lippitt and White, in Newcomb and Hartley, eds., *Readings . . .* , p. 320.) Several studies have suggested that the attachment of the German soldier to the *Wehrmacht* was essentially a loyalty to an authoritarian primary group and the father-like figure of the non-com. See Shils and Janowitz, *Public Opinion Quarterly* (1948); and H. V. Dicks, "Some Psychological Studies of the German Character," in T. H. Pear, ed., *Psychological Factor in Peace and War* (London: Hutchinson, 1950).

[23] Gardner Murphey, *In the Minds of Men* (New York: Basic Books,

Clearly a commitment to a participatory decision-making technique is not universal. The extent to which such a technique of leadership would produce higher satisfactions and productivity in cultures other than our own cannot be evaluated. The external culture of the experimental or non-experimental small group plays a major role in determining behavior within the group. Studies of small groups in cultures other than our own might be one of the most useful ways in which the relationship between small groups and the larger systems of which they are part could be explored. These studies are eagerly awaited.[24]

The last factor to be considered that limits the generality of the participation hypothesis is that of member personality. The hypothesis that an individual will be dissatisfied with a directive form of leadership because it limits his freedom of movement must be qualified by the possibility that, for some individuals, personality needs are satisfied by just such a limitation on freedom of motion. Fromm, for instance, has strongly argued the case that authoritarian relationships satisfy certain significant individual needs.[25] Haythorne *et al.* found

---

1953), pp. 114-15. Weiss reports the speculations of a German industrial psychologist as to what would happen if one tried to introduce participatory decision-making about vacation time in a German factory: "In the American factory there would be give and take, probably ending with a vote, and the agreement that the majority should rule. In the German factory, the first suggestion would be that the foreman decide. If the foreman said, 'No, you men decide,' the men would individually state the best period for them: 'May,' 'Early August,' and so on. If the foreman then said, 'We can't shut down the plant all that time; you have to decide on one time,' they would say, 'All right. You decide on the one time. We have told you our preferences.' Further insistence by the foreman on group decision would be met by increased opposition among the men. The difference is that Americans are able to see themselves as forming a group, aside from their working relationships. The Germans are a group only as they are led by their foreman. The informal group is a potentiality in America in a way it probably is not in Germany." Robert S. Weiss, "A Structure-Function Approach to Organization," *J. Soc. Issues*, 12 (1956), p. 66, n. 2.

[24] One weakness of confining work of this sort to our own society is that one too easily assumes that what is psychologically best for the individual is what accords with the value system of a democratic society. Maslow (in Kornhauser, ed., *Problems of Power in American Society*, p. 101) suggests that the characteristics of the "low scorers" on the Adorno authoritarianism scale are "aspects of general psychological health." But one wonders if the non-authoritarian would be the most healthy in a totalitarian society—or, in fact, how one would define mental health under such a circumstance.

[25] Fromm, *Escape from Freedom*, pp. 141ff.

that authoritarians (high scorers on the California F-scale) were more likely to choose directive leaders. Low scorers, on the other hand, tended to choose leaders who were friendlier and less directive.[26] And Shaw presents some evidence that performance and satisfaction in a group are a function of the agreement between personality and the structure of the group. High scorers on an acceptance-of-authority scale (a variation of the F-scale) performed better and were more satisfied in groups with a centralized communication network or a hierarchical power structure. Low scorers, on the contrary, preferred and performed better in decentralized and non-hierarchical groups.[27]

Conclusion

In political affairs there are probably no "pure types" of democratic and authoritarian leaders. Some may encourage follower participation in some decisions but not in others. Furthermore, in political systems one cannot have pure participatory or non-participatory systems. No leader in any but the smallest of groups could keep all decision-making functions in his own hands. There has to be some delegation of the functions of decision-making to others further down in the hierarchy. Nor, on the other hand, can all decision-making be exercised directly by the participants in the system. Representative structures and specialization in various fields of decision-making complicate the relatively simple picture of the experimental groups. Nevertheless, the experimental studies of democratic and autocratic leadership do indicate some of the ways in which leadership structures that tend in one of these directions will be more or less effective. Above all, some of the limitations on the generality of the participation hypothesis serve as warnings against assuming any natural superiority for democratic over autocratic methods. Though the former may be highly valued *per se*, the latter

[26] Haythorne, *et al.*, *Hum. Rel.*, 9 (1956).
[27] Marvin E. Shaw, "Acceptance of Authority, Group Structure, and the Effectiveness of Small Groups," *J. Personality*, 27 (1959), pp. 196-210.

may demonstrate much effectiveness at times. If we are committed to democracy, we must not be blind to the uses and effectiveness of authority. There is no one "best" leadership structure. What structure is best must depend upon the group setting, task, and membership—in short, upon the total situation.

Chapter XI

A CONCLUDING NOTE

WRITING in 1936, Kurt Lewin described three stages in the development of psychological theory. The first was the speculative stage. The goal of psychology was to discover ". . . the essence of things and the cause behind all occurrence." In the second, the descriptive stage, psychologists attempted ". . . to collect as many facts as possible and describe them exactly." Theoretical structures were regarded with suspicion, and facts were left to "speak for themselves." The last stage of development is the constructive. In this stage, the researcher is interested not only in broad speculative theory or in the collection of individual cases and facts, but in the relation of theory to fact and in the development of theories from which a wide range of individual facts and cases can be predicted and explained. The goal of the constructive stage is, "To discover laws. To predict individual cases."[1]

Lewin felt, in 1936, that psychology was moving from the second into the third stage of development. The study of political science is today going through a similar transition. The first half of this century saw the replacement of speculative political science by descriptive political science. The descriptive stage, marked by the accumulation of vast bodies of data and case studies on all aspects of the political process, has been followed by a new interest in theory. The concern is not with speculative theories of the nature of political society or the ideal political system, but with theories that attempt to gather some of the disparate facts of political life into a more or less general framework.

In the attempt to develop adequate theoretical models of political processes, researchers have turned to techniques not usually within the scope of political science. Attempts have been made to use mathematics or symbolic logic to create models of political relationships, and political processes have

[1] Kurt Lewin, *Principles of Topological Psychology*, p. 9.

been approximated by models borrowed from economics and game theory. This book has suggested that the small experimental group can be used as a model for the study of politics.

We have used the small experimental group as a model for the study of the leader-follower relationship in on-going social and political situations. It is hoped that, in this way, we have shed some light on problems of measurement and observation as well as on the dynamics of these relationships. Small group models of other politically relevant social processes could also be designed. Kaplan, for instance, suggests the use of small group experiments to test propositions about coalition formation among nation-states.[2] Or small group experiments might be designed to test existing propositions and to suggest new propositions about the relationship between communications and influence structures or about the processes of attitude change within a group. It is not our purpose here to suggest specific experiments that might be performed, but rather to suggest that the judicious use of small group experiments can be fruitful for political enquiry.

A model of a social system—whether it be a verbal model, a mathematical model, or a small group experimental model—is not a replication of that system. Rather, it is a simplification of it and an abstraction from it. This makes such models important tools of social analysis because it facilitates the isolation of significant relationships. Even if the simulation is unsuccessful, it can serve the useful function of leading to conceptual improvement. The power relationship between leader and follower in the small experimental group may, as we have tried to show, differ in significant ways from such relationships in on-going social and political situations, but the very process of trying to translate from one to the other requires more explicit consideration of problems of definition and measurement.

Models can thus serve useful heuristic purposes. But in the long run, we have the right to expect more from social science models than that they stimulate thinking about the creation of other models. Models of political relationships

[2] Kaplan, *System and Process in International Politics*, pp. xv-xvi.

must be developed that can be fitted to the data of politics in order better to understand and predict the processes of politics. Abstract models have a certain elegance and appeal, but unless such models can be related at some point to reality they will have a seriously limited value to social analysis. One of the major tasks of small group experimental research is that of connecting small group models more closely with actual social situations. If laboratory studies are to tell us about the behavior of "real" people, not laboratory people—and this of course is what they must do if they are to be of use to the political scientist or any other social scientist—the gap between the laboratory and the on-going social system must be bridged.

There are two ways in which the small group experimental model can be connected with actual social situations. In the first place, the way in which the experimental situation abstracts from and simplifies the actual social situation can be taken into account in extrapolating from the experimental situation. This can be done if the differences between the experimental and the real situation are systematic—i.e., under particular conditions the differences will always be of a certain type and take a uniform direction. If this is the case, the differences may be considered constants in the model and corrections can be made for them in moving from the experimental level to that of the actual social situation. Our study has described several such systematic differences between the experimental and the real worlds that can and must be taken into account in connecting the two levels.

But if the two levels are to be connected, the differences between them must not only be systematic; they must be *known* differences. Too many experimental studies have concentrated only on the laboratory processes and have ignored the way in which these processes are similar to or different from processes outside of the laboratory. This suggests that greater attention will have to be paid to the relationship between laboratory experiments and actual social situations than has been paid by many experimenters in the past.

The second way in which the small group model can be connected with actual social situations is to reduce the differences between experimental and on-going situations. This can be done by attempting closer simulation of the real world in the laboratory. The use of realistic settings, of long time-spans so that groups can develop histories, and of problems that can engage the interest of the participants would make the process of bridging the gap between the laboratory and the outside world easier. Furthermore, if we are to understand real social behavior, more attention must be paid to the population of the experimental group. A greater variety of subjects should be used, especially subjects from other cultures. Too much of small group research may be culture-bound because of the limited populations from which subjects have been selected.

More important than the mechanics of design or the selection of the population is the need for the experimentalist to work with significant social problems. The problems studied in the laboratory ought not to be uniquely laboratory problems. In survey research we do not want to know about the answers to questions given by a small sample of people. We want to know about attitudes in the population from which the sample was drawn. Similarly, in the laboratory we do not want to know how people will behave under certain controlled conditions. Ultimately we want to know how people outside of the laboratory will behave. Unless the problems faced by the laboratory populations are in some way related to significant problems faced by individuals outside, our laboratory work will tell us little.[3]

The best way to ensure that experimental studies deal with actual social problems is to make the experimental study part

[3] This is not to say that there is no room for experimental research which cannot be immediately applied to actual human affairs. There is great value in research whose only immediate goal is to develop experimental virtuosity—to improve controls or refine measurement techniques. In fact, many major advances in laboratory techniques are due to the fact that small group researchers have been unconcerned with the problem of extrapolation. But this is a question of research strategy. The long-run justification of such laboratory-oriented experimental work is that it will ultimately provide us with better tools for the understanding of actual social processes. The argument presented here for small group research that is more closely related to on-going situations should not be taken to imply an argument against concurrent small group research aimed at improving laboratory methods.

of a chain of studies. Greater efforts should be made to test in the laboratory propositions suggested by field research. Conversely, more attempts should be made to predict from the laboratory how individuals or groups will behave in actual social situations—and to test these predictions. Experimental variables should be designed with this in mind. If we want to see how groups with different types of hierarchies make decisions, it would be useful to create hierarchies similar to those found in the real world. The constant process of testing small group findings in the real world should increase our knowledge of the real world at the same time that it sharpens our use of the experimental method.

Because of the ability in the small experimental group to observe leader-follower relationships directly, the studies can suggest certain dynamic aspects of these relationships not apparent in other social situations. Thus they should be useful in suggesting field research into these relationships. Our discussion of the relationship between leaders and the norms of the group and the consequent dilemma this poses when demands for change are placed on the group should suggest ways of testing these propositions in actual social situations. The methods might have to be different—panel studies of change in attitude in response to a particular situation, for instance—but the propositions as to how the group leader can break through the limitations placed upon him should be amenable to testing in field research. Simultaneous attitude studies of leaders and non-leaders carried on over time would be one way of testing empirically in field situations the propositions about the relationship of leaders to group norms. Similarly, field research could be designed to test the proposition as to the relation between the instrumental and affective output of a system, or between participatory and non-participatory leadership. And field research of this sort should in turn feed back into experimental research, suggesting new processes to explore, new hypotheses to test. A closer integration of small group research with research into political affairs would redound to the benefit of both disciplines.

The experimental method will not replace other methods

more familiar to political science. The study of politics will never become an experimental science. Experiments will be useful only if they are adjuncts to other studies—surveys, participant observation, case studies, historical studies, and the like. Properly used, they can be of great value. Their proper use requires a full exploitation of the strengths and potentialities of the experimental laboratory. It also requires a clear realization of the limitations of the experimental approach. This study, it is hoped, has contributed to understanding both the strength and the limitations of the experimental method.

BIBLIOGRAPHY

BOOKS

Adorno, T. W., *et al. The Authoritarian Personality*. New York: Harper, 1950.

Almond, Gabriel A. *The Appeals of Communism*. Princeton: Princeton University Press, 1954.

Apter, David. *The Gold Coast in Transition*. Princeton: Princeton University Press, 1955.

Arendt, Hannah. *The Origins of Totalitarianism*. New York: Harper, 1951.

Argyle, Michael. *The Scientific Study of Human Behavior*. London: Methuen, 1957.

Argyris, Chris. *Personality and Organization*. New York: Harper, 1957.

Asch, Solomon. *Social Psychology*. New York: Prentice-Hall, 1952.

Bakke, E. W. *The Fusion Process*. New Haven: Yale University, Labor and Management Center, 1955.

Bales, Robert F. *Interaction Process Analysis*. Cambridge, Mass.: Harvard University Press, 1950.

Banfield, Edward C. *The Moral Basis of a Backward Society*. Glencoe, Ill.: Free Press, 1958.

Barnard, Chester I. *The Functions of the Executive*. Cambridge, Mass.: Harvard University Press, 1938.

Bavelas, Alex. "Morale and the Training of Leaders," in G. Watson, ed. *Civilian Morale*. Boston: Houghton-Mifflin, 1942.

———. "Communications Patterns in Task-Oriented Groups," in D. Lerner and H. Lasswell, eds. *The Policy Sciences*. Stanford, Calif.: Stanford University Press, 1951.

Berelson, Bernard R., Lazarsfeld, Paul F., and McPhee, William N. *Voting*. Chicago: University of Chicago Press, 1954.

Berenda, R. W. *The Influence of the Group on the Judgments of Children*. New York: King's Crown Press, 1950.

Blau, Peter. *The Dynamics of Bureaucracy*. Chicago: University of Chicago Press, 1955.

Brookings Institution, The. *Research Frontiers in Politics and Government: Brookings Lectures, 1955*. Washington, D.C.: Brookings Institution, 1955.

Campbell, Donald T. *A Study of Naval Leadership*. Columbus, Ohio: Ohio State University, Personnel Research Board, 1953.

Cartwright, Dorwin, ed. *Studies in Social Power.* Ann Arbor, Mich.: Institute of Social Research, 1959.

——, and Zander, Alvin, eds. *Group Dynamics.* Evanston, Ill.: Row, Peterson, 1953.

Chapin, F. Stuart. *Experimental Designs in Sociological Research.* New York: Harper, 1947.

Cole, G. D. H. *Essays in Social Theory.* London: Macmillan, 1950.

Cooley, Charles H. *Social Organization.* New York: Scribner's, 1909.

Dahl, Robert A. *A Preface to Democratic Theory.* Chicago: University of Chicago Press, 1956.

Dashiell, J. F. "Experimental Studies of the Influence of Social Situations on the Behavior of Individual Adults," in C. Murchison, ed. *Handbook of Social Psychology.* Worcester, Mass.: Clark University Press, 1935.

Dewey, John. *The Public and Its Problems.* Chicago: Gateway Books, 1946.

Dicks, H. V. "Some Psychological Studies of German Character," in T. H. Pear, ed. *Psychological Factors in Peace and War.* London: Hutchinson, 1950.

Dodd, Stuart E. *A Controlled Experiment in Rural Hygiene in Syria.* Beirut: American Press, 1934.

Faris, Robert E. "Development of the Small Group Research Movement," in M. Sherif and M. O. Wilson, eds. *Group Relations at the Crossroads.* New York: Harper, 1953.

Festinger, Leon. *A Theory of Cognitive Dissonance.* Evanston, Ill.: Row, Peterson, 1957.

——, Back, K. W., Schachter, Stanley, Kelley, H. H., and Thibault, J. W. *Theory and Experiments in Social Communications.* Ann Arbor, Mich.: University of Michigan Press, 1950.

——, and Katz, Daniel. *Research Methods in the Behavioral Sciences.* New York: Dryden Press, 1953.

——, Schachter, Stanley, and Back, K. W. *Social Pressures in Informal Groups.* New York: Harper, 1950.

Fiedler, Fred E. *Leader Attitudes and Group Effectiveness.* Urbana, Ill.: University of Illinois Press, 1958.

Follett, Mary Parker, *Freedom and Coordination.* London: Management Publications Trust, 1949.

Frenkel-Brunswik, Else. "Further Explorations by a Contributor to 'The Authoritarian Personality,'" in R. Christie and M. Jahoda, eds. *Studies in the Scope and Method of "The Authoritarian Personality."* Glencoe, Ill.: Free Press, 1954.

252

Freud, Sigmund. *Group Psychology and the Analysis of the Ego.* London: Hogarth, 1945.

Fromm, Erich. *Escape from Freedom.* New York: Farrar and Straus, 1941.

Garceau, Oliver. *The Political Life of the A.M.A.* Cambridge, Mass.: Harvard University Press, 1941.

Gordon, Thomas. *Group Centered Leadership.* Cambridge, Mass.: Riverside Press, 1955.

Gouldner, Alvin W. *Studies in Leadership: Leadership and Democratic Action.* New York: Harper, 1950.

Greenwood, Ernest. *Experimental Sociology: A Study in Method.* New York: King's Crown Press, 1945.

Grinker, Roy R., ed. *Toward a Unified Theory of Human Behavior.* New York: Basic Books, 1956.

Gross, Neal, Mason, W. S., and McEachern, A. W. *Explorations in Role Analysis.* New York: John Wiley, 1958.

Guetzkow, Harold, ed. *Groups, Leadership and Men.* Pittsburgh: Carnegie Press, 1951.

———. "Building Models About Small Groups," in Roland Young, ed. *The Study of Politics.* Evanston, Ill.: Northwestern University Press, 1958.

Halmos, Paul. *Towards a Measure of Man: The Frontiers of Normal Adjustment.* London: Routledge and Kegan Paul, 1957.

Halpin, A. W., and Winer, B. J. *The Leadership Behavior of the Airplane Commander.* Columbus, Ohio: Ohio State University, Research Foundation, 1952.

Hare, A. Paul, Borgatta, Edgar F., and Bales, Robert F., eds. *Small Groups.* New York: Alfred A. Knopf, 1955.

Harris, Henry. *The Group Approach to Leadership Testing.* London: Routledge and Kegan Paul, 1950.

Hartley, Eugene L., and Hartley, Ruth E. *Fundamentals of Social Psychology.* New York: Alfred A. Knopf, 1952.

———. *Leader Behavior Description.* Columbus, Ohio: Ohio State University, Personnel Research Board, 1950.

Homans, George. *The Human Group.* New York: Harcourt, Brace, 1950.

Hulett, J. E., Jr., and Stagner, Ross, eds. *Problems in Social Psychology: An Interdisciplinary Approach.* Urbana, Ill.: University of Illinois Press, 1952.

Hunter, Floyd A. *Community Power Structure.* Chapel Hill, N.C.: University of North Carolina Press, 1953.

Hyman, Herbert. *Survey Design and Analysis.* Glencoe, Ill.: Free Press, 1955.

Inkeles, Alex. *Public Opinion in the Soviet Union.* Cambridge, Mass.: Harvard University Press, 1951.

Jennings, Helen. *Leadership and Isolation.* New York: Longmans, Green, 1950.

Kaplan, Morton A. *System and Process in International Politics.* New York: John Wiley, 1957.

Katz, Elihu, and Lazarsfeld, Paul A. *Personal Influence: The Part Played by People in the Flow of Mass Communications.* Glencoe, Ill.: Free Press, 1955.

Kendall, Patricia C., and Lazarsfeld, Paul F. "Problems in Survey Analysis," in Robert K. Merton and Paul F. Lazarsfeld, eds. *Studies in the Scope and Method of "The American Soldier."* Glencoe, Ill.: Free Press, 1950.

Klein, Josephine. *The Study of Groups.* London: Routledge and Kegan Paul, 1956.

Laird, Donald A. and Laird, Eleanor C. *The New Psychology of Leadership.* New York: McGraw-Hill, 1956.

La Piere, Richard T. *A Theory of Social Control.* New York: McGraw-Hill, 1954.

Lasswell, Harold D. "Psychopathology and Politics," in *The Political Writings of Harold Lasswell.* Glencoe, Ill.: Free Press, 1951.

———, and Kaplan, Abraham. *Power and Society: A Framework for Political Enquiry.* New Haven: Yale University Press, 1950.

———, Lerner, Daniel, and Rothwell, C. Easton. *The Comparative Study of Elites.* Stanford, Calif.: Stanford University Press, 1952.

Lazarsfeld, Paul F., Berelson, Bernard, and Gaudet, Helen. *The People's Choice.* New York: Columbia University Press, 1948.

Lerner, Daniel. *The Passing of Traditional Society.* Glencoe, Ill.: Free Press, 1958.

Levy, David M. "Anti-Nazis: Criteria of Differentiation," in Alfred H. Stanton and Stewart E. Perry, eds. *Personality and Political Crisis.* Glencoe, Ill.: Free Press, 1951.

Lewin, Kurt. *The Conceptual Representation and Measurement of Psychological Forces.* Durham, N.C.: Duke University Press, 1938.

———. *Field Theory in Social Science.* New York: Harper, 1951.

———. *Principles of Topological Psychology.* New York: McGraw-Hill, 1936.

———. *Resolving Social Conflicts.* New York: Harper, 1948.

Likert, Rensis, and Hayes, Samuel P., Jr. *Some Applications of Behavioral Research.* Paris: UNESCO, 1957.

Lindzey, Gardner, ed. *The Handbook of Social Psychology.* Cambridge, Mass.: Addison-Wesley, 1959.

Lippitt, Ronald. *Training in Community Relations.* New York: Harper, 1949.

———, Watson, Jeanne, and Westley, Bruce. *The Dynamics of Planned Change.* New York: Harcourt, Brace, 1958.

Lipset, Seymour M. *Political Man.* Garden City, N.Y.: Doubleday, 1960.

———, Trow, Martin A., and Coleman, James S. *Union Democracy: The Internal Politics of the International Typographical Union.* Glencoe, Ill.: Free Press, 1956.

McKenzie, R. T. *British Political Parties.* London: Heinemann, 1955.

Mannheim, Karl. *Freedom, Power and Democratic Planning.* London: Routledge and Kegan Paul, 1951.

———. *Man and Society in the Age of Reconstruction.* New York: Harcourt, Brace, 1950.

———. *Systematic Sociology.* London: Routledge and Kegan Paul, 1957.

March, James, and Simon, Herbert. *Organizations.* New York: John Wiley, 1958.

Maslow, A. H. "Power Relationships and Patterns of Personal Development," in Arthur Kornhauser, ed. *Problems of Power in American Society.* Detroit: Wayne University Press, 1957.

Matthews, Donald R. *The Social Background of Political Decision Makers.* New York: Doubleday, 1954.

Merriam, Charles E. *Political Power.* New York: McGraw-Hill, 1934.

Merton, Robert K. *Social Theory and Social Structure.* Revised and enlarged edition. Glencoe, Ill.: Free Press, 1957.

Michels, Roberto. *Political Parties.* Glencoe, Ill.: Free Press, 1949.

Miller, James G., ed. *Experiments in Social Process.* New York: McGraw-Hill, 1950.

Mills, C. Wright. *The Power Elite.* New York: Oxford University Press, 1956.

Moreno, J. L. *Who Shall Survive?* Washington, D.C.: Nervous and Mental Disease Monograph, 1934.

Newcomb, Theodore M. *Personality and Social Change.* New York: Dryden Press, 1943.

———, and Hartley, Eugene L. *Readings in Social Psychology.* New York: Henry Holt, 1947.

Nisbet, Robert A. *The Quest for Community.* New York: Oxford University Press, 1953.

O.S.S. Staff Report. *The Assessment of Men.* New York: Rinehart, 1948.

Parsons, Talcott, and Bales, Robert F. *Family, Socialization, and Interaction Process Analysis.* Glencoe, Ill.: Free Press, 1955.
———, Bales, Robert F., and Shils, Edward A. *Working Papers in the Theory of Action.* Glencoe, Ill.: Free Press, 1953.
Peel, Roy V. *The Political Clubs of New York.* New York: Putnam, 1945.
Pigors, P. *Leadership or Domination.* Boston: Houghton-Mifflin, 1935.
Poston, Richard W. *Democracy Is You.* New York: Harper, 1953.

Riesman, David. *The Lonely Crowd.* New York: Doubleday, 1954.
Rodnick, David. *An Interim Report on French Culture.* Maxwell Airforce Base, Ala.: Human Resources Institute, 1953.
———. *Postwar Germans.* New Haven: Yale University Press, 1948.
Roethlisberger, F. J., and Dickson, William J. *Management and the Worker.* Cambridge, Mass.: Harvard University Press, 1939.
Ross, Murray G., and Hendry, Charles E. *New Understandings of Leadership.* New York: Association Press, 1957.

Sayles, Leonard R. *Behavior of Industrial Work Groups: Prediction and Control.* New York: John Wiley, 1958.
———, and Strauss, George. *The Local Union: Its Place in the Industrial Plant.* New York: Harper, 1953.
Schaffner, Bertram. *Fatherland: A Study of Authoritarianism in the German Family.* New York: Columbia University Press, 1948.
Scott, E. L. *Perceptions of Organization and Leadership Behavior.* Columbus, Ohio: Ohio State University Research Foundation, 1952.
Selznick, Philip. *Leadership in Administration.* Evanston, Ill.: Row, Peterson, 1957.
———. *The Organizational Weapon: A Study of Bolshevik Strategy and Tactics.* New York: McGraw-Hill, 1952.
Shartle, C. L., and Stogdill, R. M. *Studies in Naval Leadership.* Columbus, Ohio: Ohio State University Research Foundation, 1952.

Sherif, Muzafer, and Cantril, Hadley. *The Psychology of Ego-Involvements: Social Attitudes and Identifications.* New York: John Wiley, 1947.

————, and Sherif, Carolyn. *Groups in Harmony and Tension.* New York: Harper, 1953.

————, and Sherif, Carolyn. *An Outline of Social Psychology.* New York: Harper, 1956.

Shils, Edward A. "Primary Groups in the American Army," in Robert K. Merton and Paul F. Lazarsfeld, eds. *Studies in the Scope and Method of "The American Soldier."* Glencoe, Ill.: Free Press, 1950.

————. "The Study of the Primary Group," in Daniel Lerner and Harold Lasswell, eds. *The Policy Sciences.* Stanford, Calif.: Stanford University Press, 1951.

Simon, Herbert. *Administrative Behavior.* New York: Macmillan, 1957.

Snyder, Richard, Bruck, H. W., and Sapin, Burton. *Decision-Making as an Approach to the Study of International Politics.* Princeton: Princeton University, Organizational Behavior Section, 1954.

Sorokin, Pitirim A. *Fads and Foibles in Modern Sociology.* Chicago: Henry Regnery, 1956.

Stogdill, Ralph M. "Leadership and Morale in Organized Groups," in J. E. Hulett, Jr., and Ross Stagner, eds. *Problems in Social Psychology.* Urbana, Ill.: University of Illinois Press, 1952.

————, and Coons, Alvin E. *Leader Behavior: Its Measurement and Description.* Columbus, Ohio: Ohio State University, Bureau of Business Research, 1957.

————, and Koehler, K. *Measures of Leadership Structure and Organization Change.* Columbus, Ohio: Ohio State University Research Foundation, 1952.

Swanson, G. E., Newcomb, T. M., and Hartley, E. L., eds. *Readings in Social Psychology.* New York: Henry Holt, 1952.

Thibault, John W., and Kelley, Harold H. *The Social Psychology of Groups.* New York: John Wiley, 1959.

Tomasic, Dinko. *The Impact of Russian Culture on Soviet Society.* Glencoe, Ill.: Free Press, 1953.

Tönnies, Ferdinand. *Community and Society (Gemeinschaft und Gesellschaft),* Charles P. Loomis, trans. East Lansing, Mich.: Michigan State Press, 1957.

Truman, David. *The Governmental Process.* New York: Alfred A. Knopf, 1951.

Urwick, L. *The Elements of Administration.* New York: Harper, 1953.

Vinacke, W. Edgar. *The Miniature Social Situation*. Honolulu: University of Hawaii Press, 1954.

Weber, Max. *From Max Weber: Essays in Sociology*, translated, edited, and with an introduction by H. H. Gerth and C. Wright Mills. New York: Oxford University Press, 1946.
———. *General Economic History*. Glencoe, Ill.: Free Press, 1927.
Whitehead, T. N. *Leadership in a Free Society*. Cambridge, Mass.: Harvard University Press, 1936.
Whyte, William F. *Street Corner Society*. Chicago: University of Chicago Press, 1943.
Woodward, R. S. *Experimental Psychology*. New York: Henry Holt, 1938.
Wooton, Barbara. *Testament for Social Science: An Essay on the Application of Scientific Method to Human Problems*. London: Allen and Unwin, 1950.
Wylie, Lawrence. *Village in the Vaucluse*. Cambridge, Mass.: Harvard University Press, 1957.

Yanaga, Chitoshi. *Japanese People and Politics*. New York: John Wiley, 1956.

Zink, H. *City of Bosses in the United States*. Durham, N.C.: Duke University Press, 1930.

ARTICLES

Allport, Gordon W. "The Psychology of Participation," *Psychological Rev.*, 53 (1945), 117-32.
———, and Kramer, B. M. "Some Roots of Prejudice," *J. Psychology*, 22 (1946), 9-39.
Almond, Gabriel A. "Comparative Political Systems," *J. Politics*, 18 (1956), 391-409.
Ansbacher, H. L. "The History of the Leaderless Group Discussion Technique," *Psychological Bulletin*, 48 (1951), 383-90.
———. "Lasting and Passing Aspects of German Military Psychology," *Sociometry*, 12 (1949), 301-12.
Aron, Raymond. "Evidence and Inference in History," *Daedalus* (1958), 11-39.
Asch, M. J. "Non-Directive Teaching in Psychology: An Experimental Study," *Psychological Monographs*, 65 (1951), No. 4, entire.

Back, Kurt W. "Influence Through Social Communication," *J. Abnorm. Soc. Psych.*, 46 (1951), 9-23.

Baldwin, A. "Socialization and Parent-Child Relationship," *Child Development*, 19 (1948), 127-36.

Bales, Robert F., and Slater, Philip E. "Notes on 'Role Differentiation in Small Decision Making Groups': Reply to Dr. Wheeler," *Sociometry*, 20 (1957), 152-55.

———, and Strodtbeck, Fred L. "Phases in Group Problem Solving," *J. Abnorm. Soc. Psych.*, 46 (1951), 485-95; reprinted in Cartwright and Zander, eds., *Group Dynamics*.

———, et al. "Channels of Communications in Small Groups," *Am. Soc. Rev.*, 16 (1951), 461-68.

Barschak, E. "A Study of Happiness and Unhappiness in the Childhood and Adolescence of Girls in Different Cultures," *J. Psychology*, 32 (1951), 173-215.

Bass, Bernard M. "An Analysis of Leaderless Group Discussion," *J. Applied Psych.*, 33 (1949), 527-33.

———. "The Leaderless Group Discussion," *Psychol. Bull.*, 51 (1954), 465-92.

———, and Coates, C. H. "Forecasting Officer Potential Using the Leaderless Group Discussion," *J. Abnorm. Soc. Psych.*, 47 (1952), 321-25.

———, and Wurster, Cecil. "Effects of Company Rank on LGD Performance of Oil Refinery Supervisors," *J. Abnorm. Soc. Psych.*, 37 (1953), 100-04.

———, and Wurster, Cecil. "Effects of the Nature of the Problem on LGD Performance," *J. Applied Psych.*, 37 (1953), 96-99.

———, et al. "Personality Variables Related to Leaderless Group Discussion Behavior," *J. Abnorm. Soc. Psych.*, 48 (1953), 120-29.

Bates, Allen P. "Some Sociometric Aspects of Social Ranking in a Small Face-to-Face Group," *Sociometry*, 15 (1952), 330-41.

———, and Cloyd, Jerry S. "Toward the Development of Operations for Defining Group Norms and Member Roles," *Sociometry*, 19 (1956), 26-39.

Bauer, Raymond A., and Gleicher, David B. "Word-of-Mouth Communication in the Soviet Union," *Public Opinion Quarterly*, 17 (1953), 297-310.

Baumgartel, H. "Leadership Style as a Variable in Research Administration," *Administrative Science Quarterly*, 2 (1957), 344-60.

Bell, G. B., and French, R. L. "Consistency of Individual Leadership Position in Small Groups of Varying Membership," *J. Abnorm. Soc. Psych.*, 45 (1950), 764-69; reprinted in Hare, Borgatta, and Bales, eds., *Small Groups*.

———, and Hall, Henry E., Jr. "The Relationship Between Leadership and Empathy," *J. Abnorm. Soc. Psych.*, 49 (1954), 156-57.

Benne, K. D., and Sheats, P. "Functional Roles of Group Members," *J. Social Issues, 4* (1948), 41-49.

Bennett, Edith Becker. "Discussion, Commitment, Decision, and Consensus in 'Group Decision,'" *Hum. Rel., 8* (1955), 251-73.

Berelson, Bernard. "Democratic Theory and Public Opinion," *Public Opinion Quarterly, 16* (1952), 313-30.

Berkowitz, Leonard. "Personality and Group Position," *Sociometry, 19* (1956), 210-22.

———. "Sharing Leadership in Small Decision Making Groups," *J. Abnorm. Soc. Psych., 48* (1953), 231-38; reprinted in Hare, Borgatta, and Bales, eds., *Small Groups.*

Bierstedt, Robert. "An Analysis of Social Power," *Am. Soc. Rev., 15* (1950), 730-38.

Blake, Robert R., Mouton, Jane S., and Fruchter, Benjamin. "The Consistency in Interpersonal Behavior Judgments Made on the Basis of Short-Term Interactions in Three-Man Groups," *J. Abnorm. Soc. Psych., 49* (1954), 573-78.

Bloomfield, L. P., and Padelford, N. J. "Three Experiments in Political Gaming," *American Political Science Review, 53* (1959), 1105-15.

Borg, Walter R. "The Behavior of Emergent and Designated Leaders in Situational Tests," *Sociometry, 20* (1957), 95-104.

Borgatta, Edgar F., and Bales, Robert F. "Interaction of Individuals in Reconstituted Groups," *Sociometry, 16* (1953), 302-20; reprinted in Hare, Borgatta, and Bales, eds., *Small Groups.*

———, Cottrell, Leonard S., and Meyer, Henry J. "On the Dimensions of Group Behavior," *Sociometry, 19* (1956), 223-40.

Bourricaud, François. "La 'Démocratie' dans les petits groupes," *Cahiers internationaux de sociologie, 19* (1954), 104-13.

Bovard, Everett W. "Clinical Insight as a Function of Group Process," *J. Abnorm. Soc. Psych., 47* (1952), 534-39.

———. "Group Structure and Perception," *J. Abnorm. Soc. Psych., 46* (1951), 398-405; reprinted in Cartwright and Zander, eds., *Group Dynamics.*

Bradford, L. P., and French, J. R. P., issue eds. "The Dynamics of the Discussion Group," *J. Social Issues, 4* (1948), 1-75.

Brodbeck, May. "The Role of Small Groups in Mediating the Effects of Propaganda," *J. Abnorm. Soc. Psych., 52* (1956), 166-70.

Calvin, Allen D., Hoffman, Frederic K., and Harden, Edgar L. "The Effect of Intelligence and Social Atmosphere on Group Problem Solving Behavior," *J. Social Psych., 45* (1957), 61-74.

Campbell, Donald T. "An Error in Some Demonstrations of the

Superior Social Perceptiveness of Leaders," *J. Abnorm. Soc. Psych.*, *51* (1955), 694-96.

———. "Factors Relevant to the Validity of Experiments in Social Settings," *Psych. Bull.*, *54* (1957), 297-313.

Carter, Launor J. "Recording and Evaluating the Performance of Individuals as Members in Small Groups," *Personnel Psych.*, *7* (1954), 477-84; reprinted in Hare, Borgatta, and Bales, eds., *Small Groups*.

———, Haythorne, W., and Howell, M. "A Further Investigation of the Criteria of Leadership," *J. Abnorm. Soc. Psych.*, *45* (1950), 350-58; reprinted in Hare, Borgatta, and Bales, eds., *Small Groups*.

———, and Nixon, Mary. "Ability, Perception, Personality and Interest Factors Associated with Different Criteria for Leadership," *J. Psychology*, *27* (1949), 377-88.

———, and Nixon, Mary. "An Investigation of the Relationship Between Four Criteria of Leadership Ability for Three Different Tasks," *J. Psychology*, *27* (1949), 245-61.

———, et al. "The Behavior of Leaders and Other Group Members," *J. Abnorm. Soc. Psych.*, *46* (1951), 589-95; reprinted in Cartwright and Zander, eds., *Group Dynamics*.

———, et al. "A Note on a New Technique of Interaction Recording," *J. Abnorm. Soc. Psych.*, *46* (1951), 258-60.

———, et al. "The Relation of Categorization and Ratings in the Observation of Group Behavior," *Hum. Rel.*, *4* (1951), 239-54.

Cartwright, Dorwin. "Achieving Change in People: Some Applications of Group Dynamics Theory," *Hum. Rel.*, *4* (1951), 381-92.

Cattell, Raymond B. "Concepts and Method in the Measurement of Group Syntality," *Psychological Rev.*, *55* (1948), 48-63; reprinted in Hare, Borgatta, and Bales, eds., *Small Groups*.

———. "New Concepts for Measuring Leadership in Terms of Group Syntality," *Hum. Rel.*, *4* (1951), 161-84; reprinted in Cartwright and Zander, eds., *Group Dynamics*.

———, and Stice, G. F. "Four Formulae for Selecting Leaders on the Basis of Personality," *Hum. Rel.*, *7* (1954), 493-507.

Chapin, F. S. "Sociometric Stars as Isolates," *Am. J. Soc.*, *65* (1950), 263-67.

Chapple, E. D. "The Interaction Chronograph: Its Evolution and Present Application," *Personnel*, *25* (1949), 295-307.

Chowdhry, Kalma, and Newcomb, Theodore M. "The Relative Abilities of Leaders and Non-Leaders to Estimate Opinions of Their Own Groups," *J. Abnorm. Soc. Psych.*, *47* (1952), 52-57.

Coch, Lester, and French, John R. P., Jr. "Overcoming Resistance to Change," *Hum. Rel.*, *1* (1948), 512-32; reprinted in Cartwright and Zander, eds., *Group Dynamics*.

Crockett, Walter H. "Emergent Leadership in Small Decision-Making Groups," *J. Abnorm. Soc. Psych.*, *51* (1955), 378-83.

Crozier, M. "La France, terre de commandement," *Esprit*, *25* (1957), 779-98.

———. "Pour une sociologie de l'administration publique," *Revue française de science politique*, *6* (1956), 750-69.

Davies, James C., and Wada, George. "Riots and Rioters," *Western Political Quarterly*, *10* (1957), 864-74.

Demerath, Nicholas J., and Thibault, John W. "Small Groups and Administrative Organizations," *Administrative Science Quarterly*, *1* (1956), 139-54.

Easton, David. "An Approach to the Analysis of Political Systems," *World Politics*, *9* (1957), 383-400.

———. "Limits of the Equilibrium Model in Social Research," *Behavioral Science*, *1* (1956), 96-104.

Eisenstadt, S. N. "Patterns of Leadership and Social Homogeneity in Israel," *International Social Science Bulletin*, *8* (1956), 36-54.

Faw, V. "A Psychotherapeutic Method of Teaching Psychology," *American Psychologist*, *4* (1949), 104-09.

Festinger, Leon. "The Role of Group Belongingness in a Voting Situation," *Hum. Rel.*, *1* (1947), 154-80.

———. "A Theory of Social Comparative Processes," *Hum. Rel.*, *7* (1954), 117-40.

———, and J. Thibault. "Interpersonal Communications in Small Groups," *J. Abnorm. Soc. Psych.*, *46* (1951), 92-99.

———, *et al.* "The Influence Process in the Presence of Extreme Deviants," *Hum. Rel.*, *5* (1952), 327-46.

Fiedler, Fred L. "A Note on Leadership Theory: The Effect of Social Barriers on Leaders and Followers," *Sociometry*, *20* (1957), 87-94.

Flanders, Ned A. "Personal-Social Anxiety as a Factor in Experimental Learning Situations," *J. Educ. Res.*, *45* (1951), 100-10.

Fleischman, Edwin A. "Leadership Climate, Human Relations Training and Supervisory Behavior," *Personnel Psychology*, *6* (1953), 205-22.

Frank, J. D. "Experimental Studies of Personal Pressure and Resistance," *J. General Psychology*, *30* (1944), 23-56.

Fruchter, Benjamin, Blake, Robert R., and Mouton, Jane S.

"Some Dimensions of Interpersonal Relations in Three-Man Aircrews," *Psychological Monographs, 71* (1957), No. 448.

Gardner, Godfrey. "Functional Leadership and Popularity in Small Groups," *Hum. Rel., 9* (1956), 491-509.

Geiger, Kent. "Changing Political Attitudes in Totalitarian Society: A Case Study of the Role of the Family," *World Politics, 8* (1956), 187-205.

Gellhorn, Walter, and Brody, William. "Selecting Supervisory Mediators by Trial by Combat," *Public Administration Review, 8* (1948), 289-96.

Getzels, J. W., and Guba, E. G. "Role, Role Conflict and Effectiveness," *Am. Soc. Rev., 56* (1954), 164-75.

Gibb, Cecil A. "The Principles and Traits of Leadership," *J. Abnorm. Soc. Psych., 42* (1947), 267-84; reprinted in Hare, Borgatta, and Bales, eds., *Small Groups.*

———. "The Sociometry of Leadership in Temporary Groups," *Sociometry, 13* (1950), 226-43; reprinted in Hare, Borgatta, and Bales, eds., *Small Groups.*

Goldhamer, H., and Speier, H. "Some Observations on Political Gaming," *World Politics, 12* (1959), 72-83.

Guba, E. G. "Morale and Satisfaction: A Study of Past-Future Time Perspective," *Administrative Science Quarterly, 3* (1958), 194-209.

Guetzkow, Harold. "The Use of Simulation in the Study of Inter-Nation Relations," *Behavioral Science, 4* (1959), 183-91.

———, and Dill, William. "Factors in the Organizational Development of Task-Oriented Groups," *Sociometry, 20* (1957), 175-204.

Halpin, A. W. "The Leadership Behavior and Combat Performance of Airplane Commanders," *J. Abnorm. Soc. Psych., 49* (1954), 19-22.

Hare, A. Paul. "Small Group Discussion with Participatory and Supervisory Leadership," *J. Abnorm. Soc. Psych., 48* (1953), 273-75.

Haythorne, W., *et al.* "The Behavior of Authoritarian and Equalitarian Personalities in Groups," *Hum. Rel., 9* (1956), 57-74.

Heinicke, C., and Bales, R. F. "Developmental Trends in the Structure of Small Groups," *Sociometry, 16* (1953), 7-38.

Heise, George A., and Miller, George. "Problem Solving in Small Groups Using Various Communications Nets," *J. Abnorm. Soc. Psych., 46* (1951), 327-35; reprinted in Hare, Borgatta, and Bales, eds., *Small Groups.*

Hemphill, John K. "Leadership Behavior Associated with the

Administrative Reputation of College Departments," *J. Educational Psychology*, 46 (1955), 385-401.

———. "Why People Take Leadership," *Adult Leadership*, 5 (1956), 44-46.

———, *et al.* "The Relation Between the Possession of Task Relevant Information and Attempts to Lead," *Psychological Monographs*, 70 (1956), No. 414.

Homans, George C. "The Cash Posters," *Am. Soc. Rev.*, 19 (1954), 724-32.

Horowitz, E. L., and Horowitz, R. E. "Development of Social Attitudes in Children," *Sociometry*, 1 (1938), 301-38.

Horowitz, M. W., Lyons, J., and Perlmutter, H. V. "Induction of Forces in Discussion Groups," *Hum. Rel.*, 4 (1951), 57-76.

Horsfall, A. B., and Arensberg, C. M. "Teamwork and Productivity in a Shoe Factory," *Human Organization*, 8 (1949), 13-25.

Hyman, Sidney. "The Log-Cabin Myth Comes to an End," *New York Times Magazine*, September 21, 1958, p. 26.

Israel, Joachim. "Remarks Concerning Generalization in Group Experimental Research," *Acta Sociologica*, 2 (1957), 214-27.

James, J. "A Preliminary Study of the Size Determinant in Small Group Interaction," *Am. Soc. Rev.*, 16 (1951), 474-77.

Jennings, Helen H. "Leadership and Sociometric Choice," *Sociometry*, 10 (1947), 32-59.

———. "Structure of Leadership-Development and Sphere of Influence," *Sociometry*, 1 (1937), 99-143.

Kariel, Henry S. "Democracy Unlimited: Kurt Lewin's Field Theory," *Am. J. Soc.*, 62 (1956), 280-89.

Katz, Elihu. "The Two-Step Flow of Communications," *Public Opinion Quarterly*, 21 (1957), 61-78.

———, *et al.* "Leadership Stability and Social Change: An Experiment with Small Groups," *Sociometry*, 20 (1957), 36-50.

Kelley, H. H., and Shapiro, M. M. "An Experiment in Conformity to Group Norms Where Conformity Is Detrimental to Group Achievements," *Am. Soc. Rev.*, 19 (1959), 667-77.

———, and Volkhart, E. H. "The Resistance to Change of Group Anchored Attitudes," *Am. Soc. Rev.*, 17 (1952), 453-65.

Kennedy, John L. "A 'Transition-Model' Laboratory for Research in Cultural Change," *Human Organization*, 14 (1955), 16-18.

Landsberger, Henry A. "Interaction Process Analysis of Professional Behavior: A Study of Labor-Mediators in Twelve Labor-Management Disputes," *Am. Soc. Rev.*, *21* (1955), 566-75.

Lasswell, Harold D. "Current Studies of the Decision Process: Automation v. Creativity," *Western Political Quarterly*, *8* (1955), 381-99.

Lawrence, L. C., and Smith, P. C. "Group Decision and Employee Participation," *J. Applied Psych.*, *39* (1955), 334-37.

Leavitt, H. J. "Some Effects of Certain Communications Patterns on Group Performance," *J. Abnorm. Soc. Psych.*, *46* (1951), 38-50.

Leites, Nathan. "Psycho-Cultural Hypotheses About Political Acts," *World Politics*, *1* (1948), 102-19.

Levine, Jacob, and Butler, John. "Lecture v. Group Discussion in Changing Behavior," *J. Applied Psych.*, *36* (1952), 29-33.

Lewin, Kurt, and Lippitt, Ronald. "An Experimental Approach to the Study of Democracy and Autocracy: A Preliminary Note," *Sociometry*, *1* (1938), 292-300; reprinted in Hare, Borgatta, and Bales, eds., *Small Groups*.

———, Lippitt, Ronald, and White, R. "Patterns of Aggressive Behavior in Experimentally Designed Social Climates," *J. Social Psych.*, *10* (1939), 271-99.

Lippitt, Ronald. "Field Theory and Experiment in Social Psychology: Autocratic and Democratic Group Atmospheres," *Am. J. Soc.*, *45* (1939), 26-49.

———, Polanski, N., and Rosen, S. "The Dynamics of Power," *Hum. Rel.*, *5* (1952), 37-64; reprinted in Cartwright and Zander, eds., *Group Dynamics*.

McCloskey, Herbert, and Dahlgren, Harold E., "Primary Group Influence on Party Loyalty," *Am. Pol. Sci. Rev.*, *53* (1960), 757-76.

McCurdy, H. G., and Eber, H. W. "Democratic and Authoritarian: A Further Investigation of Group Problem Solving," *J. Personality*, *22* (1953), 258-69.

Maier, Norman R. F. "The Quality of Group Discussion as Influenced by the Leader," *Hum. Rel.*, *3* (1950), 155-74.

———, and Solem, A. R. "The Contribution of a Discussion Leader to the Quality of Group Thinking," *Hum. Rel.*, *5* (1952), 277-88.

March, James G. "Group Norms and the Active Minority," *Am. Soc. Rev.*, *19* (1954), 733-41.

———. "Husband-Wife Interaction over Political Issues," *Public Opinion Quarterly*, *17* (1953-54), 461-70.

———. "Influence Measurement in Experimental and Semi-experimental Groups," *Sociometry*, *19* (1956), 260-71.

March, James G. "An Introduction to the Theory and Measurement of Influence," *Am. Pol. Sci. Rev., 49* (1955), 431-51.

Medalia, Nahum. "Authoritarianism, Leader Acceptance and Group Cohesion," *J. Abnorm. Soc. Psych., 51* (1955), 207-13.

Merei, F. "Group Leadership and Institutionalization," *Hum. Rel., 2* (1949), 23-39.

Micaud, Charles A. "Organization and Leadership of the French Communist Party," *World Politics, 4* (1952), 318-55.

Mills, Theodore. "Power Relations in Three-Person Groups," *Am. Soc. Rev., 18* (1953), 351-57; reprinted in Cartwright and Zander, eds., *Group Dynamics.*

Moreno, J. L. "A Note on Cohesion in Small Groups," *Sociometry, 13* (1950), 176.

Morse, N., and Reimer, E. "The Experimental Change of a Major Organizational Variable," *J. Abnorm. Soc. Psych., 52* (1956), 120-29.

Olmsted, Michael S. "Orientation and Role in the Small Group," *Am. Soc. Rev., 19* (1954), 741-51.

Parsons, Talcott. "Suggestions for a Sociological Approach to the Theory of Organizations," *Administrative Science Quarterly, 1* (1956), 63-85, 225-39.

Pelz, D. C. "Leadership Within a Hierarchical Organization," *J. Social Issues, 71* (1951), 49-55.

Philp, Hugh, and Dunphy, Dexter. "Developmental Trends in Small Groups," *Sociometry, 22* (1959), 162-74.

Polanski, N., Lippitt, R., and Redl, F. "Problems in Interpersonal Relations in Research on Groups," *Hum. Rel., 2* (1949), 281-92.

————, Lippitt, R., and Redl, F. "An Investigation of Behavioral Contagion in Groups," *Hum. Rel., 3* (1950), 319-48.

Precker, J. A. "Similarity of Values as a Factor in Selection of Peers and Near-Authority Figures," *J. Abnorm. Soc. Psych., 47* (1952), 406-14.

Preston, M. G. and Heintz, R. K. "Effects of Participatory v. Supervisory Leadership on Group Judgments," *J. Abnorm. Soc. Psych., 44* (1949), 345-55.

Raven, Bertram H. and French, J. R. P. "Legitimate Power, Coercive Power, and Observability in Social Influence," *Sociometry, 21* (1958), 83-97.

Rieff, Philip. "Aesthetic Functions in Modern Politics," *World Politics, 5* (1953), 478-502.

Ringer, Benjamin and Sills, David L. "Political Extremists in Iran: A Secondary Analysis of Communications Data," *Public Opinion Quarterly*, *16* (1952-53), 689-701.

Schachter, Stanley. "Deviation, Rejection and Communication," *J. Abnorm. Soc. Psych.*, *46* (1951), 196-207.
———, *et al.* "Cross-Cultural Experiments in Threat and Rejection," *Hum. Rel.*, *7* (1954), 403-40.
Seeman, M. "Role Conflicts and Ambivalence in Leadership," *Am. Soc. Rev.*, *18* (1953), 373-80.
Seligman, Lester G. "Developments in the Presidency and the Conception of Political Leadership," *Am. Soc. Rev.*, *20* (1955), 706-12.
———. "The Study of Political Leadership," *Am. Pol. Sci. Rev.*, *44* (1950), 904-15.
Shaw, Marvin E. "Acceptance of Authority, Group Structure and the Effectiveness of Small Groups," *J. Personality*, *27* (1959), 196-210.
———. "A Comparison of Two Types of Leadership in Various Communications Nets," *J. Abnorm. Soc. Psych.*, *50* (1955), 127-34.
———, and Gilchrist, J. C. "Inter-group Communication and Leader Choice," *J. Soc. Psych.*, *43* (1956), 133-38.
———, Rothschild, G. H., and Strickland, J. F. "Decision Processes in Communication Nets," *J. Abnorm. Soc. Psych.*, *54* (1957), 323-30.
Sherif, Muzafer. "An Experimental Approach to the Study of Attitudes," *Sociometry*, *1* (1937), 90-98.
———. "A Study of Some Social Factors in Perception," *Archives of Psychology*, *27* (1935), No. 187.
Shils, E. A., and Janowitz, M. "Cohesion and Disintegration of the *Wehrmacht* in World War II," *Public Opinion Quarterly*, *12* (1948), 280-315.
Simon, Herbert. "Comments on the Theory of Organization," *Am. Pol. Sci. Rev.*, *46* (1952), 1130-40.
Slater, Philip E. "Role Differentiation in Small Groups," *Am. Soc. Rev.*, *20* (1955), 300-10; reprinted in Hare, Borgatta, and Bales, eds., *Small Groups.*
Snyder, Eloise. "The Supreme Court as a Small Group," *Social Forces*, *36* (1958), 232-38.
Snyder, Richard C., and Paige, Glenn D. "The United States Decision to Resist Aggression in Korea," *Administrative Science Quarterly*, *3* (1958), 341-78.
Solomon, R. L. "An Extension of Control Group Design," *Psych. Bull.*, *46* (1949), 137-50.

Stephan, F. F., and Mischler, E. G. "The Distribution of Participation in Small Groups: An Exponential Approximation," *Am. Soc. Rev.*, *17* (1952), 598-608.

Stirn, Hans. "Die 'Kleine Gruppe' in der Deutschen Soziologie und Sozialpsychologie," *Kölner Zeitschrift für Soziologie und Sozialpsychologie*, *7* (1955), 532-57.

Stogdill, Ralph M. "Personal Factors Associated with Leadership," *J. Psychology*, *25* (1948), 35-71.

———. "The Sociometry of Working Relations in Formal Organizations," *Sociometry*, *12* (1949), 276-86.

Stouffer, Samuel. "An Analysis of Conflicting Social Norms," *Am. Soc. Rev.*, *14* (1949), 707-17.

Strodtbeck, Fred L. "The Family as a Three-Person Group," *Am. Soc. Rev.*, *19* (1954), 23-29; reprinted in Hare, Borgatta, and Bales, eds., *Small Groups*.

———. "Husband-Wife Interaction over Revealed Differences," *Am. Soc. Rev.*, *16* (1951), 468-73; reprinted in Hare, Borgatta, and Bales, eds., *Small Groups*.

———. "Sex-Role Differentiation in Jury Deliberation," *Sociometry*, *19* (1956), 3-11.

———, issue editor. "Special Issue on Small Group Research," *Am. Soc. Rev.*, *19* (1954), entire.

———, James, Rita M., and Hawkins, Charles. "Social Status in Jury Deliberation," *Am. Soc. Rev.*, *22* (1957), 713-19.

Swanson, G. E. "Some Problems of Laboratory Experiments with Small Populations," *Am. Soc. Rev.*, *16* (1951), 349-58.

Talland, G. A. "The Assessment of Group Opinion by Leaders and Their Influence on Its Formation," *J. Abnorm. Soc. Psych.*, *49* (1954), 431-34.

Tannenbaum, Robert, and Massarik, Fred. "Participation by Subordinates in the Managerial Decision Making Process," *Canadian Journal of Economics and Political Science*, *18* (1950), 410-18.

Theodorson, George A. "The Relationship Between Leadership and Popularity Roles in Small Groups," *Am. Soc. Rev.*, *22* (1957), 58-67.

Thibault, John. "An Experimental Study of the Cohesiveness of Underprivileged Groups," *Hum. Rel.*, *3* (1950), 251-78; reprinted in Cartwright and Zander, eds., *Group Dynamics*.

Torrance, P. "Group Decision-Making and Disagreement," *Social Forces*, *35* (1957), 314-18.

———. "The Phenomenon of Resistance to Learning," *J. Abnorm. Soc. Psych.*, *45* (1950), 592-97.

Wapner, S., and Alper, Thelma C. "The Effect of an Audience on Behavior in a Choice Situation," *J. Abnorm. Soc. Psych.*, *47* (1952), 222-29.

Ward, Robert E. "The Socio-political Role in the Buraku (Hamlet) in Japan," *Am. Pol. Sci. Rev.*, *45* (1951), 1025-40.

Weisse, Robert S. "A Structure-Function Approach to Organization," *J. Social Issues*, *12* (1956), 61-67.

Wheeler, D. K. "Notes on 'Role Differentiation in Small Decision Making Groups,'" *Sociometry*, *20* (1957), 142-51.

Wherry, R. J., and Fryer, D. "Buddy Ratings: Popularity Contest or Leadership Criteria," *Sociometry*, *12* (1949), 179-90.

Whyte, W. F., and Gardner, B. B. "The Man in the Middle: Position and Problems of the Foreman," *Applied Anthropology*, *4* (1945), 1-28.

Williams, S. B., and Leavitt, H. J. "Group Opinions as a Predictor of Military Leadership," *J. Consulting Psychology*, *11* (1947), 283-91.

Wolman, Benjamin, "Leadership and Group Dynamics," *J. Social Psych.*, *43* (1956), 11-25.

UNPUBLISHED MATERIAL

Biel, W. C., *et al.* "The Systems Research Laboratories Air Defense Experiments." The RAND Corporation, P-1202, October 1957. Mimeographed.

Chapman, Robert L. "Description of the Air Defense Experiments, III: Data Collection and Processing." The RAND Corporation, P-658, 1955. Mimeographed.

Dupuis, Adrian Maurice. "Group Dynamics: Its Philosophical Presuppositions and Implications." Unpublished Ph.D. Dissertation, University of Minnesota, 1955.

Goldsen, J. M. "The Political Exercise: An Assessment of the Fourth Round." The RAND Corporation, 03640-RC, May 1956. Mimeographed.

Goliembiewski, Robert I. "Small Group Analysis Applied to the Study of Organization in Public Administration." Unpublished Ph.D. Dissertation, Yale University, 1958.

Hemphill, John K. "A Proposed Theory of Leadership in Small Groups," Ohio State University, Personnel Research Board, April 1954. Mimeographed.

Heyns, R. W. "Effects of Variation in Leadership on Participant Behavior in Discussion Groups." Unpublished Ph.D. Dissertation, University of Michigan, 1948.

Newell, Allan. "Description of the Air Defense Experiments, II: The Task Environment." The RAND Corporation, P-659, 1955. Mimeographed.

Strodtbeck, Fred L. "The Jury Project: Some Questions of Method Raised by Experimentation in an Institutional Study." Jury Project, The Law School, University of Chicago, September 1958. Mimeographed.

Sutton, Francis X. "Social Theory and Comparative Politics." Paper Prepared for a Conference under the Auspices of the Committee on Comparative Politics of the Social Science Research Council, Princeton, N.J., June 1955. Mimeographed.

INDEX

271